Bayesian Estimation of DSGE Models

T0342253

THE ECONOMETRIC AND TINBERGEN INSTITUTES LECTURES

Series Editors
Herman K. van Dijk and Philip Hans Franses
The Econometric Institute,
Erasmus University Rotterdam

The Econometric and Tinbergen Institutes Lecture Series is a joint project of Princeton University Press and the Econometric and Tinbergen Institutes at Erasmus University Rotterdam.

This series collects the lectures of leading researchers which they have given at the Econometric Institute for an audience of academics and students. The lectures are at a high academic level and deal with topics that have important policy implications. The series covers a wide range of topics in econometrics. It is not confined to any one area or subdiscipline.

The Econometric Institute is the leading research center in econometrics and management science in the Netherlands. The Institute was founded in 1956 by Jan Tinbergen and Henri Theil, with Theil being its first director. The Institute has received worldwide recognition with an advanced training program for various degrees in econometrics.

Other books in this series include

Anticipating Correlations: A New Paradigm for Risk Management by Robert Engle

Complete and Incomplete Econometric Models by John Geweke

Social Choice with Partial Knowledge of Treatment Response by Charles F. Manski

Yield Curve Modeling and Forecasting: The Dynamic Nelson-Siegel Approach by Francis X. Diebold and Glenn D. Rudebusch

Bayesian Non- and Semi-parametric Methods and Applications by Peter E. Rossi

Bayesian Estimation of DSGE Models

Edward P. Herbst and Frank Schorfheide

Princeton University Press
Princeton and Oxford

Published by Princeton University Press, 41 William Street, Princeton, New Jersey 08540

In the United Kingdom: Princeton University Press, 6 Oxford Street, Woodstock, Oxfordshire OX20 1TW

press.princeton.edu

Library of Congress Cataloging-in-Publication Data

Herbst, Edward P., 1984-
    Bayesian estimation of DSGE models /
    Edward P. Herbst, Frank Schorfheide.
    pages cm. – (The Econometric and Tinbergen Institutes lectures) Includes bibliographical references and index.
    ISBN 978-0-691-16108-2 (hardcover : alk. paper)
    1. Equilibrium (Economics)–Mathematical models. 2. Bayesian statistical decision theory. 3. Stochastic analysis.
    4. Econometrics.
    I. Schorfheide, Frank. II. Title.

HB145.H467 2015
339.501'519542–dc23   2015023799

British Library Cataloging-in-Publication Data is available

This book has been composed in LaTeX

The publisher would like to acknowledge the authors of this volume for providing the camera-ready copy from which this book was printed.

Printed on acid-free paper. ∞

Printed in the United States of America

    5   7   9   10   8   6   4

Hat der alte Hexenmeister
Sich doch einmal wegbegeben!
Und nun sollen seine Geister
Auch nach meinem Willen leben.
Seine Wort' und Werke
Merkt' ich und den Brauch,
Und mit Geistesstärke
Tu' ich Wunder auch.

(. . . bad things happen in between,
but eventually the master returns. . .)

"In die Ecke,
Besen! Besen!
Seid's gewesen!
Denn als Geister
Ruft euch nur zu seinem Zwecke
Erst hervor der alte Meister."

JW von Goethe, *Der Zauberlehrling*

Contents

Figures

Tables

Series Editors' Introduction

The Econometric and Tinbergen Institutes Lectures deal with topics in econometrics with important policy implications. The lectures cover a wide range of topics and are not confined to any one area or sub-discipline. Leading international scientists in the field of econometrics in which applications play a major role are invited to give three-day lectures on a topic to which they have contributed significantly.

The rise in the use and development of Dynamic Stochastic General Equilibrium (DSGE) models for macroeconomic forecasting and policy analysis has been spectacular in the past twenty years in academia and professional organizations. The present book written by Ed Herbst and Frank Schorfheide, leading researchers in this field, is very timely. It contains a clear introduction using basic New Keynesian Phillips curve models and continues to explore the inherent nonlinear structure of DSGE models. It covers a range of very novel simulation based Bayesian algorithms to handle such models. Here the reader is taken to the frontiers of modern science in the field of DSGE modeling.

This book no doubt stimulates further research in the DSGE class of models to analyze such modern economic issues as slow and imbalanced international growth, risk of deflation, and interconnectedness between real and financial sectors. This leads to the specification of a more appropriate and effective mix of fiscal and monetary policy to battle the issues mentioned.

The editors of the series are indebted to the Tinbergen Institute for continued support.

Herman K. van Dijk and Philip Hans Franses
Econometric and Tinbergen Institutes
Erasmus School of Economics

Preface

The first papers that used Bayesian techniques to estimate dynamic stochastic general equilibrium (DSGE) models were published about fifteen years ago: DeJong, Ingram, and Whiteman (2000), Schorfheide (2000), and Otrok (2001). The DSGE models at the time were relatively small in terms of the number of parameters and hidden states, and were estimated with, by today's standards, fairly simple versions of Metropolis-Hastings (MH) or importance sampling algorithms. Since then, DSGE models have grown in size, in particular the ones that are used by central banks for prediction and policy analysis. The celebrated Smets and Wouters (2003, 2007) has more than a dozen hidden states and thirty-six estimated parameters. The Smets-Wouters model forms the core of the latest vintage of DSGE models which may add a housing sector, search frictions in the labor market, or a banking sector and financial frictions to the basic set of equations. Each of these mechanisms increases the state space and the parameter space of the DSGE model.

The goal of this book is to assess the accuracy of the "standard" Bayesian computational techniques that have been applied in the DSGE model literature over the past fifteen years and to introduce and explore "new" computational tools that improve the accuracy of Monte Carlo approximations of posterior distributions associated with DSGE models. The reader will quickly notice that the tools are not really new (which is why we used quotation marks) but the application of some of these tools is: they are imported from the engineering and statistical literature and tailored toward Bayesian estimation of DSGE models. This book is based on a series of lectures on *Recent Theory and Applications of DSGE Models* which were presented as *Econometric and Tinbergen Institutes Lectures* at the Erasmus University Rotterdam in June 2012, but the material has evolved significantly since then.

The target audience of the book includes macroeconomists

in academia and central banks who are interested in applying state-of-the-art computational techniques to estimate DSGE models; econometricians who are interested in the Bayesian estimation of state-space models and nonlinear Monte Carlo filtering techniques and want to learn more about DSGE model applications in empirical macroeconomics; and PhD students who would like to conduct research at the interface of econometrics and macroeconomics.

The book has three parts. The first part consists of an introduction to DSGE modeling and Bayesian inference. We present a small-scale New Keynesian model, show how it can be solved, and turn it into a state-space model that is amenable to Bayesian estimation. Readers unfamiliar with DSGE models might have to consult a macroeconomics textbook or survey paper for more detailed background information on the specification, the solution, and the application of DSGE models. For readers unfamiliar with Bayesian econometrics, we provide a primer on Bayesian Inference. While this primer is not a substitute for a thorough textbook treatment, it shows in the context of a linear Gaussian regression model how a prior distribution is combined with a likelihood function to obtain a posterior distribution. Based on this posterior distribution one can derive point estimators, interval estimators, or solve more complicated decision problems. Moreover, we provide an introduction to important computational techniques, such as direct sampling, importance sampling, and Metropolis-Hastings algorithms.

The second part of the book is devoted to Bayesian computations for linearized DSGE models with Gaussian shocks. Thus, we focus on models for which the likelihood function can be evaluated with the Kalman filter. The starting point is the Random-Walk MH algorithm, which is the most widely used algorithm for Bayesian estimation of DSGE models in the literature. We discuss several refinements to this algorithm before proceeding with Sequential Monte Carlo (SMC) methods. While SMC algorithms are popular in the statistical literature, there are hardly any applications to the estimation of DSGE models. We provide a detailed discussion of how to tune these algorithms for DSGE model applications and examine their accuracy. The performance of MH and SMC algorithms is compared in three empirical applications.

The last part of the book focuses on computations for DSGE models solved with nonlinear techniques. The main difference is that the likelihood function can no longer be evaluated with the Kalman filter. Instead, the likelihood evaluation requires a nonlinear filter and we will focus on sequential Monte Carlo filters (also called particle filters). To avoid any disappointments, we hasten to point out that we do not estimate any nonlinear DSGE models in this book. Instead, we apply the particle filters to linear Gaussian DSGE models for which the Kalman filter delivers the exact likelihood function. This allows us to assess the accuracy of particle filter approximations. In doing so, we begin with likelihood evaluations conditional on a fixed parameter vector and subsequently embed the particle filter approximations of the likelihood function into MH and SMC algorithms to conduct posterior inference for DSGE model parameters.

In writing this book we greatly benefited (directly and indirectly) from interactions with colleagues and graduate students. We owe thanks to all of them but would like to mention a few names specifically: the series editor Herman van Dijk and two anonymous reviewers; our colleagues Frank Diebold, Jesus Fernandez-Villaverde, and Elmar Mertens; current Penn students Ross Askanazi, Jacob Warren, and the Spring 2015 Econ 722 class, who carefully combed through an earlier version of the manuscript; former Penn students Luigi Bocola, Mark Bognanni, Minchul Shin, and Dongho Song; and our collaborators on other DSGE-related projects Boragan Aruoba and Marco Del Negro. Schorfheide gratefully acknowledges financial support from the National Science Foundation. Finally, a big thanks to our wives, Sarah and Perlita, for their continued support of this project despite all the tolls it took on weeknights and weekends.

Edward Herbst, Washington DC 2015
Email: *ed.herbst@gmail.com*
Web: *edherbst.net*

Frank Schorfheide, Philadelphia 2015
Email: *schorf@ssc.upenn.edu*
Web: *sites.sas.upenn.edu/schorf*

Part I

Introduction to DSGE Modeling and Bayesian Inference

Chapter 1

DSGE Modeling

Estimated dynamic stochastic general equilibrium (DSGE) models are now widely used by academics to conduct empirical research macroeconomics as well as by central banks to interpret the current state of the economy, to analyze the impact of changes in monetary or fiscal policy, and to generate predictions for key macroeconomic aggregates. The term DSGE model encompasses a broad class of macroeconomic models that span the real business cycle models of Kydland and Prescott (1982) and King, Plosser, and Rebelo (1988) as well as the New Keynesian models of Rotemberg and Woodford (1997) or Christiano, Eichenbaum, and Evans (2005), which feature nominal price and wage rigidities and a role for central banks to adjust interest rates in response to inflation and output fluctuations. A common feature of these models is that decision rules of economic agents are derived from assumptions about preferences and technologies by solving intertemporal optimization problems. Moreover, agents potentially face uncertainty with respect to aggregate variables such as total factor productivity or nominal interest rates set by a central bank. This uncertainty is generated by exogenous stochastic processes that may shift technology or generate unanticipated deviations from a central bank's interest-rate feedback rule.

The focus of this book is the Bayesian estimation of DSGE models. Conditional on distributional assumptions for the exogenous shocks, the DSGE model generates a likelihood function, that is, a joint probability distribution for the endogenous model variables such as output, consumption, investment, and inflation that depends on the structural parameters of the model. These structural parameters characterize agents' preferences, production technologies, and the law of motion of the exogenous shocks. In a Bayesian framework, this likelihood function can be used to transform a prior distribution for the structural parameters of the DSGE model into a posterior distribution. This posterior is the basis for substantive inference and decision making. Unfortunately, it is not feasible to characterize moments and quantiles of the posterior distribution analytically. Instead, we have to use computational techniques to generate draws from the posterior and then approximate posterior expectations by Monte Carlo averages.

In Section 1.1 we will present a small-scale New Keynesian DSGE model and describe the decision problems of firms and households and the behavior of the monetary and fiscal authorities. We then characterize the resulting equilibrium conditions. This model is subsequently used in many of the numerical illustrations. Section 1.2 briefly sketches two other DSGE models that will be estimated in subsequent chapters.

1.1 A Small-Scale New Keynesian DSGE Model

We begin with a small-scale New Keynesian DSGE model that has been widely studied in the literature (see Woodford (2003) or Gali (2008) for textbook treatments). The particular specification presented below is based on An and Schorfheide (2007). The model economy consists of final goods producing firms, intermediate goods producing firms, households, a central bank, and a fiscal authority. We will first describe the decision problems of these agents, then describe the law of motion of the exogenous processes, and finally summarize the equilibrium conditions. The likelihood function for a linearized version of this model can be quickly evaluated, which makes the model an excellent showcase for the computational algorithms studied in this book.

1.1.1 Firms

Production takes place in two stages. There are monopolistically competitive intermediate goods producing firms and perfectly competitive final goods producing firms that aggregate the intermediate goods into a single good that is used for household and government consumption. This two-stage production process makes it fairly straightforward to introduce price stickiness, which in turn creates a real effect of monetary policy.

The perfectly competitive final good producing firms combine a continuum of intermediate goods indexed by $j \in [0, 1]$ using the technology

$$Y_t = \left(\int_0^1 Y_t(j)^{1-\nu} dj \right)^{\frac{1}{1-\nu}}. \tag{1.1}$$

The final good producers take input prices $P_t(j)$ and output prices P_t as given. The revenue from the sale of the final good is $P_t Y_t$ and the input costs incurred to produce Y_t are $\int_0^1 P_t(j) Y_t(j) dj$. Maximization of profits

$$\Pi_t = P_t \left(\int_0^1 Y_t(j)^{1-\nu} dj \right)^{\frac{1}{1-\nu}} - \int_0^1 P_t(j) Y_t(j) dj, \tag{1.2}$$

with respect to the inputs $Y_t(j)$ implies that the demand for intermediate good j is given by

$$Y_t(j) = \left(\frac{P_t(j)}{P_t} \right)^{-1/\nu} Y_t. \tag{1.3}$$

Thus, the parameter $1/\nu$ represents the elasticity of demand for each intermediate good. In the absence of an entry cost, final good producers will enter the market until profits are equal to zero. From the zero-profit condition, it is possible to derive the following relationship between the intermediate goods prices and the price of the final good:

$$P_t = \left(\int_0^1 P_t(j)^{\frac{\nu-1}{\nu}} dj \right)^{\frac{\nu}{\nu-1}}. \tag{1.4}$$

Intermediate good j is produced by a monopolist who has access to the following linear production technology:

$$Y_t(j) = A_t N_t(j), \tag{1.5}$$

where A_t is an exogenous productivity process that is common to all firms and $N_t(j)$ is the labor input of firm j. To keep the model simple, we abstract from capital as a factor or production for now. Labor is hired in a perfectly competitive factor market at the real wage W_t.

In order to introduce nominal price stickiness, we assume that firms face quadratic price adjustment costs

$$AC_t(j) = \frac{\phi}{2}\left(\frac{P_t(j)}{P_{t-1}(j)} - \pi\right)^2 Y_t(j), \qquad (1.6)$$

where ϕ governs the price rigidity in the economy and π is the steady state inflation rate associated with the final good. Under this adjustment cost specification it is costless to change prices at the rate π. If the price change deviates from π, the firm incurs a cost in terms of lost output that is a quadratic function of the discrepancy between the price change and π. The larger the adjustment cost parameter ϕ, the more reluctant the intermediate goods producers are to change their prices and the more rigid the prices are at the aggregate level. Firm j chooses its labor input $N_t(j)$ and the price $P_t(j)$ to maximize the present value of future profits

$$\mathbb{E}_t\left[\sum_{s=0}^{\infty} \beta^s Q_{t+s|t}\left(\frac{P_{t+s}(j)}{P_{t+s}} Y_{t+s}(j)\right.\right. \qquad (1.7)$$
$$\left.\left. -W_{t+s}N_{t+s}(j) - AC_{t+s}(j)\right)\right].$$

Here, $Q_{t+s|t}$ is the time t value of a unit of the consumption good in period $t + s$ to the household, which is treated as exogenous by the firm.

1.1.2 Households

The representative household derives utility from consumption C_t relative to a habit stock (which is approximated by the level of technology A_t)[1] and real money balances M_t/P_t.

---

[1]This assumption ensures that the economy evolves along a balanced growth path even if the utility function is additively separable in consumption, real money balances, and leisure.

The household derives disutility from hours worked H_t and maximizes

$$\mathbb{E}_t\left[\sum_{s=0}^{\infty}\beta^s\left(\frac{(C_{t+s}/A_{t+s})^{1-\tau}-1}{1-\tau}\right.\right. \tag{1.8}$$
$$\left.\left.+\chi_M\ln\left(\frac{M_{t+s}}{P_{t+s}}\right)-\chi_H H_{t+s}\right)\right],$$

where β is the discount factor, $1/\tau$ is the intertemporal elasticity of substitution, and χ_M and χ_H are scale factors that determine steady state money balances and hours worked. We will set $\chi_H = 1$. The household supplies perfectly elastic labor services to the firms, taking the real wage W_t as given. The household has access to a domestic bond market where nominal government bonds B_t are traded that pay (gross) interest R_t. Furthermore, it receives aggregate residual real profits D_t from the firms and has to pay lump-sum taxes T_t. Thus, the household's budget constraint is of the form

$$P_tC_t + B_t + M_t + T_t \tag{1.9}$$
$$= P_tW_tH_t + R_{t-1}B_{t-1} + M_{t-1} + P_tD_t + P_tSC_t,$$

where SC_t is the net cash inflow from trading a full set of state-contingent securities.

1.1.3 Monetary and Fiscal Policy

Monetary policy is described by an interest rate feedback rule of the form

$$R_t = R_t^{*\,1-\rho_R}R_{t-1}^{\rho_R}e^{\epsilon_{R,t}}, \tag{1.10}$$

where $\epsilon_{R,t}$ is a monetary policy shock and R_t^* is the (nominal) target rate:

$$R_t^* = r\pi^*\left(\frac{\pi_t}{\pi^*}\right)^{\psi_1}\left(\frac{Y_t}{Y_t^*}\right)^{\psi_2}. \tag{1.11}$$

Here r is the steady state real interest rate (defined below), π_t is the gross inflation rate defined as $\pi_t = P_t/P_{t-1}$, and π^* is the target inflation rate. Y_t^* in (1.11) is the level of output that would prevail in the absence of nominal rigidities.

We assume that the fiscal authority consumes a fraction ζ_t of aggregate output Y_t, that is $G_t = \zeta_t Y_t$, and that $\zeta_t \in [0,1]$

follows an exogenous process specified below. The government levies a lump-sum tax T_t (subsidy) to finance any shortfalls in government revenues (or to rebate any surplus). The government's budget constraint is given by

$$P_t G_t + R_{t-1} B_{t-1} + M_{t-1} = T_t + B_t + M_t. \qquad (1.12)$$

1.1.4 Exogenous Processes

The model economy is perturbed by three exogenous processes. Aggregate productivity evolves according to

$$\ln A_t = \ln \gamma + \ln A_{t-1} + \ln z_t, \quad \ln z_t = \rho_z \ln z_{t-1} + \epsilon_{z,t}. \qquad (1.13)$$

Thus, on average technology grows at the rate γ and z_t captures exogenous fluctuations of the technology growth rate. Define $g_t = 1/(1 - \zeta_t)$, where ζ_t was previously defined as the fraction of aggregate output purchased by the government. We assume that

$$\ln g_t = (1 - \rho_g) \ln g + \rho_g \ln g_{t-1} + \epsilon_{g,t}. \qquad (1.14)$$

Finally, the monetary policy shock $\epsilon_{R,t}$ is assumed to be serially uncorrelated. The three innovations are independent of each other at all leads and lags and are normally distributed with means zero and standard deviations σ_z, σ_g, and σ_R, respectively.

1.1.5 Equilibrium Relationships

We consider the symmetric equilibrium in which all intermediate goods producing firms make identical choices so that the j subscript can be omitted. The market clearing conditions are given by

$$Y_t = C_t + G_t + AC_t \quad \text{and} \quad H_t = N_t. \qquad (1.15)$$

Because the households have access to a full set of state-contingent claims, it turns out that $Q_{t+s|t}$ in (1.7) is

$$Q_{t+s|t} = (C_{t+s}/C_t)^{-\tau} (A_t/A_{t+s})^{1-\tau}. \qquad (1.16)$$

Thus, in equilibrium households and firms are using the same stochastic discount factor. Moreover, it can be shown that output, consumption, interest rates, and inflation have to satisfy the following optimality conditions:

$$1 = \beta \mathbb{E}_t \left[\left(\frac{C_{t+1}/A_{t+1}}{C_t/A_t} \right)^{-\tau} \frac{A_t}{A_{t+1}} \frac{R_t}{\pi_{t+1}} \right] \tag{1.17}$$

$$1 = \phi(\pi_t - \pi) \left[\left(1 - \frac{1}{2\nu} \right) \pi_t + \frac{\pi}{2\nu} \right] \tag{1.18}$$

$$-\phi \beta \mathbb{E}_t \left[\left(\frac{C_{t+1}/A_{t+1}}{C_t/A_t} \right)^{-\tau} \frac{Y_{t+1}/A_{t+1}}{Y_t/A_t} (\pi_{t+1} - \pi) \pi_{t+1} \right]$$

$$+\frac{1}{\nu} \left[1 - \left(\frac{C_t}{A_t} \right)^{\tau} \right].$$

Equation (1.17) is the consumption Euler equation which reflects the first-order condition with respect to the government bonds B_t. In equilibrium, the household equates the marginal utility of consuming a dollar today with the discounted marginal utility from investing the dollar, earning interest R_t, and consuming it in the next period. Equation (1.18) characterizes the profit maximizing choice of the intermediate goods producing firms. The first-order condition for the firms' problem depends on the wage W_t. We used the households' labor supply condition to replace W_t by a function of the marginal utility of consumption. In the absence of nominal rigidities ($\phi = 0$) aggregate output is given by

$$Y_t^* = (1 - \nu)^{1/\tau} A_t g_t, \tag{1.19}$$

which is the target level of output that appears in the monetary policy rule (1.11).

In Section 2.1 of Chapter 2 we will use a solution technique for the DSGE model that is based on a Taylor series approximation of the equilibrium conditions. A natural point around which to construct this approximation is the steady state of the DSGE model. The steady state is attained by setting the innovations $\epsilon_{R,t}$, $\epsilon_{g,t}$, and $\epsilon_{z,t}$ to zero at all times. Because technology $\ln A_t$ evolves according to a random walk with drift $\ln \gamma$, consumption and output need to be detrended for a steady state to exist. Let $c_t = C_t/A_t$ and $y_t = Y_t/A_t$, and $y_t^* = Y_t^*/A_t$. Then the steady state is given by

$$
\pi = \pi^*, \quad r = \frac{\gamma}{\beta}, \quad R = r\pi^*, \tag{1.20}
$$

$$
c = (1-\nu)^{1/\tau}, \quad y = gc = y^*.
$$

Steady state inflation equals the targeted inflation rate π_*; the real rate depends on the growth rate of the economy γ and the reciprocal of the households' discount factor β; and finally steady state output can be determined from the aggregate resource constraint. The nominal interest rate is determined by the Fisher equation; the dependence of the steady state consumption on ν reflects the distortion generated by the monopolistic competition among intermediate goods producers. We are now in a position to rewrite the equilibrium conditions by expressing each variable in terms of percentage deviations from its steady state value. Let $\hat{x}_t = \ln(x_t/x)$ and write

$$
1 = \beta \mathbb{E}_t \left[e^{-\tau \hat{c}_{t+1} + \tau \hat{c}_t + \hat{R}_t - \hat{z}_{t+1} - \hat{\pi}_{t+1}} \right] \tag{1.21}
$$

$$
0 = \left(e^{\hat{\pi}_t} - 1 \right) \left[\left(1 - \frac{1}{2\nu} \right) e^{\hat{\pi}_t} + \frac{1}{2\nu} \right] \tag{1.22}
$$
$$
- \beta \mathbb{E}_t \left[\left(e^{\hat{\pi}_{t+1}} - 1 \right) e^{-\tau \hat{c}_{t+1} + \tau \hat{c}_t + \hat{y}_{t+1} - \hat{y}_t + \hat{\pi}_{t+1}} \right]
$$
$$
+ \frac{1-\nu}{\nu \phi \pi^2} \left(1 - e^{\tau \hat{c}_t} \right)
$$

$$
e^{\hat{c}_t - \hat{y}_t} = e^{-\hat{g}_t} - \frac{\phi \pi^2 g}{2} \left(e^{\hat{\pi}_t} - 1 \right)^2 \tag{1.23}
$$

$$
\hat{R}_t = \rho_R \hat{R}_{t-1} + (1 - \rho_R)\psi_1 \hat{\pi}_t \tag{1.24}
$$
$$
+ (1 - \rho_R)\psi_2 \left(\hat{y}_t - \hat{g}_t \right) + \epsilon_{R,t}
$$

$$
\hat{g}_t = \rho_g \hat{g}_{t-1} + \epsilon_{g,t} \tag{1.25}
$$

$$
\hat{z}_t = \rho_z \hat{z}_{t-1} + \epsilon_{z,t}. \tag{1.26}
$$

The equilibrium law of motion of consumption, output, interest rates, and inflation has to satisfy the expectational difference equations (1.21) to (1.26).

1.2 Other DSGE Models Considered in This Book

In addition to the small-scale New Keynesian DSGE model, we consider two other models: the widely used Smets-Wouters (SW) model, which is a more elaborate version of the small-scale DSGE model that includes capital accumulation as well as wage rigidities, and a real business cycle model with a detailed characterization of fiscal policy. We will present a brief overview of these models below and provide further details as needed in Chapter 6.

1.2.1 The Smets-Wouters Model

The Smets and Wouters (2007) model is a more elaborate version of the small-scale DSGE model presented in the previous section. In the SW model capital is a factor of intermediate goods production, and in addition to price stickiness the model features nominal wage stickiness. In order to generate a richer autocorrelation structure, the model also includes investment adjustment costs, habit formation in consumption, and partial dynamic indexation of prices and wages to lagged values. The model is based on work by Christiano, Eichenbaum, and Evans (2005), who added various forms of frictions to a basic New Keynesian DSGE model in order to capture the dynamic response to a monetary policy shock as measured by a structural vector autoregression (VAR). In turn (the publication dates are misleading), Smets and Wouters (2003) augmented the Christiano-Eichenbaum-Evans model by additional exogenous structural shocks (among them price markup shocks, wage markup shocks, preference shocks, and others) to be able to capture the joint dynamics of Euro Area output, consumption, investment, hours, wages, inflation, and interest rates.

The Smets and Wouters (2003) paper has been highly influential, not just in academic circles but also in central banks because it demonstrated that a modern DSGE model that is usable for monetary policy analysis can achieve a time series fit that is comparable to a less restrictive vector autoregression (VAR). The 2007 version of the SW model contains a number of minor modifications of the 2003 model in order to optimize its fit on U.S. data. We will use the 2007 model exactly as it is presented in Smets and Wouters (2007) and refer the reader to that article for details. The log-linearized equilibrium conditions are reproduced in Appendix A.1. By now, the SW model has become one of the workhorse models in the DSGE model literature and in central banks around the world. It forms the core of most large-scale DSGE models that augment the SW model with additional features such as a multi-sector production structure or financial frictions. Because of its widespread use, we will consider its estimation in this book.

1.2.2 A DSGE Model for the Analysis of Fiscal Policy

In the small-scale New Keynesian DSGE model and in the SW model, fiscal policy is passive and non-distortionary. The level of government spending as a fraction of GDP is assumed to evolve exogenously and an implicit money demand equation determines the amount of seignorage generated by the interest rate feedback rule. Fiscal policy is passive in the sense that the government raises lump-sum taxes (or distributes lump-sum transfers) to ensure that its budget constraint is satisfied in every period. These lump-sum taxes are non-distortionary, because they do not affect the decisions of households and firms. The exact magnitude of the lump-sum taxes and the level of government debt are not uniquely determined, but they also do not matter for macroeconomic outcomes. Both the small-scale DSGE model and the SW model were explicitly designed for the analysis of monetary policy and abstract from a realistic representation of fiscal policy.

In order to provide a careful and realistic assessment of the effects of exogenous changes in government spending and tax rates, a more detailed representation of the fiscal sector is necessary. An example of such a model is the one studied by Leeper, Plante, and Traum (2010). While the authors abstract from monetary policy, they allow for capital, labor, and consumption tax rates that react to the state of the economy, in particular the level of output and debt, and are subject to exogenous shocks, which reflect unanticipated changes in fiscal policy. In addition to consumption, investment, and hours worked, the model is also estimated based on data on tax revenues, government spending, and government debt to identify the parameters of the fiscal policy rules. The estimated model can be used to assess the effect of counterfactual fiscal policies.

We selected the fiscal policy model because during and after the 2007–09 recession, the DSGE model-based analysis of government spending and tax changes has received considerable attention and because the model gives rise to complicated, multi-modal posterior distributions which require sophisticated posterior samplers – such as the ones discussed in this book – to implement the Bayesian estimation. For a detailed model description we refer the reader to Leeper, Plante, and Traum (2010). The log-linearized equilibrium conditions are reproduced in Appendix A.2.

Chapter 2

Turning a DSGE Model into a
Bayesian Model

Formally, a Bayesian model consists of a joint distribution of data Y and parameters θ. In the context of a DSGE model application Y might comprise time series for GDP growth, inflation, and interest rates, and θ stacks the structural parameters that, for instance, appeared in the description of the small-scale DSGE model in Section 1.1 of Chapter 1. Throughout this book we will represent distributions by densities and denote the joint distribution by $p(Y, \theta)$. The joint distribution can be factored into a distribution of the data given the parameters, $p(Y|\theta)$, and a prior distribution $p(\theta)$. The density $p(Y|\theta)$ as function of θ is called likelihood function. In a Bayesian framework the likelihood function is used to update *a priori* beliefs about the parameter vector θ, represented by the prior $p(\theta)$, in view of the sample information Y. After the updating, the state of knowledge about the parameter vector θ is summarized by the posterior distribution $p(\theta|Y)$ and Bayes Theorem provides the formal link between prior distribution, likelihood function, and posterior distribution.

In order to turn the DSGE models of Chapter 1 into Bayesian models, we need to specify a probability distribution for the innovations of the exogenous shock processes, solve for the equilibrium law of motion of the endogenous variables conditional on the DSGE model parameter vector θ, develop an algorithm that evaluates the likelihood function $p(Y|\theta)$ for a given set of data Y and parameter vector θ, and specify a prior distribution for the DSGE model parameters. We will subsequently illustrate these steps in the context of the small-scale New Keynesian DSGE model that was introduced in Section 1.1.

There exist a wide variety of numerical techniques to solve DSGE models (approximately). Throughout this book we will focus on a technique that involves the log-linearization of the equilibrium conditions and the solution of the resulting linear rational expectations difference equations. This method is described in Section 2.1. The approximate solution takes the form of a vector autoregressive process for the model variables, which is driven by the innovations to the exogenous shock processes, and is used as a set of state-transition equations in the state-space representation of the DSGE model. The state-transition equations are augmented by a set of measurement equations that express observed macroeconomic and financial time series used to estimate the DSGE model as function of the (potentially unobserved) state variables. To complete the specification of the empirical model, we make a distributional assumption for the exogenous shock innovations. Under the assumption that these innovations are normally distributed, the log-linearized DSGE model takes the form of a linear Gaussian state-space model with system matrices that are highly nonlinear functions of the structural parameter vector θ.

The state-space representation of the DSGE model and the evaluation of the likelihood function are described in Section 2.2. The evaluation of the likelihood function associated with the state-space representation of the DSGE model requires a filter that integrates out the hidden state variables of the DSGE model. We first present a general characterization of the filtering algorithm. If the DSGE model is solved by a linear approximation technique and the innovations to the exogenous shock processes are assumed to be Gaussian, as is the case for the DSGE models considered in this book, then the filtering problem simplifies considerably and the likelihood function can be evaluated with the Kalman filter. Thus, we also provide a summary of the Kalman filter recursions. Finally, we discuss the specification of prior distributions $p(\theta)$ in Section 2.3.

2.1 Solving a (Linearized) DSGE Model

Log-linearization and straightforward manipulation of Equations (1.21) to (1.23) yield the following representation for the consumption Euler equation, the New Keynesian Phillips curve, and the monetary policy rule:

$$\hat{y}_t = \mathbb{E}_t[\hat{y}_{t+1}] - \frac{1}{\tau}\left(\hat{R}_t - \mathbb{E}_t[\hat{\pi}_{t+1}] - \mathbb{E}_t[\hat{z}_{t+1}]\right) \qquad (2.1)$$
$$+\hat{g}_t - \mathbb{E}_t[\hat{g}_{t+1}]$$
$$\hat{\pi}_t = \beta\mathbb{E}_t[\hat{\pi}_{t+1}] + \kappa(\hat{y}_t - \hat{g}_t)$$
$$\hat{R}_t = \rho_R\hat{R}_{t-1} + (1 - \rho_R)\psi_1\hat{\pi}_t + (1 - \rho_R)\psi_2\left(\hat{y}_t - \hat{g}_t\right) + \epsilon_{R,t}$$

where

$$\kappa = \tau\frac{1 - \nu}{\nu\pi^2\phi}. \qquad (2.2)$$

Iterating the consumption Euler equation forward implies that output is a function of the sum of expected future real returns on bonds. Provided prices are sticky, the central bank is able to influence aggregate output by manipulating the real rate indirectly through adjustments of the nominal interest rate. The New Keynesian Phillips curve links inflation to real activity. Iterating the New Keynesian Phillips curve forward implies that inflation is a function of the expected discounted sum of the future output gap $\hat{y}_t - \hat{g}_t$. Recall that we previously defined the (detrended) output in the absence of nominal rigidities as $y_t^* = (1 - \nu)^{1/\tau}A_tg_t$ or $\hat{y}_t^* = \hat{g}_t$ in log-linear terms. If we call $\hat{y}_t^*$ potential output, then $\hat{y}_t - \hat{g}_t = \hat{y}_t - \hat{y}_t^*$ can be interpreted as an output gap.

Equations (2.1) combined with the law of motion of the exogenous shocks in (1.25) and (1.26) form a linear rational expectations system that determines the evolution of

$$x_t = [\hat{y}_t, \hat{\pi}_t, \hat{R}_t, \epsilon_{R,t}, \hat{g}_t, \hat{z}_t]'.$$

In order to solve for the law of motion of x_t it is convenient to augment x_t by the expectations $\mathbb{E}_t[\hat{y}_{t+1}]$ and $\mathbb{E}_t[\hat{\pi}_{t+1}]$, defining the $n \times 1$ vector

$$s_t = \left[x_t', \mathbb{E}_t[\hat{y}_{t+1}], \mathbb{E}_t[\hat{\pi}_{t+1}]\right]'. \qquad (2.3)$$

We are now in a position to cast the log-linearized DSGE model in the canonical linear rational expectations form that underlies the solution method proposed by Sims (2002):[1]

$$\Gamma_0 s_t = \Gamma_1 s_{t-1} + \Psi \epsilon_t + \Pi \eta_t, \qquad (2.4)$$

where $\epsilon_t = [\epsilon_{z,t}, \epsilon_{g,t}, \epsilon_{R,t}]'$. The vector η_t captures one-step-ahead rational expectations forecast errors. To write the equilibrium conditions of the small-scale New Keynesian model in the form of (2.4), we begin by replacing $\mathbb{E}_t[\hat{g}_{t+1}]$ and $\mathbb{E}_t[\hat{z}_{t+1}]$ in the first equation of (2.1) with $\rho_g \hat{g}_t$ and $\rho_z \hat{z}_t$, respectively. We then introduce expectational errors for inflation and output. Let

$$\eta_{y,t} = y_t - \mathbb{E}_{t-1}[\hat{y}_t], \quad \eta_{\pi,t} = \pi_t - \mathbb{E}_{t-1}[\hat{\pi}_t], \qquad (2.5)$$

and define $\eta_t = [\eta_{y,t}, \eta_{\pi,t}]$. Using these definitions, the set of equations (2.1), (1.25), (1.26), and (2.5) can be written as (2.4). The system matrices Γ_0, Γ_1, Ψ, and Π are functions of the DSGE model parameters θ.

For the linearized equilibrium conditions (2.1) to characterize a solution to the underlying dynamic programming problems of the households and firms in the DSGE model, a set of transversality conditions needs to be satisfied. It turns out that these conditions are satisfied if the law of motion is non-explosive. This stability requirement restricts the set of solutions to (2.4). Depending on the system matrices Γ_0, Γ_1, Ψ, and Π the system may have no non-explosive solution (non-existence), exactly one stable solution (uniqueness), or many stable solutions (indeterminacy). Sims (2002) provides a general method to construct stable solutions for the canonical system (2.4). The system can be transformed through a generalized complex Schur decomposition (QZ) of Γ_0 and Γ_1. There exist $n \times n$ matrices Q, Z, Λ, and Ω, such that $Q'\Lambda Z' = \Gamma_0$, $Q'\Omega Z' = \Gamma_1$, $QQ' = ZZ' = I$, and Λ and Ω are upper-triangular. Let $w_t = Z's_t$ and pre-multiply (2.4) by Q

---

[1]There exist many alternative solution methods for linear rational expectations systems, e.g., Blanchard and Kahn (1980), Binder and Pesaran (1997), Anderson (2000), Klein (2000), Christiano (2002), and King and Watson (1998). Each of these solution methods is associated with its own canonical form of the rational expectations system.

to obtain:

$$\begin{bmatrix} \Lambda_{11} & \Lambda_{12} \\ 0 & \Lambda_{22} \end{bmatrix} \begin{bmatrix} w_{1,t} \\ w_{2,t} \end{bmatrix} \quad (2.6)$$

$$= \begin{bmatrix} \Omega_{11} & \Omega_{12} \\ 0 & \Omega_{22} \end{bmatrix} \begin{bmatrix} w_{1,t-1} \\ w_{2,t-1} \end{bmatrix} + \begin{bmatrix} Q_1 \\ Q_2 \end{bmatrix} (\Psi \epsilon_t + \Pi \eta_t).$$

The second set of equations can be rewritten as:

$$w_{2,t} = \Lambda_{22}^{-1} \Omega_{22} w_{2,t-1} + \Lambda_{22}^{-1} Q_2 (\Psi \epsilon_t + \Pi \eta_t). \quad (2.7)$$

Without loss of generality, we assume that the system is ordered and partitioned such that the $m \times 1$ vector $w_{2,t}$ is purely explosive, where $0 \le m \le n$.

A non-explosive solution of the LRE model (2.4) for s_t exists if $w_{2,0} = 0$ and for every $l \times 1$ vector of structural shock innovations ϵ_t, one can find a $k \times 1$ vector of rational expectations errors η_t that offsets the impact of ϵ_t on $w_{2,t}$:

$$\underbrace{Q_2 \Psi}_{m \times l} \underbrace{\epsilon_t}_{l \times 1} + \underbrace{Q_2 \Pi}_{m \times k} \underbrace{\eta_t}_{k \times 1} = \underbrace{0}_{m \times 1}. \quad (2.8)$$

If $m = k$ and the matrix $Q_2 \Pi$ is invertible, then the unique set of expectational errors that ensure the stability of the system is given by

$$\eta_t = -\left(Q_2 \Pi\right)^{-1} Q_2 \Psi \epsilon_t.$$

In general, it is not guaranteed that the vector η_t need is uniquely determined by ϵ_t. An example of non-uniqueness (or indeterminacy) is the case in which the number of expectation errors k exceeds the number of explosive components m and (2.8) does not provide enough restrictions to uniquely determine the elements of η_t. In this case it is possible to introduce expectation errors (martingale difference sequences) ζ_t that are unrelated to the fundamental uncertainty ϵ_t without destabilizing the system. Using a singular value decomposition of $Q_2 \Pi$ of the form:

$$Q_2 \Pi = \underbrace{U_1}_{m \times r} \underbrace{D_{11}}_{r \times r} \underbrace{V_1'}_{r \times k},$$

we can express

$$\eta_t = (-V_1 D_{11}^{-1} U_1' Q_2 \Psi + V_2 M_1) \epsilon_t + V_2 M_2 \zeta_t, \quad (2.9)$$

where V_2 is a matrix composed of orthonormal columns that are orthogonal to V_1 (this matrix is a by-product of the singular value decomposition of $Q_2\Pi$), M_1 is an arbitrary $(k-r) \times l$ matrix, and M_2 is an arbitrary $(k-r) \times p$ matrix. The matrices M_1 and M_2 and the vector of so-called sunspot shocks ζ_t capture the potential multiplicity of non-explosive solutions (indeterminacy) of (2.8). A derivation of (2.9) is provided in Lubik and Schorfheide (2003).

The overall set of non-explosive solutions (if it is non-empty) to the linear rational expectations system (2.4) can be obtained from $s_t = Zw_t$, (2.7), and (2.9). If the system has a unique stable solution, then it can be written as a VAR in s_t:

$$s_t = \Phi_1(\theta)s_{t-1} + \Phi_\epsilon(\theta)\epsilon_t. \qquad (2.10)$$

Here the coefficient matrices $\Phi_1(\theta)$ and $\Phi_\epsilon(\theta)$ are functions of the structural parameters of the DSGE model. The vector autoregressive representation in (2.10) forms the basis for our empirical model.

2.2 The Likelihood Function

In order to construct a likelihood function, we have to relate the model variables s_t in (2.3) to a set of observables y_t. Thus, the specification of the empirical model is completed by a set of measurement equations. For the small-scale New Keynesian DSGE model we assume that the time period t in the model corresponds to one quarter and that the following observations are available for estimation: quarter-to-quarter per capita GDP growth rates (YGR), annualized quarter-to-quarter inflation rates (INFL), and annualized nominal interest rates (INT). The three series are measured in percentages and their relationship to the model variables is given by the following set of equations:

$$
\begin{aligned}
YGR_t &= \gamma^{(Q)} + 100(\hat{y}_t - \hat{y}_{t-1} + \hat{z}_t) \qquad (2.11)\\
INFL_t &= \pi^{(A)} + 400\hat{\pi}_t\\
INT_t &= \pi^{(A)} + r^{(A)} + 4\gamma^{(Q)} + 400\hat{R}_t.
\end{aligned}
$$

The parameters $\gamma^{(Q)}$, $\pi^{(A)}$, and $r^{(A)}$ are related to the steady states of the model economy as follows:

$$\gamma = 1 + \frac{\gamma^{(Q)}}{100}, \quad \beta = \frac{1}{1 + r^{(A)}/400}, \quad \pi = 1 + \frac{\pi^{(A)}}{400}.$$

The structural parameters are collected in the vector θ. Since in the first-order approximation the parameters ν and ϕ are not separately identifiable, we express the model in terms of κ, defined in (2.2). Let

$$\begin{aligned} \theta &= [\tau, \kappa, \psi_1, \psi_2, \rho_R, \rho_g, \rho_z, \quad (2.12) \\ &\quad r^{(A)}, \pi^{(A)}, \gamma^{(Q)}, \sigma_R, \sigma_g, \sigma_z]'. \end{aligned}$$

More generically, the measurement equation (2.11) can be expressed as

$$y_t = \Psi_0(\theta) + \Psi_1(\theta)t + \Psi_2(\theta)s_t + u_t, \quad (2.13)$$

where we allow for a vector of measurement errors u_t.[2]

Equations (2.10) and (2.13) provide a state-space representation for the linearized DSGE model. The challenge in evaluating the likelihood function is that the states s_t are (at least partially) unobserved. Let $X_{t_1:t_2} = \{x_{t_1}, x_{t_1+1}, \ldots, x_{t_2}\}$. The state-space representation provides a joint density for the observations and latent states given the parameters:

$$\begin{aligned} p(Y_{1:T}, S_{1:T}|\theta) &= \prod_{t=1}^{T} p(y_t, s_t|Y_{1:t-1}, S_{1:t-1}, \theta) \quad (2.14) \\ &= \prod_{t=1}^{T} p(y_t|s_t, \theta)p(s_t|s_{t-1}, \theta), \end{aligned}$$

where $p(y_t|s_t, \theta)$ and $p(s_t|s_{t-1}, \theta)$ represent the measurement and state-transition equations, respectively. However, Bayesian Inference has to be based on the likelihood function that

---

[2]The DSGE model solution method implies that certain linear combinations of model variables, namely $w_{2,t}$ in (2.7), are equal to zero. If some elements of $w_{2,t}$ only depend on variables that can be measured in the data, this implication is most likely violated. To cope with this problem, one can either limit the number of observables included in y_t, as we do in the New Keynesian model, or include so-called measurement errors as, for instance, in Sargent (1989), Altug (1989), and Ireland (2004).

is constructed only from the observables, $p(Y_{1:T}|\theta)$, which means that the hidden states $S_{1:T}$ have to be integrated out. A filter generates the sequence of conditional distributions $s_t|Y_{1:t}$ and densities $p(y_t|Y_{1:t-1}, \theta)$. In turn, the desired likelihood function can be obtained as:

$$p(Y_{1:T}|\theta) = \prod_{t=1}^{T} p(y_t|Y_{1:t-1}, \theta). \qquad (2.15)$$

Algorithm 1 (Generic Filter)

Let $p(s_0|Y_{1:0}, \theta) = p(s_0|\theta)$. For $t = 1$ to T:

1. *From iteration $t - 1$ we have $p(s_{t-1}|Y_{1:t-1}, \theta)$.*

2. *Forecasting t given $t - 1$:*

   (a) Transition equation:

   $$p(s_t|Y_{1:t-1}, \theta)$$
   $$= \int p(s_t|s_{t-1}, Y_{1:t-1}, \theta)p(s_{t-1}|Y_{1:t-1}, \theta)ds_{t-1}$$

   (b) Measurement equation:

   $$p(y_t|Y_{1:t-1}, \theta)$$
   $$= \int p(y_t|s_t, Y_{1:t-1}, \theta)p(s_t|Y_{1:t-1}, \theta)ds_t$$

3. *Updating with Bayes Theorem. Once y_t becomes available:*

   $$p(s_t|Y_{1:t}, \theta) = p(s_t|y_t, Y_{1:t-1}, \theta)$$
   $$= \frac{p(y_t|s_t, Y_{1:t-1}, \theta)p(s_t|Y_{1:t-1}, \theta)}{p(y_t|Y_{1:t-1}, \theta)}.$$

If the DSGE model is log-linearized and the errors are Gaussian, then the distributions that appear in Algorithm 1 are Gaussian. In this case the Kalman filter can be used to recursively compute the means and covariance matrices of these distributions and thereby to evaluate the likelihood function. Thus, to complete the model specification we make the following distributional assumptions about the distribution of the structural innovations ϵ_t, the measurement errors u_t, and the initial state s_0:

$$\epsilon_t \quad \sim \quad iidN(0, \Sigma_\epsilon), \quad u_t \sim iidN(0, \Sigma_u), \qquad (2.16)$$
$$s_0 \quad \sim \quad N(\bar{s}_{0|0}, P_{0|0}).$$

In stationary models it is common to assume that $\bar{s}_{0|0}$ and $P_{0|0}$ correspond to the invariant distribution associated with the law of motion of s_t in (2.10). The four conditional distributions in the description of Algorithm 1 for a linear Gaussian state-space model are summarized in Table 2.1. Detailed derivations can be found in textbook treatments of the Kalman filter, e.g., Hamilton (1994) or Durbin and Koopman (2001).

2.3 Priors

Bayesian Inference combines the likelihood function with a prior distribution to form a posterior distribution. Prior distributions are used to describe the state of knowledge about the parameter vector θ before observing the sample Y. They play an important role in the estimation of DSGE models because they allow researchers to incorporate information not contained in the estimation sample into the empirical analysis. For concreteness, consider the small-scale New Keynesian DSGE model with parameter vector θ defined in (2.12). The specification of a joint probability distribution for a 13-dimensional parameter vector may appear to be a daunting task.

As a first step in the elicitation of a prior distribution, it is useful to group the elements of θ into three different categories (see Del Negro and Schorfheide (2008)). The first group, denoted by $\theta_{(ss)}$, contains parameters that affect the steady state of the DSGE model. In the small-scale New Keynesian model $\theta_{(ss)} = [r^{(A)}, \pi^{(A)}, \gamma^{(Q)}]'$. These three parameters determine the steady state real interest rate, inflation rate, and overall growth rate of the economy. The second group of parameters characterizes the law of motion of the exogenous shock processes: $\theta_{(exo)} = [\rho_g, \rho_z, \sigma_g, \sigma_z, \sigma_R]'$. Finally, the last

Table 2.1: Conditional Distributions for Kalman Filter

	Distribution	Mean and Variance
$s_{t-1} \vert (Y_{1:t-1}, \theta)$	$N\left(\bar{s}_{t-1\vert t-1}, P_{t-1\vert t-1}\right)$	Given from Iteration $t-1$
$s_t \vert (Y_{1:t-1}, \theta)$	$N\left(\bar{s}_{t\vert t-1}, P_{t\vert t-1}\right)$	$\bar{s}_{t\vert t-1} = \Phi_1 \bar{s}_{t-1\vert t-1}$
		$P_{t\vert t-1} = \Phi_1 P_{t-1\vert t-1} \Phi_1' + \Phi_\epsilon \Sigma_\epsilon \Phi_\epsilon'$
$y_t \vert (Y_{1:t-1}, \theta)$	$N\left(\bar{y}_{t\vert t-1}, F_{t\vert t-1}\right)$	$\bar{y}_{t\vert t-1} = \Psi_0 + \Psi_1 t + \Psi_2 \bar{s}_{t\vert t-1}$
		$F_{t\vert t-1} = \Psi_2 P_{t\vert t-1} \Psi_2' + \Sigma_u$
$s_t \vert (Y_{1:t}, \theta)$	$N\left(\bar{s}_{t\vert t}, P_{t\vert t}\right)$	$\bar{s}_{t\vert t} = \bar{s}_{t\vert t-1} + P_{t\vert t-1} \Psi_2' F_{t\vert t-1}^{-1} \left(y_t - \bar{y}_{t\vert t-1}\right)$
		$P_{t\vert t} = P_{t\vert t-1} - P_{t\vert t-1} \Psi_2' F_{t\vert t-1}^{-1} \Psi_2 P_{t\vert t-1}$

group of parameters controls the endogenous propagation mechanisms without affecting the steady state of the model: $\theta_{(endo)} = [\tau, \kappa, \psi_1, \psi_2, \rho_R]'$.

Once the parameters are grouped into the three categories, one can contemplate *a priori* plausible ranges for these parameters. While priors could in principle be formed by pure introspection, in reality most priors (as well as most model specifications) are based on some empirical observations. To indicate this dependence on non-sample (meaning other than Y) information, we could write $p(\theta|\mathcal{X}^0)$ instead of $p(\theta)$, but for notational convenience we omit the dependence on $\mathcal{X}^0$. The tacit assumption underlying posterior inference with a prior that is constructed (at least in part) from non-sample information is that $p(Y|\mathcal{X}^0, \theta) \approx p(Y|\theta)$, that is, the two sources of information are approximately independent conditional on θ. This assumption is a reasonable approximation if the observations in $\mathcal{X}^0$ pre-date the observations in Y or if Y consists of macroeconomic time series and $\mathcal{X}^0$ contains micro-level data from an overlapping time period.

Priors for $\theta_{(ss)}$ are often based on pre-sample averages. For instance, if the estimation sample starts in 1983:I, the prior distribution for $r^{(A)}$, $\pi^{(A)}$, and $\gamma^{(Q)}$ may be informed by data from the 1970s. Priors for $\theta_{(endo)}$ may be partly based on microeconometric evidence. For instance, in a version of the New Keynesian model that replaces the quadratic price adjustment costs with a Calvo mechanism (intermediate good producers can re-optimize their prices with an exogenous probability $1 - \zeta_p$ and are unable to change their prices with probability ζ_p), the slope of the Phillips curve κ is related to the frequency of price changes, which can be measured from micro-level data. Ríos-Rull, Schorfheide, Fuentes-Albero, Kryshko, and Santaeulalia-Llopis (2012) provide a very detailed discussion of the prior elicitation for a Frisch labor supply elasticity (a parameter that is implicitly set to infinity in the small-scale New Keynesian DSGE model).

Priors for $\theta_{(exo)}$ are the most difficult to specify, because the exogenous processes tend to be unobserved. Del Negro and Schorfheide (2008) suggest to elicit priors for $\theta_{(exo)}$ indirectly. Conditional on $\theta_{(ss)}$ and $\theta_{(endo)}$, the exogenous shock parameters determine the volatility and persistence of y_t.

Thus, beliefs—possibly informed by pre-sample observations—about the volatility, autocorrelations, and cross-correlation of output growth, inflation, and interest rates, could be mapped into beliefs about the persistence and volatility of the exogenous shocks. This could be achieved by an iterative procedure in which (i) a prior for θ_{exo} is specified; (ii) draws are generated from this prior; (iii) data y_t are simulated from the DSGE model and sample moments are computed based on the simulated trajectories; (iv) the plausibility of the prior predictive distribution of the sample moment is assessed and the prior for θ is adjusted until the prior predictive distribution of the sample moment is consistent with the prior beliefs.

After one has determined a plausible range for each of the DSGE model parameters, one has to represent the *a priori* beliefs by probability distributions. In most applications in the DSGE model literature, researchers start by choosing a family of probability distributions for each element of θ. Distributions are often chosen based on the domain of the parameters. For instance, prior distributions for parameters on the real line could be Normal, priors for non-negative parameters could be log Normal, Gamma, or Inverse Gamma, and priors for parameters on a bounded interval could follow a truncated normal or a Beta distribution. The distributions are typically parameterized such that the plausible range for each parameter corresponds to a 90% or 95% credible interval. A joint prior distribution for θ could then be obtained from the product of marginal distributions, possibly truncated to ensure the existence of a unique stable DSGE model solution over the domain of the prior.

Generating prior distributions for a high-dimensional parameter vector as the product of marginal distributions could have undesirable consequences. While each of the marginal distributions may appear plausible in view of the non-sample information $\mathcal{X}^0$, the joint prior may place a lot of mass on parameter combinations that imply implausible dynamics of the DSGE model. For instance, in the SW model the capital-output ratio and the consumption-output ratio are complicated functions of the households' discount factor, the capital share parameter in a Cobb-Douglas production function, and the capital depreciation rate. Seemingly plausible marginal distributions for these three parameters could generate an implausible (i.e., inconsistent with pre-sample evidence) prior distribution for the implied steady state ratios. This problem can be partly circumvented by re-parameterizing the DSGE model in terms of steady states rather than $\theta_{(ss)}$.

In general, it is good practice to generate draws from the prior distribution of θ; compute important transformations of θ such as steady-state ratios and possibly impulse-response functions or variance decompositions; and examine the implied prior distributions for economically important nonlinear transformations of θ. Moreover, as mentioned above, conditional on the draws of θ from the prior, one should simulate trajectories for y_t from the DSGE model and calculate sample moments of interest to understand the implications of the θ prior. In an informal iterative procedure, the prior for θ could be respecified until the implied prior for important parameter transformations and the sample moments of simulated data have the desired features. To some extent, such an iterative procedure can be replaced by the approach proposed in Del Negro and Schorfheide (2008), which represents beliefs about steady states and the dynamics of the endogenous variables through artificial dummy observations.

Table 2.2 summarizes the prior distribution that we will use for the estimation of the small-scale New Keynesian DSGE model. Similar priors have been used elsewhere in the empirical DSGE model literature. The priors for the steady state parameters are based on averages of output growth, inflation, and interest rates from a pre-1983:I sample. While presample averages determine the location of the prior distribution, e.g., its mean, some judgment is required in the specification of the standard deviations. The prior standard deviations partly reflect estimation uncertainty and partly data uncertainty. For instance, estimates of average inflation and real rates are sensitive to the choice of interest and inflation rate series.

The prior credible interval for the risk-aversion parameter τ covers logarithmic preferences and a risk-aversion of up to $\tau = 3$. It excludes the very large values that are often used in the asset-pricing literature because we are not trying to match the equity premium with this model. We as-

Table 2.2: Prior Distribution

Name	Domain	Prior		
		Density	Para (1)	Para (2)
Steady State Related Parameters $\theta_{(ss)}$				
$r^{(A)}$	$\mathbb{R}^+$	Gamma	0.50	0.50
$\pi^{(A)}$	$\mathbb{R}^+$	Gamma	7.00	2.00
$\gamma^{(Q)}$	$\mathbb{R}$	Normal	0.40	0.20
Endogenous Propagation Parameters $\theta_{(endo)}$				
τ	$\mathbb{R}^+$	Gamma	2.00	0.50
κ	$[0,1]$	Uniform	0.00	1.00
ψ_1	$\mathbb{R}^+$	Gamma	1.50	0.25
ψ_2	$\mathbb{R}^+$	Gamma	0.50	0.25
ρ_R	$[0,1)$	Uniform	0.00	1.00
Exogenous Shock Parameters $\theta_{(exo)}$				
ρ_G	$[0,1)$	Uniform	0.00	1.00
ρ_Z	$[0,1)$	Uniform	0.00	1.00
$100\sigma_R$	$\mathbb{R}^+$	InvGamma	0.40	4.00
$100\sigma_G$	$\mathbb{R}^+$	InvGamma	1.00	4.00
$100\sigma_Z$	$\mathbb{R}^+$	InvGamma	0.50	4.00

Notes: Marginal prior distributions for each DSGE model parameter. Para (1) and Para (2) list the means and the standard deviations for Beta, Gamma, and Normal distributions; the upper and lower bound of the support for the Uniform distribution; s and ν for the Inverse Gamma distribution, where $p_{\mathcal{IG}}(\sigma|\nu, s) \propto \sigma^{-\nu-1}e^{-\nu s^2/2\sigma^2}$. The joint prior distribution of θ is truncated at the boundary of the determinacy region.

sume a uniform distribution for the slope coefficient κ of the Phillips curve, which covers both very flat as well as very steep Phillips curves. The priors for the parameters of the monetary policy rule are loosely centered around values typically associated with the Taylor rule. While many researchers use Beta distributions centered around 0.8 or 0.9 for the autocorrelation coefficients of the exogenous shocks, we are using uniform distributions for the small-scale New Keynesian model. Finally, the distributions for the innovation standard deviations of the exogenous shock processes are chosen to obtain realistic magnitudes for the volatilities of output growth, inflation, and interest rates. The low degree of freedom of the inverse Gamma distributions creates fairly dispersed priors for the σ-s. The joint prior distribution is the product of the marginal densities. The domain of the prior is truncated to ensure that the linearized rational expectations model has a unique stable solution.

Chapter 3

A Crash Course in Bayesian Inference

In a Bayesian setting the calculus of probability is used to characterize and update an individual's state of knowledge or degree of beliefs with respect to quantities such as model parameters or future observations. The prior distribution $p(\theta)$ discussed in the previous section is meant to describe the initial state of knowledge about the model parameter vector θ—before observing the sample Y, e.g., data on output growth, inflation, and nominal interest rates. The Bayesian approach prescribes consistency among the beliefs held by an individual and their reasonable relation to any kind of objective data. Learning about θ takes place by updating the prior distribution in light of the data Y. The likelihood function $p(Y|\theta)$ summarizes the information about the parameter contained in the sample Y. According to Bayes Theorem, the conditional distribution of θ given Y is given by

$$p(\theta|Y) = \frac{p(Y|\theta)p(\theta)}{p(Y)}. \tag{3.1}$$

This distribution is called posterior distribution. The term in the denominator is called marginal likelihood. It is defined as

$$p(Y) = \int p(Y|\theta)p(\theta)d\theta \tag{3.2}$$

and normalizes the posterior density such that it integrates to one.

In a nutshell, Bayesian inference amounts to characterizing properties of the posterior distribution $p(\theta|Y)$. Unfortunately, for many interesting models, including the DSGE models considered in this book, it is not possible to evaluate the moments and quantiles of the posterior $p(\theta|Y)$ analytically. In general, we are only able to numerically evaluate the prior density $p(\theta)$ and the likelihood function $p(Y|\theta)$. In order to compute posterior quantiles and moments of functions $h(\theta)$ we have to rely on numerical techniques. Throughout this book we will use posterior samplers that generate sequences of draws θ^i, $i = 1, \ldots, N$ from $p(\theta|Y)$. The algorithms are designed such that they only require the evaluation of prior density and likelihood function, which appear in the numerator of (3.1), but not the marginal likelihood that appears in the denominator. We will show that (Monte Carlo) averages of these draws typically satisfy a strong law of large numbers (SLLN) and often also a central limit theorem (CLT). The SLLN provides a formal justification for using averages of posterior draws to approximate posterior means and the CLT gives a characterization of the accuracy of this approximation.

While this chapter is not meant to be a substitute for a textbook treatment of Bayesian econometrics (see, for instance, Koop (2003), Lancaster (2004), or Geweke (2005)), we nonetheless try to provide a self-contained review of Bayesian inference and decision making. We begin in Section 3.1 with a discussion of Bayesian inference for a simple autoregressive (AR) model, which takes the form of a Gaussian linear regression. For this model, the posterior distribution can be characterized analytically and closed-form expressions for its moments are readily available. Draws from the posterior distribution can be easily generated using a direct sampling algorithm. Section 3.2 discusses how to turn posterior distributions—or draws from posterior distributions—into point estimates, interval estimates, forecasts, and how to solve general decision problems. In Section 3.3 we modify the parameterization of an AR(1) model to introduce some identification problems. Lack of or weak identification of key structural parameters is a common occurrence in the context of DSGE models. In our AR(1) example the posterior distribution of the parameter of interest becomes non-Gaussian, and sampling from this posterior is now less straightforward. We proceed by introducing two important posterior samplers. In Chapters 4 and 5 we will employ variants of these samplers to implement the Bayesian analysis of DSGE models.

Section 3.4 focuses on importance sampling, whereas Section 3.5 provides an introduction to the Metropolis-Hastings algorithm.

3.1 The Posterior of a Linear Gaussian Model

We illustrate some of the mechanics of Bayesian inference in the context of the following AR(p) model:

$$y_t = \theta_1 y_{t-1} + \ldots + \theta_p y_{t-p} + u_t, \quad u_t | Y_{1:t-1} \sim iidN(0,1), \quad (3.3)$$

for $t = 1, \ldots, T$. Let $\theta = [\theta_1, \ldots, \theta_p]'$. Conditional on the initial observations $y_{1-p:0}$ the likelihood function is of the form

$$p(Y_{1:T} | Y_{1-p:0}, \theta) \qquad (3.4)$$

$$= \prod_{t=1}^{T} p(y_t | Y_{1:t-1}, Y_{1-p:0}, \theta)$$

$$= (2\pi)^{-T/2} \exp\left\{ -\frac{1}{2}(Y - X\theta)'(Y - X\theta) \right\},$$

where $Y_{1:t} = \{y_1, \ldots, y_t\}$ and the $T \times 1$ matrices Y and X are composed of the elements y_t and $x_t' = [y_{t-1}, \ldots, y_{t-p}]$. Let $\mathcal{I}$ denote the identity matrix. Suppose the prior distribution is of the form

$$\theta \sim N\left(0, \tau^2 \mathcal{I}\right) \qquad (3.5)$$

with density

$$p(\theta) = (2\pi\tau^2)^{-p/2} \exp\left\{ -\frac{1}{2\tau^2}\theta'\theta \right\}. \qquad (3.6)$$

The hyperparameter τ controls the variance of the prior distribution and can be used to illustrate the effect of the prior variance on the posterior distribution.

According to Bayes Theorem the posterior distribution of θ is proportional ($\propto$) to the product of prior density and likelihood function

$$p(\theta|Y) \propto p(\theta)p(Y|\theta). \qquad (3.7)$$

To simplify the notation we dropped $Y_{1-p:0}$ from the conditioning set and we replaced $y_{1:t}$ by the matrix Y. Absorbing terms that do not depend on θ into the proportionality constant, the right-hand side of (3.7) can be written as

$$p(\theta)p(Y|\theta) \propto \exp\left\{ -\frac{1}{2}[Y'Y - \theta'X'Y - Y'X\theta \right. \quad (3.8)$$

$$\left. -\theta'X'X\theta - \tau^{-2}\theta'\theta] \right\}.$$

Straightforward algebraic manipulations let us express the exponential term as

$$
\begin{aligned}
Y'Y &- \theta'X'Y - Y'X\theta - \theta'X'X\theta - \tau^{-2}\theta'\theta \quad (3.9)\\
&= \left(\theta - (X'X + \tau^{-2}\mathcal{I})^{-1}X'Y\right)'\left(X'X + \tau^{-2}\mathcal{I}\right)\\
&\quad \times \left(\theta - (X'X + \tau^{-2}\mathcal{I})^{-1}X'Y\right)\\
&\quad + Y'Y - Y'X(X'X + \tau^{-2}\mathcal{I})^{-1}X'Y.
\end{aligned}
$$

Note that the terms in the last line of (3.9) do not depend on θ and after taking an exponential transformation can be absorbed in the proportionality constant in (3.8). Because the term in the second line of (3.9) is a quadratic function of θ, we can deduce that the posterior distribution is Normal

$$\theta|Y \sim \mathcal{N}(\bar{\theta}, \bar{V}_\theta). \quad (3.10)$$

The posterior mean and covariance matrix are given by

$$\bar{\theta} = (X'X + \tau^{-2}\mathcal{I})^{-1}X'Y, \quad \bar{V}_\theta = (X'X + \tau^{-2}\mathcal{I})^{-1}.$$

The posterior mean of θ can be expressed as a weighted average of the maximum likelihood estimator (MLE), given by $\hat{\theta}_{mle} = (X'X)^{-1}X'Y$, and the prior mean, which is equal to zero:

$$\bar{\theta} = (X'X + \tau^{-2}\mathcal{I})^{-1}\left(X'X\hat{\theta}_{mle} + \tau^{-2} \cdot 0\right). \quad (3.11)$$

The weights depend on the information contents of the likelihood function, $X'X$, and the prior precision τ^{-2}. To better understand the properties of the posterior distribution, we can conduct two thought experiments. In the first thought experiment we hold the data fixed and consider a change in the prior distribution. A decrease in the prior variance

τ shifts the posterior mean toward the prior mean and reduces the posterior variance. Vice versa, an increase in τ
makes the prior distribution more diffuse and shifts the posterior mean toward the maximum of the likelihood function.
As $\tau \longrightarrow \infty$, the posterior variance approaches the negative
inverse Hessian of the log-likelihood function evaluated at the
MLE, which is given by $(X'X)^{-1}$. In the second thought experiment, we hold the prior distribution fixed and increase
the sample size. If $|\theta| < 1$, then $X'X/T$ is convergent in prob-
ability as the sample size $T \longrightarrow \infty$. Suppose we divide the
terms in parentheses on the right-hand side of (3.11) by T,
then we can deduce that the discrepancy between the posterior mean and the MLE converges in probability to zero. Thus,
the influence of the prior distribution on the posterior mean
vanishes as the sample size increases.

In our derivation of the posterior distribution we have de-
liberately ignored all the normalization constants and only
focused on terms that depend on θ. This approach served us
well because based on the general shape of the posterior density we were able to determine that it belongs to the family
of Gaussian densities, for which the normalization constants
are well known. We can use this information to easily derive
the marginal data density $p(Y)$ that appears in the denominator of Bayes Theorem in (3.1). Write

$$
\begin{aligned}
p(Y) &= \frac{p(Y|\theta)p(\theta)}{p(\theta|Y)} \qquad\qquad (3.12) \\
&= \exp\left\{-\frac{1}{2}[Y'Y - Y'X(X'X + \tau^{-2}\mathcal{I})^{-1}X'Y]\right\} \\
&\quad \times (2\pi)^{-T/2}|1 + \tau^2 X'X|^{-1/2}.
\end{aligned}
$$

The second expression on the right-hand side is obtained by
replacing $p(Y|\theta)$, $p(\theta)$, and $p(\theta|Y)$ in the first line by (3.4),
(3.6), and the probability density function (pdf) of the Gaus-
sian posterior distribution in (3.10), respectively.

The exponential term in (3.12) measures the goodness-of-
fit, whereas $|1 + \tau^2 X'X|$ is a penalty for model complexity. If τ
is close to zero, our model has essentially no free parameters
because the tight prior distribution forces the posterior to be
close to zero as well. In this case the goodness-of-fit term

tends to be small but the penalty for model complexity is also small. If, on the other hand, τ is large, then the goodness-of-fit term is large, as it approximately equals (minus) the sum of squared residuals from an OLS regression. The penalty tends to be large as well. Thus, neither specifications with a very concentrated prior or a very diffuse prior tend to be associated with a high marginal data density.

Now suppose that τ is fixed and the sample size T tends to infinity. In this case $1/\tau^2$ is negligible and the goodness-of-fit term corresponds to the sum-of-squared residuals associated with the MLE estimator. Under the assumption that the autoregressive process is stationary and $X'X/T \xrightarrow{a.s.} \mathbb{E}[x_t x_t']$, we can approximate the log penalty term as $-(1/2)\ln|1 + \tau^2 X'X| \approx -(p/2)\ln T - (1/2)\ln|1/T + \tau^2 \mathbb{E}[x_t x_t']|$. The combination of the log goodness-of-fit term with the dominating term of the penalty, $-(p/2)\ln T$, delivers the Schwarz (1978) model selection criterion, which penalizes models by the number of estimated parameters. Thus, the marginal data density incorporates a penalty for estimated model parameters. Marginal data density plays an important role in the computation of posterior model probabilities. A detailed discussion will be provided in the next section.

To economize on notation we often abbreviate posterior distributions $p(\theta|Y)$ by $\pi(\theta)$ and posterior expectations of a function $h(\theta)$ by

$$\mathbb{E}_\pi[h] = \mathbb{E}_\pi[h(\theta)] = \int h(\theta)\pi(\theta)d\theta = \int h(\theta)p(\theta|Y)d\theta. \quad (3.13)$$

The remainder of this book focuses on comparing algorithms that generate draws $\{\theta^i\}_{i=1}^N$ from posterior distributions of parameters in DSGE models. These draws can then be transformed into objects of interest, $h(\theta^i)$, and a Monte Carlo average of the form

$$\bar{h}_N = \frac{1}{N} \sum_{i=1}^N h(\theta^i) \quad (3.14)$$

may be used to approximate the posterior expectation of $\mathbb{E}_\pi[h]$. For the approximation to be useful, it should satisfy a a SLLN and a CLT. In the simple linear regression model with Gaussian posterior given by (3.10) it is possible to sample directly from the posterior distribution and obtain independently and identically distributed (iid) draws from $\pi(\cdot)$.

Algorithm 2 (Direct Sampling) *For $i = 1$ to N, draw θ^i from $N(\bar{\theta}, \bar{V}_\theta)$.*

Provided that $\mathbb{V}_\pi[h(\theta)] < \infty$ we can deduce from Kolmogorov's SLLN and the Lindeberg-Levy CLT that

$$\bar{h}_N \xrightarrow{a.s.} \mathbb{E}_\pi[h]$$
$$\sqrt{N}\left(\bar{h}_N - \mathbb{E}_\pi[h]\right) \implies N\left(0, \mathbb{V}_\pi[h(\theta)]\right). \qquad (3.15)$$

Thus, the posterior variance of $h(\theta)$, scaled by $1/N$, determines the accuracy of the Monte Carlo approximation. In the context of DSGE models, direct iid sampling from the posterior is generally infeasible and the variance of the Monte Carlo approximation is (much) larger than $\mathbb{V}_\pi[h(\theta)]/N$. Below, we will use the ratio of the actual variance to the infeasible variance $\mathbb{V}_\pi[h(\theta)]/N$ as a measure of efficiency of an algorithm.

3.2 Bayesian Inference and Decision Making

The posterior distribution $p(\theta|Y)$ summarizes the information about θ after having observed the data Y and can be used for inference and decision making. From a Bayesian perspective it is optimal to make decisions that minimize the posterior expected loss of the decision maker. It turns out that many inferential problems, e.g., point or interval estimation, can be restated as decision problems. Let $\mathcal{L}(h(\theta), \delta)$ denote the loss function under which the decision δ is evaluated.[1] We are interested in deriving the decision rule $\delta^*(Y)$ that minimizes the posterior expected loss. In the remainder of this section we provide a brief overview of a decision-theoretic approach to Bayesian inference. A textbook treatment is provided by Robert (1994).

The posterior expected loss associated with a decision rule $\delta(Y)$ is given by

$$\rho\big(\delta(Y)|Y\big) = \int_\Theta \mathcal{L}\big(h(\theta), \delta(Y)\big)p(\theta|Y)d\theta. \qquad (3.16)$$

---

[1] Alternatively, the loss function could depend on future or counterfactual values of y_t, i.e., $\mathcal{L}(y_*, \delta)$.

Note that in this calculation the observations Y are fixed and we are integrating over the unknown parameter θ under the posterior distribution. A Bayes decision is a decision that minimizes the posterior expected loss:

$$\delta^*(Y) = \text{argmin}_{\delta \in \mathcal{D}} \ \rho(\delta|Y). \tag{3.17}$$

Because all calculations are conditional on Y, we simply write δ instead of $\delta(Y)$ from now on. For some decision problems, e.g., point estimation under a quadratic loss function (see below), it is possible to solve for δ^* analytically, expressing the optimal decision as a function of moments or quantiles of the posterior distribution of θ. A Monte Carlo approximation can then be used to evaluate δ. For other decision problems it might not be feasible to derive δ^* analytically. In these cases one can replace the posterior risk for each choice of δ by a Monte Carlo approximation of the form

$$\bar{\rho}_N(\delta|Y) = \frac{1}{N} \sum_{i=1}^{N} \mathcal{L}\big(h(\theta^i), \delta\big), \tag{3.18}$$

where the θ^i's are draws from the posterior $p(\theta|Y)$. If the draws are generated by importance sampling, then the losses have to be reweighted using the importance weights as in (3.49) below. A numerical approximation to the Bayes decision $\delta^*(\cdot)$ is then given by

$$\delta_N^*(Y) = \text{argmin}_{\delta \in \mathcal{D}} \ \bar{\rho}_N\big(\delta(\cdot)|Y\big). \tag{3.19}$$

According to the frequentist large sample theory for extremum estimators (see for instance the textbook treatment in van der Vaart (1998)), $\delta_N^*(Y) \xrightarrow{a.s.} \delta^*(Y)$ provided that $\bar{\rho}_N(\delta|Y)$ converges to $\rho(\delta|Y)$ uniformly in δ as $N \longrightarrow \infty$.

3.2.1 Point Estimation

Suppose that $h(\theta)$ is scalar. The most widely used loss functions are the quadratic loss function $\mathcal{L}_2\big(h(\theta), \delta\big) = \big(h(\theta) - \delta\big)^2$ and the absolute error loss function $\mathcal{L}_1\big(h(\theta), \delta\big) = \big|h(\theta) - \delta\big|$. The Bayes estimator associated with the quadratic loss function is the posterior mean $\mathbb{E}_\pi[\theta]$ which can be approximated by the Monte Carlo average

$$\bar{h}_N = \frac{1}{N} \sum_{i=1}^{N} h(\theta^i). \tag{3.20}$$

The Bayes estimator associated with the absolute error loss function is the posterior median, which can be approximated by the sample median of the posterior draws $h(\theta^i)$.

3.2.2 Interval Estimation

Casting an interval estimation problem into a decision-theoretic framework requires a bit more work, because Bayesian interval estimates have to satisfy a constraint on the posterior coverage probability. Suppose that $h(\theta)$ is scalar. In this case the interval estimate could correspond to a single connected interval or a collection of disjoint intervals. In the former case, it consists of a lower bound δ_l and an upper bound δ_u. Let $\delta = [\delta_l, \delta_u]'$ and consider the following two-player game between the econometrician and an adversary. The econometrician chooses δ and the adversary chooses a scalar parameter $\lambda \in \mathbb{R}^-$. The econometrician's loss function is

$$\begin{aligned} &\mathcal{L}_E(\theta, \delta, \lambda) &(3.21)\\ &= \max_{\lambda \in \mathbb{R}^-} (\delta_u - \delta_l) + \lambda \big(\mathbb{I}\{\delta_l \le h(\theta) \le \delta_u\} - (1 - \alpha) \big) \end{aligned}$$

and the adversary's loss function is

$$\mathcal{L}_A(\theta, \delta, \lambda) = -\lambda \big(\mathbb{I}\{\delta_l \le h(\theta) \le \delta_u\} - (1 - \alpha) \big), \tag{3.22}$$

where $\mathbb{I}\{x \le a\}$ is the indicator function that equals one if $x \ge a$ and equals zero otherwise. If $\delta_l \le \theta \le \delta_u$ then the factor post-multiplying λ is positive for $\alpha > 0$ and the adversary minimizes his loss by setting $\lambda = 0$. Vice versa, if $h(\theta)$ is outside of the interval $[\delta_l, \delta_u]$, then the best choice for the adversary is to set $\lambda = -\infty$. The econometrician has an incentive to choose a short interval that covers $h(\theta)$.

Now suppose neither player knows $h(\theta)$ and both players minimize their posterior expected loss under the same distribution $p(h(\theta)|Y)$. Taking the optimal choice of the adversary as given, the posterior risk of the econometrician is given by

$$\rho(\delta_l(Y), \delta_u(Y)|Y) \tag{3.23}$$
$$= (\delta_u - \delta_l) + \max_{\lambda \in \mathbb{R}^-} \lambda(\mathbb{P}(\delta_l \leq h(\theta) \leq \delta_u|Y) - (1 - \alpha)).$$

The interval $[\delta_l(Y), \delta_u(Y)]$ that minimizes the posterior risk in (3.23) is the shortest *connected* interval with coverage probability $1 - \alpha$. The shortest connected interval can be computed based on equally weighted draws as follows: sort the draws $h(\theta^i)$ in ascending order to obtain the sequence $h^{(i)}$; for $i = 1$ to $\lfloor N\alpha \rfloor$ minimize $h^{(\lfloor N(1-\alpha) \rfloor + i)} - h^{(i)}$ with respect to i.

To allow for disjoint credible intervals, the difference $\delta_u - \delta_l$ in the above loss function has to be replaced by the sum of the lengths of the disjoint intervals. The credible interval that minimizes the posterior risk under the loss function that penalizes the total length of the disjoint segments has the property that $p(\delta_l|Y) = p(\delta_u|Y) = \kappa$. It is called the highest-posterior-density (HPD) set because the density of all values of θ that are included in this set exceeds the threshold κ. The HPD set is formally defined as $CS_{HPD} = \{h \, |p(h|Y) \geq \kappa\}$. The threshold κ is chosen to guarantee that the set has a $1 - \alpha$ coverage probability. If the posterior density is multi-modal then the HPD interval may consist of disjoint segments. If it does, the combined length of the disjoint intervals is smaller than the length of the shortest connected interval.

In practice researchers often replace the shortest connected credible interval or the HPD interval by equal-tail-probability sets that satisfy

$$\int_{-\infty}^{\delta_l} p(h|Y)d\theta = \int_{\delta_u}^{\infty} p(h|Y)d\theta = \alpha/2.$$

While these intervals tend to be longer than the other two intervals, they are easier to compute because δ_l and δ_u are simply the $\alpha/2$ and $1 - \alpha/2$ quantiles which can be obtained by solving the simplified quantile regression problem

$$\hat{\theta}_\tau = \text{argmin}_q \left[(1 - \tau) \frac{1}{N} \sum_{h(\theta^i) < q} (q - h(\theta^i)) \right. \tag{3.24}$$
$$\left. + \tau \frac{1}{N} \sum_{h(\theta^i) \geq q} (h(\theta^i) - q) \right]$$

for $\tau = \alpha/2$ and $\tau = 1 - \alpha/2$. The quantiles can also be computed directly by sorting the posterior draws θ^i.

3.2.3 Forecasting

In forecasting applications the argument $h(\theta)$ of the loss function is replaced by a future observation y_{T+h}: $L(y_{T+h}, \delta)$. Moreover, the expected loss is computed under the posterior predictive distribution $p(y_{T+h}|Y_{1:T})$. By setting $p = 1$ in (3.3) we obtain the AR(1) model and can write

$$y_{T+h} = \theta^h y_T + \sum_{s=0}^{h-1} \theta^s u_{T+h-s}, \qquad (3.25)$$

which implies that the h-step ahead conditional distribution of y_{T+h} is

$$y_{T+h}|(Y_{1:T}, \theta) \sim N\left(\theta^h y_T, \frac{1 - \theta^h}{1 - \theta}\right). \qquad (3.26)$$

To simplify the subsequent notation, we dropped the initial observations y_0 from the conditioning set. The posterior predictive density of y_{T+h} is obtained by integrating out θ using the posterior distribution $p(\theta|Y)$:

$$p(y_{T+h}|Y_{1:T}) = \int p(y_{T+h}|y_T, \theta)p(\theta|Y_{1:T})d\theta. \qquad (3.27)$$

Draws from the predictive distribution can be easily generated with the following algorithm:

Algorithm 3 (Sampling from Predictive Distribution) *For each draw θ^i from the posterior distribution $p(\theta|Y_{1:T})$ sample a sequence of innovations $u_{T+1}^i, \ldots, u_{T+h}^i$ and compute y_{T+h}^i as a function of θ^i, $u_{T+1}^i, \ldots, u_{T+h}^i$, and $Y_{1:T}$, e.g., according to (3.25).*

Moments and quantiles of the predictive distribution can be approximated based on the draws y_{T+h}^i. The posterior expected loss is given by

$$\rho(\delta|Y_{1:T}) = \int_{y_{T+h}} \mathcal{L}(y_{T+h}, \delta)p(y_{T+h}|Y_{1:T})dy_{T+h}, \qquad (3.28)$$

which can be approximated by the Monte Carlo average

$$\bar{\rho}(\delta|Y_{1:T}) = \frac{1}{N} \sum_{i=1}^{N} \mathcal{L}(y_{T+h}^i, \delta) \qquad (3.29)$$

under suitable regularity conditions. The convergence of this Monte Carlo average can be studied using the decomposition

$$\bar{\rho}(\delta|Y_{1:T}) - \rho(\delta|Y_{1:T}) \qquad (3.30)$$

$$= \frac{1}{N} \sum_{i=1}^{N} \mathcal{L}(y_{T+h}^i, \delta) - \mathbb{E}[\mathcal{L}(y_{T+h}^i, \delta)|\theta^i, Y_{1:T}]$$

$$+ \frac{1}{N} \sum_{i=1}^{N} \mathbb{E}[\mathcal{L}(y_{T+h}^i, \delta)|\theta^i, Y_{1:T}] - \rho(\delta|Y).$$

The first term is a Monte Carlo average of a function of the y_{T+h}^i draws conditional on the $\{\theta^i\}_{i=1}^N$ draws generated by Algorithm 3 and the second term is a Monte Carlo average of functions of θ^i. Point and interval predictions can be easily obtained by following the steps in the preceding subsections.

3.2.4 Model Selection and Averaging

The Bayesian framework is well suited to account for model uncertainty. In the context of the AR(p) model introduced in Section 3.1, there is uncertainty about the number of lags p. In the context of a DSGE model, a researcher might be uncertain whether price stickiness, wage stickiness, informational frictions, or monetary frictions are quantitatively important for business cycle fluctuations and policy interventions. To capture model uncertainty, a researcher can assign prior probabilities $\gamma_{j,0}$ to models M_j, $j = 1, \ldots, J$, which are then updated in view of the data Y. The posterior model probabilities are given by

$$\gamma_{j,T} = \frac{\gamma_{j,0} p(Y|M_j)}{\sum_{j=1}^{J} \gamma_{j,0} p(Y|M_j)}, \qquad (3.31)$$

where

$$p(Y|M_j) = \int p(Y|\theta_{(j)}, M_j) p(\theta_{(j)}|M_j) d\theta_{(j)}$$

is the marginal data density associated with model M_j. In the context of the AR(p) model, a formula for the marginal data density was given in (3.12). For models that cannot be cast in the form of a linear Gaussian regression model, the evaluation of the marginal data density often imposes computational challenges. We will discussion numerical approximations of $p(Y|M_j)$ in more detail in subsequent chapters.

The log marginal data density can be interpreted as the sum of one-step-ahead predictive scores. Adding time subscripts, we can write

$$\ln p(Y|M_j) \tag{3.32}$$
$$= \sum_{t=1}^{T} \ln \int p(y_t|\theta_{(j)}, Y_{1:t-1}, M_j) p(\theta_{(j)}|Y_{1:t-1}, M_j) d\theta_{(j)}.$$

The summands on the right-hand side provide a decomposition of the one-step-ahead predictive densities, which highlights that the inference about $\theta_{(j)}$ is based on time $t-1$ information, when making the prediction for y_t. The predictive score is small, whenever the predictive density assigns a low value to the observed y_t. If the predictive distribution is Gaussian, then the log score is a function of the mean-squared prediction error.

It is beyond the scope of this book to provide a general discussion of the use of posterior model probabilities for model comparison. An excellent survey is provided by Kass and Raftery (1995). We simply highlight a few issues that are important in DSGE model applications. Once the posterior model probabilities have been obtained, they can be used for model selection or averaging. Bayesian model selection typically refers to the solution of a decision problem in which the loss associated with selecting the correct model is zero and the loss associated with choosing an incorrect model is one. It can be verified that the solution that minimizes the posterior expected loss is to select the model with the highest posterior probability. Bayesian model selection assumes that the model space is complete, in the sense that one of the models included in the calculation of the posterior probabilities is believed to be the correct one. If one among the J models is randomly selected to generate a sequence of observations

$Y_{1:T}$, then under fairly general conditions the posterior probability assigned to that model will converge to one as $T \longrightarrow \infty$. An early version of this result for general linear regression models was proved by Halpern (1974). The result has subsequently been extended to other model classes and to account for misspecification of all models $M_1, \ldots, M_j$. For instance, Fernandez-Villaverde and Rubio-Ramirez (2004) show in the context of DSGE models that if all models are misspecified, the model that is closest in Kullback-Leibler distance to the "true" data generating process will asymptotically receive posterior probability one.

Bayesian model averaging (BMA) refers to a procedure in which posterior distributions from a single model are replaced by the mixture of distribution obtained by averaging across all available models, using the posterior model probabilities as weights. BMA was advocated by Leamer (1978) as a way of accounting for model uncertainty. Hoeting, Madigan, Raftery, and Volinsky (1999) provide a review of BMA techniques. Suppose that $h_j(\theta_{(j)})$ transforms the model-specific parameters into a common object, e.g., the impulse response to a monetary policy shock, then we can form

$$p(h|Y) = \sum_{j=1}^{J} \gamma_{j,T} p(h_j(\theta_{(j)})|Y, M_j). \qquad (3.33)$$

Similarly, the predictive distribution for a future observation y_{T+h} takes the form

$$p(y_{T+h}|Y_{1:T}) = \sum_{j=1}^{J} \gamma_{j,T} p(y_{T+h}|Y_{1:T}, M_j). \qquad (3.34)$$

Forecasting applications of Bayesian model averaging in the econometrics literature include, among others, Min and Zellner (1993) and Wright (2008). For example, Del Negro, Hasegawa, and Schorfheide (2014) compare density forecasts from a Bayesian model average of DSGE models with and without financial frictions to forecasts obtained by using alternative methods of combining predictive densities.

3.3 A Non-Gaussian Posterior of a Set-Identified Model

Unfortunately, in most applications posterior distributions are non-Gaussian and direct sampling is often impossible. Before studying the complicated posterior distributions that arise in DSGE model applications, we will take an intermediate step and consider a stylized set-identified model that leads to a non-Gaussian posterior distribution for its parameter θ. Considering an illustrative example in which point identification of θ fails is useful, because there are many DSGE model applications in which some of the structural parameters are difficult to identify or not at all identifiable. Identification problems in DSGE models typically come in two varieties: (i) local identification problems in which the likelihood function is fairly flat in certain directions of the parameter space; (ii) global identification problems in which the likelihood function is multi-modal. The example in this section is designed to showcase a problem in which the information in the likelihood function can at most deliver a lower and an upper bound on the parameter θ. The resulting posterior distribution is non-Gaussian and it remains non-Gaussian as the sample size increases. In Section 3.4 we will use the posterior of the set-identified model to illustrate the importance sampling algorithm.

Suppose that y_t follows an AR(1) process with autoregressive coefficient that we now denote by ϕ. However, unlike in Section 3.1, we now assume that the object of interest is not the autoregressive parameter, but instead a parameter θ that can be bounded based on ϕ as follows:

$$\phi \leq \theta \quad \text{and} \quad \theta \leq \phi + 1. \tag{3.35}$$

Strictly speaking, the parameter θ is set identified. The interval $\Theta(\phi) = [\phi, \ \phi + 1]$ is called the identified set and in this simple example its length is equal to one. To complete the model specification we specify a prior for θ conditional on ϕ of the form

$$\theta|\phi \sim U[\phi, \phi + 1]. \tag{3.36}$$

The joint posterior distribution of θ and ϕ can be characterized as follows:

$$p(\theta, \phi | Y) = p(\phi | Y) p(\theta | \phi, Y) \propto p(Y | \phi) p(\theta | \phi) p(\phi). \quad (3.37)$$

Because θ does not enter the likelihood function, we can deduce that

$$\begin{aligned} p(\phi | Y) &= \int p(\theta, \phi | Y) d\theta \propto \int p(Y | \phi) p(\theta | \phi) p(\phi) d\theta \\ &\propto p(Y | \phi) p(\phi). \end{aligned}$$

The second line follows from $\int p(\theta | \phi) d\theta = 1$ for all ϕ. Therefore,

$$p(\phi | Y) = \frac{p(Y | \phi) p(\phi)}{\int p(Y | \phi) p(\phi) d\phi}, \quad (3.38)$$

that is, the conditional distribution of $\theta | \phi$ has no influence on the posterior distribution of ϕ. Moreover,

$$\begin{aligned} p(\theta | \phi, Y) &\propto p(\theta, \phi | Y) \propto p(Y | \phi) p(\theta | \phi) p(\phi) \\ &\propto p(\theta | \phi). \end{aligned}$$

Because $p(\theta | \phi)$ is a properly normalized conditional density, we deduce that

$$p(\theta | \phi, Y) = p(\theta | \phi), \quad (3.39)$$

that is, the distribution of θ conditional on ϕ is not updated in view of the sample information Y, because the parameter θ does not enter the likelihood function.

According to (3.10) the posterior distribution of the AR(1) parameter ϕ (recall that the AR(1) model is now parameterized in terms of ϕ: $y_t = \phi y_{t-1} + u_t$) takes the form $\phi | Y \sim N(\bar{\phi}, \bar{V}_\phi)$. We showed in (3.39) that the posterior distribution of θ conditional on ϕ is simply equal to the prior distribution of θ, which is uniform on the set $\Theta(\phi)$ (see (3.36)). Thus, the marginal posterior distribution of θ is given by

$$\begin{aligned} \pi(\theta) &= \int p(\phi | Y) \mathbb{I}\{\phi \le \theta \le \phi + 1\} d\phi \quad (3.40) \\ &= \int_{\theta-1}^{\theta} p(\phi | Y) d\phi \\ &= \Phi_N \left(\frac{\theta - \bar{\phi}}{\sqrt{\bar{V}_\phi}} \right) - \Phi_N \left(\frac{\theta - 1 - \bar{\phi}}{\sqrt{\bar{V}_\phi}} \right), \end{aligned}$$

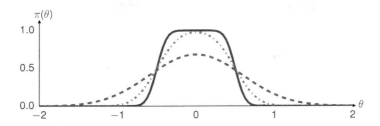

Figure 3.1: Posterior Distribution for Set-Identified Model. The figure depicts the posterior distribution $\pi(\theta)$ in (3.40) for $\bar{\phi} = -0.5$ and $\bar{V}_\phi$ equal to $1/4$ (dotted), $1/20$ (dashed), and $1/100$ (solid).

where $\Phi_N(x)$ is the cumulative density function of a $N(0,1)$ and $\mathbb{I}\{x \le a\}$ is the indicator function that equals one if $x \le a$.

Figure 3.1 depicts the posterior of θ for three choices of $\bar{V}_\phi$. If the posterior variance of the reduced-form parameter ϕ is large, the posterior looks almost Gaussian. However, as $\bar{V}_\phi$ decreases, the posterior starts to resemble the shape of a step function that increases from zero to one at $\theta = -0.5$ and then drops to zero around $\theta = 0.5$. The flatness of the posterior density on the interval $[\bar{\phi}, \bar{\phi} + 1]$ gets more pronounced as the sample size increases and the uncertainty about the parameter ϕ vanishes. In this stylized example, it is possible to sample from the posterior distribution of θ directly by first sampling $\phi^i \sim N(\bar{\phi}, \bar{V}_\phi)$ and then sampling $\theta^i | \phi^i \sim U[\phi^i, \phi^i + 1]$. This scheme generates *iid* draws from the joint posterior $(\phi, \theta)|Y$. The θ^i draws can then be used to construct Monte Carlo approximations for moments associated with the marginal posterior distribution $\theta|Y$. As an alternative to direct sampling we will use the posterior in (3.40) to illustrate the importance sampling algorithm introduced in the next section. Importance sampling is an important building block of the sequential Monte Carlo algorithm considered in Chapter 5.

3.4 Importance Sampling

Instead of attempting to sample directly from the posterior $\pi(\theta)$ in (3.40), we could approximate $\pi(\cdot)$ by using a different, tractable density $g(\theta)$ that is easy to sample from and then reweight the draws. This approach is called importance sampling, a term due to Hammersley and Handscomb (1964) who were among the first to propose the method. Kloek and van Dijk (1978) introduced importance sampling into the econometrics literature, and Geweke (1989) studies the asymptotic properties of importance sampling approximations. Because in many applications the posterior density can only be evaluated up to a constant of proportionality, we write

$$\pi(\theta) = \frac{f(\theta)}{Z}. \tag{3.41}$$

Typically, $f(\theta)$ corresponds to the product of likelihood function and prior density $p(Y|\theta)p(\theta)$ in the numerator of Bayes Theorem (3.1) and Z corresponds to the marginal likelihood $p(Y)$ in the denominator. We subsequently describe the importance sampling algorithm, discuss the convergence of posterior mean approximations as the number of draws from this algorithm tends to infinity, and provide a numerical illustration based on the set-identified model introduced in Section 3.3. The basic idea of importance sampling is, of course, completely unrelated to the identification problem discussed in the previous section. In Chapter 5 we will embed an importance sampler in a more general sequential Monte Carlo algorithm that allows us to generate draws from very complicated DSGE model posteriors.

3.4.1 The Importance Sampling Algorithm

Importance sampling (IS) is based on the following identity:

$$\mathbb{E}_\pi[h(\theta)] = \int h(\theta)\pi(\theta)d\theta = \frac{1}{Z}\int_\Theta h(\theta)\frac{f(\theta)}{g(\theta)}g(\theta)d\theta. \tag{3.42}$$

Because $\mathbb{E}_\pi[1] = 1$ we can deduce that the normalization constant Z is given by

$$Z = \int_\Theta \frac{f(\theta)}{g(\theta)}g(\theta)d\theta. \tag{3.43}$$

The ratio

$$w(\theta) = \frac{f(\theta)}{g(\theta)} \tag{3.44}$$

is called the (unnormalized) importance weight. We can also define a normalized importance weight as

$$v(\theta) = \frac{w(\theta)}{\int w(\theta)g(\theta)d\theta} = \frac{w(\theta)}{\int Z\pi(\theta)d\theta} = \frac{w(\theta)}{Z}. \tag{3.45}$$

It is straightforward to verify based on (3.42) and the definition in (3.44) that

$$\mathbb{E}_\pi[h(\theta)] = \int v(\theta)h(\theta)g(\theta)d\theta. \tag{3.46}$$

The importance sampling algorithm generates iid draws from the proposal density $g(\theta)$. These draws are reweighted by $w(\theta)$ and the average of the importance weights can be used to approximate the normalization constant Z.

Algorithm 4 (Importance Sampling)

1. *For $i = 1$ to N, draw $\theta^i \stackrel{iid}{\sim} g(\theta)$ and compute the unnormalized importance weights*

$$w^i = w(\theta^i) = \frac{f(\theta^i)}{g(\theta^i)}. \tag{3.47}$$

2. *Compute the normalized importance weights*

$$W^i = \frac{w^i}{\frac{1}{N}\sum_{i=1}^N w^i}. \tag{3.48}$$

An approximation of $\mathbb{E}_\pi[h(\theta)]$ is given by

$$\bar{h}_N = \frac{1}{N}\sum_{i=1}^N W^i h(\theta^i). \tag{3.49}$$

Note that according to our definitions W^i is different from $v(\theta^i)$. W^i is normalized by the sample average of the unnormalized weights w^i, whereas $v(\theta)$ is normalized by the population normalization constant Z. By construction, the sample average $\frac{1}{N}\sum_{i=1}^N W^i = 1$.

3.4.2 Convergence and Accuracy

Throughout this book we will discuss the accuracy of Monte Carlo approximations of posterior moments. In practice, one can assess the accuracy by computing a Monte Carlo approximation $\bar{h}_N$ multiple times and examine its variability across repeated runs of the posterior sampler. If $\bar{h}_N$ satisfies a CLT and the number of draws N is sufficiently large, then the variance across repeated runs of the algorithm (provided this variance is finite for the given N) will approximately coincide with the asymptotic variance implied by the CLT. Moreover, this variance will decay at rate $1/N$. Combined with some information about the run time of the posterior sampler, the user will be able to trade off computational accuracy and time. We provide a discussion of CLTs for various posterior samplers and use repeated independent runs to document their accuracy in practical application. We start with a relatively detailed derivation of a CLT for the importance sampler and then, in later chapters, provide a more informal discussion for the more elaborate posterior samplers.

If $\mathbb{E}_g[|hf/g|] < \infty$ and $\mathbb{E}_g[|f/g|] < \infty$, see Geweke (1989), the Monte Carlo estimate $\bar{h}_N$ defined in (3.49) converges almost surely (a.s.) to $E_\pi[h(\theta)]$ as $N \longrightarrow \infty$. In Chapter 5 we will refer to the collection of pairs $\{(\theta^i, W^i)\}_{i=1}^N$ as a particle approximation of $\pi(\theta)$. The accuracy of the approximation is driven by the "closeness" of $g(\cdot)$ to $f(\cdot)$ and is reflected in the distribution of the weights. If the distribution of weights is very uneven, the Monte Carlo approximation $\bar{h}$ is inaccurate. Uniform weights arise if $g(\cdot) \propto f(\cdot)$, which means that we are sampling directly from $\pi(\theta)$.

The limit distribution of the Monte Carlo approximation can be derived as follows. Define the population analogue of the normalized importance weights as $v(\theta) = w(\theta)/Z$ and write

$$\bar{h}_N = \frac{\frac{1}{N}\sum_{i=1}^N (w^i/Z)h(\theta^i)}{\frac{1}{N}\sum_{i=1}^N (w^i/Z)} = \frac{\frac{1}{N}\sum_{i=1}^N v(\theta^i)h(\theta^i)}{\frac{1}{N}\sum_{i=1}^N v(\theta^i)}. \quad (3.50)$$

Now consider a first-order Taylor series expansion in terms of deviations of the numerator from $\mathbb{E}_\pi[h]$ and deviations of the denominator around 1:

$$\sqrt{N}(\bar{h}_N - \mathbb{E}_\pi[h]) \tag{3.51}$$

$$= \sqrt{N}\left(\frac{1}{N}\sum_{i=1}^{N} v(\theta^i)h(\theta^i) - \mathbb{E}_\pi[h]\right)$$

$$-\mathbb{E}_\pi[h]\sqrt{N}\left(\frac{1}{N}\sum_{i=1}^{N} v(\theta^i) - 1\right) + o_p(1)$$

$$= (I) - \mathbb{E}_\pi[h] \cdot (II) + o_p(1).$$

Provided that $\sup_\theta \pi(\theta)/g(\theta) < \infty$ and $\mathbb{E}_g[h^2] < \infty$, we can apply a multivariate extension of the Lindeberg-Levy CLT to the terms (I) and (II). Using straightforward but tedious algebra it can be shown that the variances and covariance of (I) and (II) are given by

$$\begin{aligned}
\mathbb{V}_g[hv] &= \mathbb{E}_\pi[(\pi/g)h^2] - \mathbb{E}_\pi^2[h], \\
\mathbb{V}_g[v] &= \mathbb{E}_\pi[(\pi/g)] - 1, \\
COV_g(hv, v) &= \left(\mathbb{E}_\pi[(\pi/g)h] - \mathbb{E}_\pi[h]\right).
\end{aligned}$$

In turn we can deduce that

$$\sqrt{N}(\bar{h}_N - \mathbb{E}_\pi[h]) \Longrightarrow N\big(0, \Omega(h)\big), \tag{3.52}$$

where

$$\Omega(h) = \mathbb{V}_g[(\pi/g)(h - \mathbb{E}_\pi[h])].$$

We can now define the following inefficiency factor (relative to iid sampling):[2]

$$\text{InEff}_\infty = \frac{\Omega(h)}{\mathbb{V}_\pi[h]}. \tag{3.53}$$

Here the ∞ subscript indicates that the inefficiency factor is computed based on the ratio of asymptotic variances.

While the inefficiency factor can in principle be less than one, it is typically greater than one. Using a crude approximation (see, e.g., Liu (2001)), one can factorize $\Omega(h)$ as follows:

$$\Omega(h) \approx \mathbb{V}_\pi[h]\big(\mathbb{V}_g[\pi/g] + 1\big), \tag{3.54}$$

---

[2]To compute the asymptotic inefficiency factor for a particular application we rely on estimates of $\Omega(h)$ and $\mathbb{V}_\pi$, but we will not make a notational distinction between the "true" asymptotic inefficiency factor and an estimate of it.

which implies that

$$\text{InEff}_\infty \approx 1 + \mathbb{V}_g[\pi/g]. \tag{3.55}$$

The approximation of the asymptotic inefficiency factor is independent of the function $h(\cdot)$ and highlights that the larger the variance of the importance weights, the less accurate the Monte Carlo approximation relative to the accuracy that could be achieved with an iid sample from the posterior.

3.4.3 A Numerical Illustration

Figure 3.2 provides a numerical illustration of the importance sampling algorithm in the context of the posterior density (3.40) associated with the set-identified model in Section 3.3. Panel (i) depicts the posterior density for $\bar{\phi} = -0.5$ and $\bar{V} = 100$. We consider two importance sampling densities. Both are centered at $\theta = 0.5$. The first density ("concentrated") has a variance of 0.125, whereas the second density ("diffuse") has a larger variance of 0.5. The concentrated importance sampling density assigns a very small probability to the interval $[-0.5, -0.25]$ which has a large probability under the posterior distribution.

The accuracy of the importance sampling approximations are illustrated in Panels (ii) and (iii) as a function of the number of draws N. We depict the asymptotic inefficiency factor InEff_∞ defined in (3.53) as well as a simulation-based inefficiency factor InEff_N in which we replace the asymptotic variance of the importance sampler by a finite sample estimate computed from multiple runs of the algorithm. More specifically, we run the importance sampling algorithm $N_{run} = 1,000$ times and compute the variance of the Monte Carlo approximations of $\mathbb{E}_\pi[\theta]$ and $\mathbb{E}_\pi[\theta^2]$ across the runs, denoted by $\mathbb{V}[\bar{h}_N]$. We divide this variance by $\mathbb{V}_\pi[h]/N$ so that it is on the same scale as the asymptotic inefficiency factor:

$$\text{InEff}_N = \frac{\mathbb{V}[\bar{h}_N]}{\mathbb{V}_\pi[h]/N}. \tag{3.56}$$

In general, the asymptotic approximation is very accurate. A comparison between Panels (ii) and (iii) highlights that the

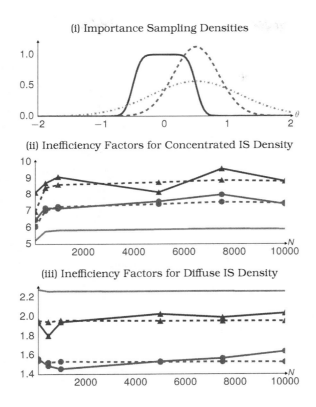

Figure 3.2: IS Approximations of $\mathbb{E}_\pi[\theta]$ and $\mathbb{E}_\pi[\theta^2]$. Panel (i) depicts the posterior density $\pi(\theta)$ (solid) as well as two importance sampling densities ("concentrated" (dashed) and "diffuse" (dotted)) $g(\theta)$. Panels (ii) and (iii) depict large sample inefficiency factors InEff$_\infty = \Omega(h)/\mathbb{V}_\pi[h]$ (dashed) as well as their small sample approximations (solid) based on $N_{run} = 1,000$. We consider $h(\theta) = \theta$ (triangles) and $h(\theta) = \theta^2$ (circles). The solid line (no symbols) depicts the approximate inefficiency factor $1 + \mathbb{V}_g[\pi/g]$.

approximation with the "concentrated" importance sampling density is a lot less accurate than the approximation obtained with the "diffuse" importance sampling densities, which does a much better job of covering the tails of the posterior distribution. Finally, we also plot the approximate asymptotic inefficiency factor defined in (3.55), which provides a crude measure of accuracy.

To ensure that the importance sampling algorithm delivers accurate approximations of posterior moments, it is important that the importance density g is well-tailored toward the target distribution π. Equation (3.55) highlights that one has to choose g to achieve a small variance of the importance weights. In applications with approximately elliptical posterior, a good importance density can be obtained by centering a fat-tailed t distribution at the mode of π and using a scaled version of the inverse Hessian of $\ln \pi$ at the mode to align the contours of the importance density with the contours of the posterior π. However, for highly irregular and non-elliptical posteriors, other approaches of generating an efficient g may be necessary. The sequential Monte Carlo algorithm discussed in Chapter 5 constructs the importance densities in a sequential manner.

3.5   Metropolis-Hastings Algorithms

The Metropolis-Hastings (MH) algorithm belongs to the class of Markov chain Monte Carlo (MCMC) algorithms. The algorithm constructs a Markov chain such that the stationary distribution associated with this Markov chain is unique and equals the posterior distribution of interest. A first version of such an algorithm had been constructed by Metropolis, Rosenbluth, Rosenbluth, Teller, and Teller (1953) to solve a minimization problem and was later generalized by Hastings (1970). Tierney (1994) proved important convergence results for MCMC algorithms and Monte Carlo averages computed based on their output. Chib and Greenberg (1995) provide an excellent introduction to MH algorithms. Detailed textbook treatments can be found, for instance, in Robert and Casella (2004) or Geweke (2005).

While the importance sampler generates a sequence of independent draws from the posterior distribution $\pi(\theta)$, the MH algorithm generates a sequence of serially correlated draws. As long as the correlation in the Markov chain is not too strong, Monte Carlo averages of these draws can accurately approximate posterior means of $h(\theta)$. We subsequently introduce a generic MH algorithm, show why the target posterior distribution arises as an invariant distribution under the Markov chain generated by the MH algorithm, analytically solve for the Markov transition kernel of the MH algorithm in a very simple example, and provide a numerical illustration.

3.5.1 A Generic MH Algorithm

A key ingredient of the MH algorithm is a proposal distribution $q(\vartheta|\theta^{i-1})$, which potentially depends on the draw θ^{i-1} in iteration $i-1$ of the algorithm. The proposed draw is always accepted if it raises the posterior density (relative to θ^{i-1}) and it is sometimes accepted even if it lowers the posterior density. If the proposed draw is not accepted, then the chain does not move and $\theta^i = \theta^{i-1}$. The indexacceptance probability is chosen to ensure that the distribution of the draws converges to the target posterior distribution. The algorithm takes the following form:

Algorithm 5 (Generic MH Algorithm) *For $i = 1$ to N:*

1. *Draw ϑ from a density $q(\vartheta|\theta^{i-1})$.*

2. *Set $\theta^i = \vartheta$ with probability*

$$\alpha(\vartheta|\theta^{i-1}) = \min\left\{1, \frac{p(Y|\vartheta)p(\vartheta)/q(\vartheta|\theta^{i-1})}{p(Y|\theta^{i-1})p(\theta^{i-1})/q(\theta^{i-1}|\vartheta)}\right\}$$

and $\theta^i = \theta^{i-1}$ otherwise.

Because $p(\theta|Y) \propto p(Y|\theta)p(\theta)$ we can replace the posterior densities in the calculation of the acceptance probabilities $\alpha(\vartheta|\theta^{i-1})$ by the product of likelihood and prior, which does not require the evaluation of the marginal data density $p(Y)$. Algorithm 5 describes how to generate a parameter draw θ^i conditional on a parameter draw θ^{i-1}. Thus, implicitly it characterizes a Markov transition kernel $K(\theta|\tilde{\theta})$, where the conditioning value $\tilde{\theta}$ corresponds to the parameter draw from iteration $i-1$.

3.5.2 An Important Property of the MH Algorithm

The probability theory underlying the convergence of Monte Carlo averages constructed from the output of the MH algorithm is considerably more complicated than the theory for the importance sampler. The key questions are the following: (i) suppose that θ^0 is generated from some arbitrary density $g(\cdot)$ and θ^N is obtained by iterating the Markov transition kernel forward N times, then is it true that θ^N is approximately distributed according to $p(\theta|Y)$ and the approximation error vanishes as $N \longrightarrow \infty$? (ii) Suppose that (i) is true, is it also true that sample averages of θ^i, $i = 1, \ldots, N$ satisfy a SLLN and a CLT?

For Algorithm 5 to generate a sequence of draws from the posterior distribution $p(\theta|Y)$ a necessary condition is that the posterior distribution is an invariant distribution under the transition kernel $K(\cdot|\cdot)$, that is,

$$p(\theta|Y) = \int K(\theta|\tilde{\theta})p(\tilde{\theta}|Y)d\tilde{\theta}. \tag{3.57}$$

Thus, if θ^{i-1} is a draw from the posterior distribution $p(\theta|Y)$ then θ^i is also a draw from this distribution. We will limit our theoretical analysis of the general MH algorithm to the verification of this invariance property. For a comprehensive exposition of the convergence theory for Markov chains and MCMC algorithms, we refer the interested reader to Tierney (1994) or textbook treatments such as Robert and Casella (2004) or Geweke (2005).

Verifying the invariance property is relatively straightforward. The transition kernel can be expressed as follows:

$$K(\theta|\tilde{\theta}) = u(\theta|\tilde{\theta}) + r(\tilde{\theta})\delta_{\tilde{\theta}}(\theta). \tag{3.58}$$

Here $u(\theta|\tilde{\theta})$ is the density kernel (note that $u(\theta|\cdot)$ does not integrate to one) for accepted draws:

$$u(\theta|\tilde{\theta}) = \alpha(\theta|\tilde{\theta})q(\theta|\tilde{\theta}). \tag{3.59}$$

Recall from Algorithm 5 above that $q(\cdot|\cdot)$ is the density for the proposed draw and $\alpha(\cdot|\cdot)$ is the probability that the draw is accepted. The term $r(\tilde{\theta})$ is the probability that conditional on $\tilde{\theta}$ the proposed draw will be rejected:

$$r(\tilde{\theta}) = \int \left[1 - \alpha(\theta|\tilde{\theta}) \right] q(\theta|\tilde{\theta}) d\theta = 1 - \int u(\theta|\tilde{\theta}) d\theta. \quad (3.60)$$

Here $1 - \alpha(\theta|\tilde{\theta})$ is the rejection probability of the proposed draw θ and $q(\theta|\tilde{\theta})$ describes the distribution of the proposed draw given $\tilde{\theta}$. If the proposed draw is rejected, then the algorithm sets $\theta^i = \theta^{i-1}$, which means that conditional on the rejection, the transition density degenerates to a pointmass at $\theta = \tilde{\theta}$, which is captured by the Dirac delta function $\delta_{\tilde{\theta}}(\theta)$ in (3.58).[3]

The MH step is constructed to be reversible in the following sense. Conditional on the sampler not rejecting the proposed draw, the density associated with a transition from $\tilde{\theta}$ to θ is identical to the density associated with a transition from θ to $\tilde{\theta}$:

$$p(\tilde{\theta}|Y)u(\theta|\tilde{\theta}) \quad (3.61)$$

$$= p(\tilde{\theta}|Y)q(\theta|\tilde{\theta}) \min \left\{ 1, \frac{p(\theta|Y)/q(\theta|\tilde{\theta})}{p(\tilde{\theta}|Y)/q(\tilde{\theta}|\theta)} \right\}$$

$$= \min \left\{ p(\tilde{\theta}|Y)q(\theta|\tilde{\theta}), \, p(\theta|Y)q(\tilde{\theta}|\theta) \right\}$$

$$= p(\theta|Y)q(\tilde{\theta}|\theta) \min \left\{ \frac{p(\tilde{\theta}|Y)/q(\tilde{\theta}|\theta)}{p(\theta|Y)/q(\theta|\tilde{\theta})}, \, 1 \right\}$$

$$= p(\theta|Y)u(\tilde{\theta}|\theta).$$

Using the reversibility result, we can now verify the invariance property in (3.57):

$$\int K(\theta|\tilde{\theta})p(\tilde{\theta}|Y)d\tilde{\theta} \quad (3.62)$$

$$= \int u(\theta|\tilde{\theta})p(\tilde{\theta}|Y)d\tilde{\theta} + \int r(\tilde{\theta})\delta_{\tilde{\theta}}(\theta)p(\tilde{\theta}|Y)d\tilde{\theta}$$

$$= \int u(\tilde{\theta}|\theta)p(\theta|Y)d\tilde{\theta} + r(\theta)p(\theta|Y)$$

$$= p(\theta|Y).$$

---

[3]The Dirac delta function has the property that $\delta_{\tilde{\theta}}(\theta) = 0$ for $\theta \neq \tilde{\theta}$ and $\int \delta_{\tilde{\theta}}(\theta)d\theta = 1$.

The second equality follows from (3.61) and the properties of the Dirac delta function. The last equality follows from (3.60).

The invariance property in (3.58) is by no means sufficient to guarantee that the Monte Carlo average of draws $h(\theta^i)$ from Algorithm 5 converges to the posterior expectation $\mathbb{E}_\pi[h]$. In particular, one needs to ensure that the transition kernel $K(\cdot|\cdot)$ has a unique invariant distribution, that repeated application of the transition kernel leads to convergence to the unique invariant distribution regardless of the chain's initialization, and that the autocorrelation of the draws θ^i generated by the Markov chain decays sufficiently fast such that sample averages converge to population means. Rather than providing a general treatment of convergence, we will examine a specific example, in which we can solve for the transition kernel analytically.

3.5.3 An Analytical Example

Suppose the parameter space is discrete and θ can only take two values: τ_1 and τ_2. The posterior distribution then simplifies to two probabilities which we denote as $\pi_l = \mathbb{P}\{\theta = \tau_l|Y\}$, $l = 1, 2$. The proposal distribution in Algorithm 5 can be represented as a two-stage Markov process with transition matrix

$$Q = \left[\begin{array}{cc} q_{11} & q_{12} \\ q_{21} & q_{22} \end{array} \right], \tag{3.63}$$

where q_{lk} is the probability of drawing $\vartheta = \tau_k$ conditional on $\theta^{i-1} = \tau_l$. For illustrative purposes, we will assume that

$$q_{11} = q_{22} = q, \quad q_{12} = q_{21} = 1 - q$$

and that the posterior distribution has the property

$$\pi_2 > \pi_1.$$

We now derive a transition matrix for the Markov chain generated by Algorithm 5. Suppose that $\theta^{i-1} = \tau_1$. Then with probability q, $\vartheta = \tau_1$. The probability that this draw will be accepted is

$$\alpha(\tau_1|\tau_1) = \min\left\{1, \frac{\pi_1/q}{\pi_1/q}\right\} = 1.$$

With probability $1 - q$ the proposed draw is $\vartheta = \tau_2$. The probability that this draw will be rejected is

$$1 - \alpha(\tau_2|\tau_1) = 1 - \min\left\{1, \frac{\pi_2/(1-q)}{\pi_1/(1-q)}\right\} = 0$$

because we previously assumed that $\pi_2 > \pi_1$. Thus, the probability of a transition from $\theta^{i-1} = \tau_1$ to $\theta^i = \tau_1$ is

$$k_{11} = q \cdot 1 + (1 - q) \cdot 0 = q.$$

Using similar calculations for the three other possible transitions it can be verified that the Markov transition matrix for the process $\{\theta^i\}_{i=1}^{N}$ is given by

$$K = \begin{bmatrix} k_{11} & k_{12} \\ k_{21} & k_{22} \end{bmatrix} \tag{3.64}$$

$$= \begin{bmatrix} q & (1-q) \\ (1-q)\frac{\pi_1}{\pi_2} & q + (1-q)\left(1 - \frac{\pi_1}{\pi_2}\right) \end{bmatrix}.$$

Straightforward calculations reveal that the transition matrix K has two eigenvalues λ_1 and λ_2:

$$\lambda_1(K) = 1, \quad \lambda_2(K) = q - (1-q)\frac{\pi_1}{1-\pi_1}. \tag{3.65}$$

The eigenvector associated with $\lambda_1(K)$ determines the invariant distribution of the Markov chain, which, as we have seen in Section 3.5.2, equals the posterior distribution. Provided that the second eigenvalue is different from one, the posterior is the unique invariant distribution of the Markov chain. The persistence of the Markov chain is characterized by the eigenvalue $\lambda_2(K)$. In fact, we can represent the Markov chain by an AR(1) process (see, for instance, Hamilton (1994)). Define the transformed parameter

$$\xi^i = \frac{\theta^i - \tau_1}{\tau_2 - \tau_1}, \tag{3.66}$$

which takes the values 0 or 1. ξ^i follows the first-order autoregressive process

$$\xi^i = (1 - k_{11}) + \lambda_2(K)\xi^{i-1} + \nu^i. \tag{3.67}$$

Conditional on $\xi^{i-1} = j - 1$, $j = 1, 2$, the innovation ν^i has support on k_{jj} and $(1 - k_{jj})$, its conditional mean is equal to zero, and its conditional variance is equal to $k_{jj}(1 - k_{jj})$.

The persistence of the Markov chain depends on the proposal distribution, which in our discrete example is characterized by the probability q. One could easily obtain an *iid* sample from the posterior by setting $q = \pi_1$ (which implies $\lambda_2(K) = 0$). While in general it is not feasible to tailor the proposal density to generate serially uncorrelated draws, the goal of MCMC design is to keep the persistence of the chain as low as possible. As q approaches one, the autocorrelation of the Markov chain increases and converges to one. In the limit, if $q = 1$, then $\theta^i = \theta^1$ for all i and the equilibrium distribution of the chain is no longer unique.

As in Section 3.4, we will now examine the convergence of Monte Carlo averages of $h(\theta^i)$. Based on the autoregressive representation in (3.67) it is straightforward to compute the autocovariance function of ξ^i, which then can be converted into the autocovariance function of $h(\theta^i)$:

$$\text{COV}(h(\theta^i), h(\theta^{i-l})) \qquad (3.68)$$

$$= \ \left(h(\tau_2) - h(\tau_1)\right)^2 \pi_1(1 - \pi_1) \left(q - (1 - q)\frac{\pi_1}{1 - \pi_1}\right)^l$$

$$= \ \mathbb{V}_\pi[h] \left(q - (1 - q)\frac{\pi_1}{1 - \pi_1}\right)^l.$$

Defining the Monte Carlo estimate

$$\bar{h}_N = \frac{1}{N} \sum_{i=1}^{N} h(\theta^i) \qquad (3.69)$$

we deduce from a central limit theorem for dependent random variables that

$$\sqrt{N}(\bar{h}_N - \mathbb{E}_\pi[h]) \Longrightarrow N\big(0, \Omega(h)\big), \qquad (3.70)$$

where $\Omega(h)$ is now the long-run covariance matrix

$$\Omega(h) = \lim_{L \longrightarrow \infty} \mathbb{V}_\pi[h] \left(1 + 2 \sum_{l=1}^{L} \frac{L - l}{L} \left(q - (1 - q)\frac{\pi_1}{1 - \pi_1}\right)^l\right).$$

In turn, the asymptotic inefficiency factor is given by

$$\text{InEff}_\infty = \frac{\Omega(h)}{\mathbb{V}_\pi[h]} \tag{3.71}$$

$$= 1 + 2 \lim_{L \to \infty} \sum_{l=1}^{L} \frac{L-l}{L} \left(q - (1-q)\frac{\pi_1}{1-\pi_1} \right)^l.$$

For $q = \pi_1$ the inefficiency factor is one. For $q > \pi_1$ the inefficiency factor is greater than one because the draws are positively correlated, whereas for $q < \pi_1$ the algorithm produces negatively correlated draws which lead to an inefficiency factor that is less than one.

3.5.4 A Numerical Illustration

We now provide a numerical illustration using the discrete example, assuming that the posterior takes the form of a Bernoulli distribution ($\tau_1 = 0, \tau_2 = 1$) with $\pi_1 = 0.2$. To assess the effectiveness of different MH settings, we vary $q \in [0, 1)$. Panel (i) of Figure 3.3 displays the autocorrelations up to 9 lags for $q = \{0, 0.2, 0.5, 0.99\}$. When $q = 0.99$ the chain generated by the MH algorithm is extremely autocorrelated. According to (3.64) the probability of moving from $\theta^{i-1} = \tau_1$ to $\theta^i = \tau_2$ is $1 - q$, or 0.01. Similarly, the probability of moving from $\theta^{i-1} = \tau_2$ to $\theta^i = \tau_1$ is $(1-q)\pi_1/\pi_2 = 0.0025$. Thus, if the initial draw is $\theta^0 = \tau_1$, one would expect 100 draws before encountering τ_2. However, recall that 80% of the realized draws from the invariant distribution should be τ_2.

Intuitively, the high autocorrelation reflects the fact that it will take a high number of draws to accurately reflect the target distribution, or that the chain is "moving" extremely slowly around the parameter space. This will manifest itself in a high variance of Monte Carlo estimates, as we will see below. If $q = 0.5$, then the autocorrelation is substantially weaker than under the $q = 0.99$ sampler, but still positive. If $\theta^{i-1} = \tau_1$, the sampler will set $\theta^i = \tau_1$ with probability greater than $\pi_1 = 0.2$, inducing a positive autocorrelation in the chain. If $q = \pi_1 = 0.2$, the autocorrelation is exactly equal to zero. Finally, if $q = 0$, the MH chain actually has a negative first-order autocorrelation. For $\theta^{i-1} = \tau_1$ the probability of τ_1 for θ^i

(i) Autocorrelation Function of θ^i

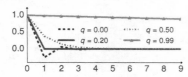

(ii) Asymptotic Inefficiency InEff$_\infty$

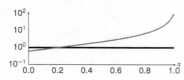

(iii) Small-Sample Variance $\mathbb{V}[\bar{h}_N]$ versus HAC Estimates of $\Omega(h)$

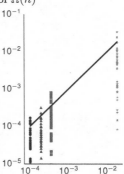

Figure 3.3: Performance of Discrete MH Algorithm for $\pi_1 = 0.2$. Panel (iii) depicts the small-sample variance $\mathbb{V}[\bar{h}_N]$ computed across $N_{run} = 50$ MCMC runs (x-axis) versus HAC estimates of $\Omega(h)/N$ (y-axis) computed for each chain based on (3.72) with $L = 400$. Circles are $q = 0$, triangles are $q = 0.2$, squares are $q = 0.5$, stars are $q = 0.99$. The solid line represents the 45-degree line.

is zero, which is much less than one would expect under *iid* draws. Induced negative autocorrelation can actually serve to reduce Monte Carlo variance relative to theoretical variance, which the next panel highlights.

Panel (ii) depicts the inefficiency factor InEff$_\infty$ as a function of q. The horizontal line indicates an inefficiency factor of one. The y coordinates are rescaled in log terms. Consistent with the autocorrelations discussed above, for large values of q, the variance of Monte Carlo estimates of h drawn from the MH chain are much larger than the variance of estimates derived from *iid* draws. Indeed, when $q = 0.99$ the variance is about 100 times larger. As q moves closer to π_1 the relative variance shrinks. Indeed, when $q = \pi_1$ the Monte Carlo estimates from the MH sampler and an *iid* sampler have the same variance, as the chain generated by the MH sampler mimics the *iid* sampler. Finally, if $q < \pi_1$, the Monte Carlo variance from the MH sampler is smaller than that under *iid* draws. While the reduction in MC variance found for $q < \pi_1$ is obviously desirable, it is unrealistic in practice. The design of a good MH sampler—here, this amounts to picking q—is highly dependent on the target distribution, indexed by π_1. Unfortunately, the reason one often resorts to MCMC techniques is that important features of the target distribution, i.e, π_1, are not well understood.

In an environment where asymptotic variances are not known in closed form, it is difficult to know when the chain generated by an MH algorithm has converged. There are many diagnostics available for this, some of which we will discuss in more detail in the next section. At the heart of most of the measures, though, is whether the empirical variability of an estimate computed across many runs of an MH sampler is consistent with estimates within each chain. With an eye toward between-chain and within-chain measurement, we run $N_{run} = 50$ replications of the MH sampler for $q = \{0, 0.2, 0.5, 0.99\}$. The length of each simulation is $N = 1,000$. We set $h(\theta) = \theta$, i.e., we are interested in the variance of Monte Carlo estimates of the mean of the distribution. For each replication, we compute an estimate of $\Omega(h)/N$, using a simple Newey-West heteroskedastic- and autocorrelation-consistent (HAC) estimator,

$$\text{HAC}[\bar{h}] = \frac{1}{N}\left(\hat{\gamma}_0 + 2\sum_{l=1}^{L}\left(1 - \frac{l}{L+1}\right)\hat{\gamma}_l\right), \qquad (3.72)$$

where $\gamma_l = \text{COV}(h(\theta^i), h(\theta^{i-l}))$, with L set to 400. We also compute an estimate of the variance of $\bar{h}_N$ across the fifty replications, denoted by $\mathbb{V}[\bar{h}_N]$. Panel (iii) of Figure 3.3 examine the relationships between these two estimates. The y-coordinate of the dots represents the HAC estimates for each q, while the x-coordinate indicates an estimate of the small-sample variance $\mathbb{V}[\bar{h}_N]$ for each q. The solid line gives the 45-degree line. One can see that relative ordering for the q-s is preserved in small samples, with $q = 0$ having the lowest small-sample variance and $q = 0.99$ having the highest. More importantly, the small-sample variance for each of the simulators is bracketed by the HAC estimates, indicated by the solid line bisecting the dots for each q. That is, the within-chain estimates appear consistent with the between-chain measures, though on average the HAC estimator underestimates the variance of the Monte Carlo approximation.

Part II

Estimation of Linearized DSGE Models

Chapter 4

Metropolis-Hastings Algorithms for DSGE Models

To date, the most widely used method to generate draws from posterior distributions of a DSGE model is the random walk MH (RWMH) algorithm. This algorithm is a special case of the generic Algorithm 5 introduced in Section 3.5 in which the proposal distribution $q(\vartheta|\theta^{i-1})$ can be expressed as the random walk $\vartheta = \theta^{i-1} + \eta$ and η is drawn from a distribution that is centered at zero. We introduce a benchmark RWMH algorithm in Section 4.1 and apply it to the small-scale New Keynesian DSGE model in Section 4.2. The DSGE model likelihood function in combination with the prior distribution presented in Section 2.3 leads to a posterior distribution that has a fairly regular elliptical shape. In turn, the draws from a simple RWMH algorithm can be used to obtain an accurate numerical approximation of posterior moments.

Unfortunately, in many other applications, in particular those involving medium- and large-scale DSGE models, the posterior distributions could be very non-elliptical. Irregularly shaped posterior distributions are often caused by identification problems or misspecification. The DSGE model may suffer from a local identification problem that generates a posterior that is very flat in certain directions of the parameter space, similar to the posterior encountered in the simple set-identified model of Section 3.3. Alternatively, the posterior may exhibit multimodal features. Multimodality could be caused by the data's inability to distinguish between the role of a DSGE model's external and internal propagation mechanisms. For instance, inflation persistence can be generated by highly autocorrelated cost-push shocks or by firms' inability to frequently re-optimize their prices in view of fluctuating marginal costs. We use a very stylized state-space model to illustrate these challenges for posterior simulators in Section 4.3.

In view of the difficulties caused by irregularly shaped posterior surfaces, we review a variety of alternative MH samplers in Section 4.4. These algorithms differ from the RWMH algorithm in two dimensions. First, they use alternative proposal distributions $q(\vartheta|\theta^{i-1})$. In general, we consider distributions of the form

$$q(\cdot|\theta^{i-1}) = p_t(\cdot|\mu(\theta^{i-1}), \Sigma(\theta^{i-1}), \nu), \qquad (4.1)$$

where $p_t(\cdot)$ refers to the density of a student-t distribution. Thus, our exploration of proposal densities concentrates on different ways of forming the location parameter $\mu(\cdot)$ and the scale matrix $\Sigma(\cdot)$. For $\nu = \infty$ this notation nests Gaussian proposal distributions. The second dimension in which we generalize the algorithm is blocking, i.e., we group the parameters into subvectors, and use a Block MH sampler to draw iteratively from conditional posterior distributions.

While the alternative MH samplers are designed for irregular posterior surfaces for which the simple RWMH algorithm generates inaccurate approximations, we illustrate the performance gains obtained through these algorithms using the simple New Keynesian DSGE model in Section 4.5. Similar to the illustrations in Section 3.5, we evaluate the accuracy of the algorithms by computing the variance of Monte Carlo approximations across multiple chains. Our simulations demonstrate that careful tailoring of proposal densities $q(\vartheta|\theta^{i-1})$ as well as blocking the parameters can drastically improve the accuracy of Monte Carlo approximations. Finally, Section 4.6 takes a brief look at the numerical approximation of marginal data densities that are used to compute posterior model probabilities.

In Section 3.5, we showed directly that the Monte Carlo estimates associated with the discrete MH algorithm satisfied a SLLN and CLT for dependent, identically distributed random variables. All of the MH algorithms here give rise to Markov chains that are recurrent, irreducible, and aperiodic for the target distribution of interest. These properties are sufficient for a SLLN to hold. However, validating conditions for a CLT to hold is much more difficult and beyond the scope of this book.

4.1 A Benchmark Algorithm

The most widely used MH algorithm for DSGE model applications is the *random walk MH* (RWMH) algorithm. The mean of the proposal distribution in (4.1) is simply the current location in the chain and its variance is prespecified:

$$\mu(\theta^{i-1}) = \theta^{i-1} \text{ and } \Sigma(\theta^{i-1}) = c^2 \hat{\Sigma}. \tag{4.2}$$

The name of the algorithm comes from the random walk form of the proposal, which can be written as

$$\vartheta = \theta^{i-1} + \eta,$$

where η is mean zero with variance $c^2 \hat{\Sigma}$. Given the symmetric nature of the proposal distribution, the acceptance probability becomes

$$\alpha = \min \left\{ \frac{p(\vartheta|Y)}{p(\theta^{i-1}|Y)}, 1 \right\}.$$

A draw, ϑ, is accepted with probability one if the posterior at ϑ has a higher value than the posterior at θ^{i-1}. The probability of acceptance decreases as the posterior at the candidate value decreases relative to the current posterior.

To implement the RWMH, the user still needs to specify ν, c, and $\hat{\Sigma}$. For all of the variations of the RWMH we implement, we set $\nu = \infty$ in (4.1), that is, we use a multivariate normal proposal distribution in keeping with most of the literature. Typically, the choice of c is made conditional on $\hat{\Sigma}$, so we first discuss the choice for $\hat{\Sigma}$. The proposal variance controls the relative variances and correlations in the proposal distribution. As we have seen in Section 3.5, the sampler can work very poorly if q is strongly at odds with the target distribution. This intuition extends to the multivariate setting here. Suppose θ comprises two parameters, say β and δ, that are highly correlated in the posterior distribution. If the variance of the proposal distribution does not capture this correlation, e.g., the matrix $\hat{\Sigma}$ is diagonal, then the draw ϑ is unlikely to reflect the fact that if β is large then δ should also be large, and vice versa. Therefore, $p(\vartheta|Y)$ is likely to be smaller than $p(\theta^{i-1}|Y)$, and so the proposed draw will be rejected with high probability. As a consequence, the chain will have a high rejection rate, exhibit a high autocorrelation, and the Monte Carlo estimates derived from it will have a high variance.

A good choice for $\hat{\Sigma}$ seeks to incorporate information from the posterior, to potentially capture correlations discussed above. Obtaining this information can be difficult. A popular approach, used in Schorfheide (2000), is to set $\hat{\Sigma}$ to be the negative of the inverse Hessian at the mode of the log posterior, $\hat{\theta}$, obtained by running a numerical optimization routine before running MCMC. Using this as an estimate for the covariance of the posterior is attractive, because it can be viewed as a large sample approximation to the posterior covariance matrix as the sample size $T \longrightarrow \infty$. There exists a large literature on the asymptotic normality of posterior distributions. Fundamental conditions can be found, for instance, in Johnson (1970).

Unfortunately, in many applications the maximization of the posterior density is tedious and the numerical approximation of the Hessian may be inaccurate. These problems may arise if the posterior distribution is very non-elliptical and possibly multimodal, or if the likelihood function is replaced by a non-differentiable particle filter approximation (see Chapter 8). In both cases, a (partially) adaptive approach may work well: First, generate a set of posterior draws based on a reasonable initial choice for $\hat{\Sigma}$, e.g., the prior covariance matrix. Second, compute the sample covariance matrix from the first sequence of posterior draws and use it as $\hat{\Sigma}$ in a second run of the RWMH algorithm. In principle, the covariance matrix $\hat{\Sigma}$ can be adjusted more than once. However, $\hat{\Sigma}$ must be fixed eventually to guarantee the convergence of the posterior simulator. Samplers which constantly (or automatically) adjust $\hat{\Sigma}$ are known as adaptive samplers and require substantially more elaborate theoretical justifications.

Instead of strictly following one of the two approaches of tuning $\hat{\Sigma}$ that we just described, we use an estimate of the posterior covariance, $\mathbb{V}_\pi[\theta]$, obtained from an earlier estimation in the subsequent numerical illustrations. While this approach is impractical in empirical work, it is useful for the purpose of comparing the performance of different posterior samplers, because it avoids a distortion due to a mismatch between the Hessian-based estimate and the posterior covariance. Thus, it is a best-case scenario for the algorithm. To summarize, we examine the following variant of the RWMH algorithm:

$$\text{RWMH-V} \quad : \quad \hat{\Sigma} = \mathbb{V}_\pi[\theta].$$

The final parameter of the algorithm is the scaling factor c. This parameter is typically adjusted to ensure a "reasonable" acceptance rate. Given the opacity of the posterior, it is difficult to derive a theoretically optimal acceptance rate. If the sampler accepts too frequently, it may be making very small movements, resulting in large serial correlation and a high variance of the resulting Monte Carlo estimates. Similarly, if the chain rejects too frequently, it may get stuck in one region of the parameter space, again resulting in accurate estimates. However, for the special case of a target distribution which is multivariate normal, Roberts, Gelman, and Gilks (1997) have derived a limit (in the size of parameter vector) optimal acceptance rate of 0.234. Most practitioners target an acceptance rate between 0.20 and 0.40. The scaling factor c can be tuned during the burn-in period or via pre-estimation chains. We will discuss the relationship between the accuracy of Monte Carlo approximations and the choice of c in more detail in Section 4.2.2.

4.2 The RWMH-V Algorithm at Work

We now apply the RWMH-V algorithm to the estimation of the small-scale New Keynesian model introduced in Chapter 1.1. The model is solved using a log-linear approximation as described in Chapter 2.1. This model has been previously used to illustrate the Bayesian analysis of DSGE models by An and Schorfheide (2007). We begin with this DSGE model on account of its simplicity. We can be confident that all of

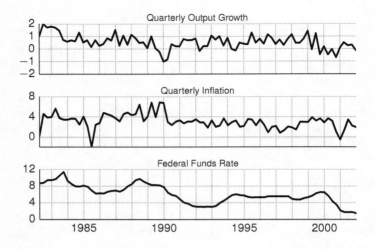

Figure 4.1: Observables for the Small-Scale Model. Output growth per capita is measured in quarter-on-quarter (Q-o-Q) percentages. Inflation is CPI inflation in annualized Q-o-Q percentages. Federal funds rate is the average annualized effective funds rate for each quarter.

our samplers converge to the posterior in reasonable time, allowing us to execute the estimation repeatedly under various configurations of the posterior samplers and to concentrate on the variance of the Monte Carlo approximations of posterior moments as a measure of success. In later chapters, we will examine more elaborate models where some simulators have trouble replicating key features of the posterior. The New Keynesian DSGE model is estimated based on three observables: quarterly per capita GDP growth, quarterly inflation, and the annualized federal funds rate, whose measurement equations were defined in Equation (2.13). The observations (see Appendix for detailed definitions) used in the estimation range from 1983:I to 2002:IV, giving us a total of $T = 80$ observations. The three time series are plotted in Figure 4.1. We use the prior distribution presented in Table 2.2.

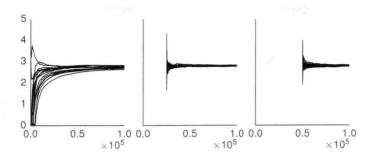

Figure 4.2: Convergence of Monte Carlo Average $\bar{\tau}_{N|N_0}$. The x-axis indicates the number of draws N.

4.2.1 Burn-in and Computation of Posterior Estimates

In general, the initial draws obtained from an MH algorithm do not reflect the posterior distribution. Indeed, there may be a large number of draws before the sampler has "converged," that is, when a draw from the Markov chain has approximately the same distribution as a direct draw from the posterior. For this reason, it is common practice to drop a substantial part (say the first N_0 draws) of the initial simulations of the MH chain, known as the burn-in. Figure 4.2 depicts

$$\bar{\theta}_{N|N_0} = \frac{1}{N - N_0} \sum_{i=N_0+1}^{N} \theta^i$$

as a function of N for multiple runs of the RWMH-V algorithm and three choices of N_0 for a particular element of θ, namely, the risk-aversion parameter τ. Initial draws are generated from the prior distribution. The dispersion of initial recursive mean after burn-in corresponds roughly to posterior variance to the extent that the chain converged to its equilibrium distribution after N_0 draws. Each recursive mean appears to approach the same limit point. For the remainder of this section we set $N = 100,000$ and $N_0 = 50,000$.

While the draws generated by the posterior simulator represent the joint posterior distribution of the parameter vector

Table 4.1: Posterior Estimates of DSGE Model Parameters

	Mean	[0.05, 0.95]		Mean	[0.05,0.95]
τ	2.83	[1.95, 3.82]	ρ_r	0.77	[0.71, 0.82]
κ	0.78	[0.51, 0.98]	ρ_g	0.98	[0.96, 1.00]
ψ_1	1.80	[1.43, 2.20]	ρ_z	0.88	[0.84, 0.92]
ψ_2	0.63	[0.23, 1.21]	σ_r	0.22	[0.18, 0.26]
$r^{(A)}$	0.42	[0.04, 0.95]	σ_g	0.71	[0.61, 0.84]
$\pi^{(A)}$	3.30	[2.78, 3.80]	σ_z	0.31	[0.26, 0.36]
$\gamma^{(Q)}$	0.52	[0.28, 0.74]			

Notes: We generated $N = 100,000$ draws from the posterior and discarded the first 50,000 draws. Based on the remaining draws we approximated the posterior mean and the 5th and 95th percentiles.

θ, researchers typically start the empirical analysis by reporting summary statistics for the marginal posterior distribution of each parameter. The draws for individual elements of the vector θ, say the draws of the risk aversion parameter τ^i, $i = 1, \ldots, N$, approximate the marginal posterior distribution of that particular parameter. Table 4.1 provides posterior mean parameter estimates and 90% credible intervals. Instead of computing HPD intervals, we report the 5th and the 95th percentiles of the posterior distribution, which can be easily obtained after sorting the posterior draws for each parameter (see Chapter 3). The estimated annualized steady state growth rate of the economy is 2%, the estimated steady state inflation rate for the sample period is 3.3%, and the implied steady state nominal interest rate is 5.8%. The risk aversion parameter τ is estimated to be 2.83. The estimated slope of the New Keynesian Phillips curve is fairly large, $\bar{\kappa} = 0.78$, implying a low degree of price rigidity and a small effect of monetary policy shocks on output. The central bank reacts strongly to inflation movements as well as to deviations of output from flexible price output.

4.2.2 The Effect of Scaling the Proposal Covariance Matrix

Given the widespread use of the RWMH-V algorithm, it is instructive to investigate the effect of the scaling constant c. To do so, we run the benchmark RWMH-V algorithm for different choices of c. For each choice of c, we run $N_{run} = 50$ Monte Carlo chains. Unlike before, the chains are now initialized with draws from the posterior distribution (obtained from a preliminary estimation of the DSGE model). Nonetheless, we still use a burn-in period equal to half of the chain length. Here we are taking for granted that for all but the very extreme choices of c the runs have converged to the posterior; detailed examination of the draws generated by each chain confirms this.

The results for the risk-aversion parameter τ are depicted in Figure 4.3. The acceptance rate of the RWMH-V sampler is decreasing in c. If c is small, the proposed random walk steps of the sampler are tiny and the probability that the proposed draws are accepted is very high. As c increases, the average proposed step sizes get larger and the probability of acceptance decreases because it becomes more likely to propose a parameter value that is associated with a low posterior density. We measure the variance of the Monte Carlo approximation using estimates of InEff$_\infty$ (HAC$[\bar{\tau}]/(\mathbb{V}_\pi[\tau]/N)$) and the small-sample inefficiency factor InEff$_N = \mathbb{V}[\bar{\tau}]/(\mathbb{V}_\pi[\tau]/N)$, where $\mathbb{V}[\bar{\tau}]$ is the small-sample variance of $\bar{\tau}$ across the multiple chains.

The two inefficiency measures are very similar and indicate that the accuracy of the posterior mean approximation has a U-shape as a function of c. The minimum, i.e., the highest precision, is attained for $c = 0.5$. Intuitively, for small values of c, the serial correlation and hence the inefficiency factors are large because the step-sizes are very small. For very large values of c the serial correlation is high because the probability that a proposed parameter draw is rejected, i.e., $\theta^i = \theta^{i-1}$, is very high. The bottom panel of Figure 4.3 depicts the relationship between the acceptance rate and the accuracy of the Monte Carlo approximation. For the posterior mean of τ the Monte Carlo approximation error is smallest for acceptance rates between 20% and 40%. While Figure 4.3 focuses on τ,

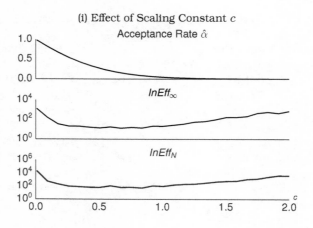

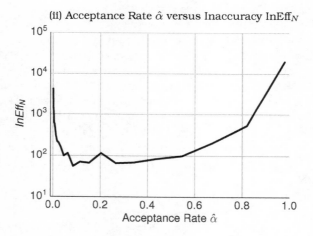

Figure 4.3: Effect of Scaling on Accuracy. Results are for posterior mean of τ, based on $N_{run} = 50$ independent Markov chains. Panel (i): The acceptance rate (average across multiple chains), HAC-based estimate of $\text{InEff}_\infty[\bar{\tau}]$ (average across multiple chains), and $\text{InEff}_N[\bar{\tau}]$ are shown as a function of the scaling constant c. Panel (ii): $\text{InEff}_N[\bar{\tau}]$ versus the acceptance rate $\hat{\alpha}$.

the results for the other parameters are qualitatively similar.

4.2.3 Transformations of Parameters: Impulse Responses

The parameter draws θ^i can be transformed into other statistics of interest $h(\theta^i)$. For instance, the DSGE model can be used to study the propagation of exogenous shocks. Conditional on a parameter vector θ, it is straightforward to compute impulse response functions (IRFs) from the state-space representation of the DSGE model given by (2.10) and (2.13). The mapping from the parameters to the IRFs is an example of a function $h(\theta)$ that is of interest in many DSGE model applications. (Pointwise) Bayesian inference for IRFs can be implemented by first converting each draw θ^i into $h(\theta^i)$ and then computing posterior means and credible intervals for each element of the $h(\cdot)$ vector. Results for the small-scale DSGE model are depicted in Figures 4.4 and 4.5. The first figure shows the response of the exogenous shock processes $\hat{g}_t$ and $\hat{z}_t$ to one-standard deviation innovations. Both shocks follow AR(1) processes, but the government spending shock ($\bar{\rho}_g = 0.98$) is much more persistent than the technology growth shock ($\bar{\rho}_z = 0.88$). The three columns of Figure 4.5 indicate the responses to the government spending shock $\epsilon_{g,t}$, the technology growth shock $\epsilon_{z,t}$, and the monetary policy shock $\epsilon_{R,t}$, respectively. The three rows depict the responses of output, inflation, and interest rates to the three shocks. The solid lines depict posterior mean responses and the shaded areas are 90% credible bands.

The log-linearized equilibrium conditions for the small-scale DSGE model were summarized in (2.1). A positive government spending (or, more generally, demand) shock raises output, but leaves inflation and interest rates unchanged. In this simple model, consumption deviations from the stochastic trend, $\hat{c}_t$, is the difference between output deviations $\hat{y}_t$ and the government spending shock $\hat{g}_t$. Moreover, $\hat{g}_t$ equals potential output, i.e., the output that would prevail in the absence of price rigidities, and $\hat{c}_t = \hat{y}_t - \hat{g}_t$ can be interpreted as the output gap. If the log-linearized equilibrium conditions are rewritten in terms of $\hat{c}_t$, then the government spending shock drops out of the Euler equation, the New Keynesian

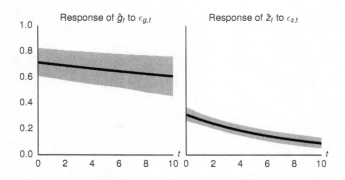

Figure 4.4: Impulse Responses of Exogenous Processes. The figure depicts pointwise posterior means and 90% credible bands. The responses are in percent relative to the initial level.

Phillips curve, and the monetary policy rule. This implies that the government spending shock only affects output, but not the output gap, i.e., consumption, inflation, and interest rate.

In response to a technology growth shock $\hat{z}_t$, output and consumption react proportionally, i.e., $\hat{y} = \hat{c}_t$. While the level of output will adjust to the new level of technology in the long run, expectations of increasing productivity lead agents to increase consumption initially by more than $\hat{z}_t$, meaning that $\hat{y}_t = \hat{c}_t > 0$. According to the Phillips curve, the positive output gap is associated with an increase in inflation, which in turn triggers a rise in interest rate. In the long run, the levels of output and consumption rise permanently while both inflation and interest rates revert back to their steady state values.

Finally, an unanticipated increase in nominal interest rates raises the real rate because inflation is slow to adjust. According to the Euler equation, current consumption is minus the sum of future expected real rates, which means that consumption and output fall. According to the price setting equation, a drop in output and consumption leads to a fall in inflation. Our Phillips curve slope estimate $\hat{\kappa} = 0.78$ implies that the output response is smaller than the inflation response.

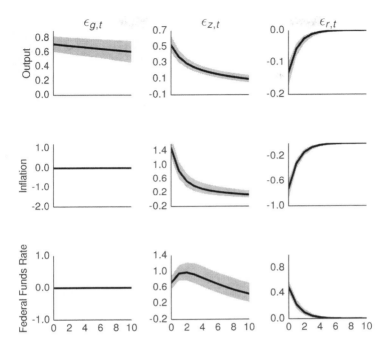

Figure 4.5: Impulse Responses of Endogenous Variables. The figure depicts pointwise posterior means and 90% credible bands. The responses of output are in percent relative to the initial level, whereas the responses of inflation and interest rates are in annualized percentages.

In the remainder of this chapter, we will not focus on posterior estimates per se but rather on the accuracy with which various posterior samplers can generate approximations of posterior moments.

4.3 Challenges Due to Irregular Posteriors

The benchmark RWMH-V algorithm performed well on the posterior distribution of the small-scale New Keynesian DSGE model. Unfortunately, as the size of the DSGE model increases (in terms of number of structural parameters and number of observables in the measurement equation) or if the DSGE model is estimated under a more diffuse prior distribution, the performance of the RWMH-V algorithm often deteriorates. The advanced computational techniques that we will present subsequently provide an important alternative to the benchmark algorithm in cases in which the posterior distribution is very non-elliptical. Irregular posterior distributions tend to arise if the DSGE model is too stylized to be able to fit the data (misspecification) or if its parameters lack identification.

This subsection focuses on irregularities arising from identification problems. Whereas the early literature on DSGE model estimation paid little attention to identification (because the models seemed to be tightly parameterized compared to, say, VARs), researchers eventually began to realize that estimation objective functions, including the likelihood function, are often uninformative with respect to important structural parameters. Canova and Sala (2009), for instance, documented identification problems in popular New Keynesian DSGE models. These identification problems may arise from the data set's inability to distinguish endogenous sources of persistence in DSGE models, e.g., due to price adjustment costs, from exogenous sources of persistence, i.e., highly correlated exogenous shocks. Moreover, they may arise from the rational expectations equilibrium logic of the model. A large coefficient ψ_1 on inflation in the monetary policy rule of the small-scale New Keynesian DSGE model implies a low volatility of inflation in equilibrium. If, in turn, the observed inflation volatility is very low, it becomes very difficult to determine the policy rule coefficient precisely.

Subsequent work by Iskrev (2010) and Komunjer and Ng (2011) provides criteria that allow researchers to check *ex ante* whether the parameters of a DSGE model are locally identifiable in population. These criteria are important for Bayesian analysis because if it turns out that certain parameters are not locally identifiable, the researcher may want to add external information (not contained in the estimation sample Y) to sharpen inference and should use extra care ensuring that the output of the posterior simulator is accurate.

We now highlight some of the challenges for Bayesian computations arising from local or global identification issues. For illustrative purposes, consider the following stylized state-space model discussed in Schorfheide (2010):

$$y_t = [1 \; 1]s_t, \quad s_t = \begin{bmatrix} \phi_1 & 0 \\ \phi_3 & \phi_2 \end{bmatrix} s_{t-1} + \begin{bmatrix} 1 \\ 0 \end{bmatrix} \epsilon_t, \qquad (4.3)$$

where

$$\epsilon_t \sim iidN(0,1).$$

The mapping between some structural parameters $\theta = [\theta_1, \theta_2]'$ and the reduced-form parameters $\phi = [\phi_1, \phi_2, \phi_3]'$ is assumed to be

$$\phi_1 = \theta_1^2, \quad \phi_2 = (1 - \theta_1^2), \quad \phi_3 - \phi_2 = -\theta_1 \theta_2. \qquad (4.4)$$

We further assume that the structural parameters are restricted to the unit square:

$$0 \leq \theta_1 \leq 1, \quad 0 \leq \theta_2 \leq 1.$$

The first state, $s_{1,t}$, looks like a typical exogenous driving force of a DSGE model, e.g., total factor productivity, while the second state $s_{2,t}$ evolves like an endogenous state variable, e.g., the capital stock, driven by the exogenous process and past realizations of itself. The mapping from structural to reduced-form parameters is chosen to highlight the identification problems endemic to DSGE models. First, θ_2 is not identifiable if θ_1 is 0, because θ_2 enters the model only multiplicatively. Second, letting L denote the lag operator with the property that $Ly_t = y_{t-1}$, we can write the law of motion of y_t as a restricted ARMA(2,1) process:

$$\left(1 - \theta_1^2 L\right)\left(1 - (1 - \theta_1^2)L\right)y_t = \left(1 - \theta_1 \theta_2 L\right)\epsilon_t. \qquad (4.5)$$

Given θ_1 and θ_2, we obtain an observationally equivalent process by switching the values of the two roots of the autoregressive lag polynomial. Choose $\tilde{\theta}_1$ and $\tilde{\theta}_2$ such that

$$\tilde{\theta}_1 = \sqrt{1 - \theta_1^2}, \quad \tilde{\theta}_2 = \theta_1 \theta_2 / \tilde{\theta}_1.$$

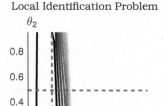

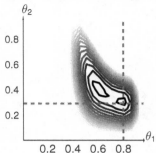

Figure 4.6: Posteriors for Stylized State-Space Model. Intersections of the solid lines indicate parameter values that were used to generate the data from which the posteriors are constructed. Left panel: $\theta_1 = 0.1$ and $\theta_2 = 0.5$. Right panel: $\theta_1 = 0.8$, $\theta_2 = 0.3$.

This observational equivalence can cause a bimodality in the likelihood function.

Figure 4.6 depicts posterior contours for two hypothetical posteriors based on $T = 200$ observations each. Both posteriors are based on a prior distribution that is uniform on the unit square. The contours in the left panel highlight the local identification problem that arises if θ_1 is close to zero. The data underlying the posterior were generated by setting $\theta_1 = 0.1$ and $\theta_2 = 0.5$. Given the small value of θ_1, it is difficult to identify θ_2. Thus, the posterior is very flat in the direction of θ_2. The contours depicted in the right panel highlight the global identification problem. We simulated observations based on $\theta = [0.8, 0.3]'$. This parameterization is observationally equivalent to $\theta = [0.6, 0.4]'$.

For the MH algorithm to be efficient, the posterior on the left requires that the algorithm tries to make relatively large steps in the θ_2 direction and small steps in the θ_1 direction. As discussed in Section 4.1, this can be achieved by aligning the contours of the proposal density of the RWMH-V algorithm with the contours of the posterior. Sampling from the posterior depicted in the right panel is considerably more challenging, because the sampler has to travel from one modal region to the other, crossing a valley. This turns out to be difficult for the benchmark RWMH-V algorithm. Blocking, i.e., sampling from the posterior of $\theta_2|(\theta_1, Y)$ and $\theta_1|(\theta_2, Y)$, can help and so can a more careful tailoring of the proposal densities for the conditional distributions.

4.4 Alternative MH Samplers

The benchmark RWMH algorithm can be improved in two directions. First, it is often helpful to split the parameters into blocks, and sample from the posterior distribution of each block, conditional on the most recent draws of all the other parameters. Block MH algorithms are discussed in Section 4.4.1. Second, one can tailor the proposal distribution to reduce the persistence in the Markov chain. We consider two algorithms that have this feature: the Metropolis-Adjusted Langevin algorithm in Section 4.4.2 and the Newton MH algorithm in Section 4.4.3. This list is not exhaustive. For instance, Kohn, Giordani, and Strid (2010) propose an adaptive MH algorithm in which the proposal distribution is a mixture of a random walk proposal, an independence proposal, and a t-copula estimated from previous draws of the chain. While this is a promising approach, it requires the user to specify a large set of tuning parameters, which may be daunting to the applied macroeconomist.

4.4.1 Block MH Algorithm

Despite a careful choice of the proposal distribution $q(\cdot|\theta^{i-1})$, it is natural that the efficiency of the MH algorithm decreases as dimension of the parameter vector θ increases. This problem is particularly pronounced for the RWMH-V algorithm, as we will see below. The success of the proposed random walk move decreases as the dimension d of the parameter space increases. One way to alleviate this problem is to break the parameter vector into blocks. Suppose the dimension of the parameter vector θ is d. A partition of the parameter space, B, is a collection of N_{blocks} sets of indices. These sets are mutually exclusive and collectively exhaustive. Call the subsectors that correspond to the index sets θ_b, $b = 1, \ldots, N_{blocks}$. In the context of a sequence of parameter draws, let θ_b^i refer to the bth block of ith draw of θ and let $\theta_{<b}^i$ refer to the ith draw of all of the blocks before b and similarly for $\theta_{>b}^i$. Algorithm 6 describes a generic block MH algorithm.

Algorithm 6 (Block MH Algorithm) *Draw $\theta^0 \in \Theta$ and then for $i = 1$ to N:*

1. *Create a partition B^i of the parameter vector into N_{blocks} blocks $\theta_1, \ldots, \theta_{N_{blocks}}$ via some rule (perhaps probabilistic), unrelated to the current state of the Markov chain.*

2. *For $b = 1, \ldots, N_{blocks}$:*

   (a) Draw $\vartheta_b \sim q(\cdot | \left[\theta_{<b}^i, \theta_b^{i-1}, \theta_{\geq b}^{i-1} \right])$.

   (b) With probability,

   $$\alpha = \max \left\{ \frac{p(\left[\theta_{<b}^i, \vartheta_b, \theta_{>b}^{i-1} \right] | Y) q(\theta_b^{i-1}, | \theta_{<b}^i, \vartheta_b, \theta_{>b}^{i-1})}{p(\theta_{<b}^i, \theta_b^{i-1}, \theta_{>b}^{i-1} | Y) q(\vartheta_b | \theta_{<b}^i, \theta_b^{i-1}, \theta_{>b}^{i-1})}, 1 \right\},$$

   set $\theta_b^i = \vartheta_b$, otherwise set $\theta_b^i = \theta_b^{i-1}$.

In order to make the Block MH algorithm operational, the researcher has to decide how to allocate parameters to blocks in each iteration and how to choose the proposal distribution $q(\cdot | \left[\theta_{<b}^i, \theta_b^{i-1}, \theta_{>b}^{i-1} \right])$ for parameters of block b.

In general, the optimal block structure is not known outside of a few special cases—discussed in, for example, Roberts and Sahu (1997). A good rule of thumb, however, is that we want the parameters *within* a block, say, θ^b, to be as correlated as possible, while we want the parameters between blocks, say, θ_b and θ_{-b}, to be "as independent as possible," according to Robert and Casella (2004). The intuition for this rule is the following: if θ_1 and θ_2 are independent, then sampling $p(\theta_1 | \theta_2)$ and $p(\theta_2 | \theta_1)$ iteratively will directly produce draws from $p(\theta_1, \theta_2)$, because $p(\theta_1 | \theta_2) = p(\theta_1)$ and $p(\theta_2 | \theta_1) = p(\theta_2)$. On the other hand, if θ_1 and θ_2 are of the same dimension and perfectly correlated, then sampling $p(\theta_1 | \theta_2)$ amounts to solving a deterministic function for θ_1 in θ_2. The subsequent draw from $P(\theta_2 | \theta_1)$ will amount to solving for θ_2 as a function of θ_1, that is, θ_2 will be the same value as before and the chain will not move throughout the parameter space. Unfortunately, picking the "optimal" blocks to minimize dependence across blocks requires *a priori* knowledge about the posterior and is therefore often infeasible.

The first three papers in the DSGE model literature to consider blocking were Curdia and Reis (2009), Chib and Ramamurthy (2010), and Herbst (2011). Curdia and Reis (2009) group the parameters by type: economic—those related to agents' preferences and production technologies, and statistical—those governing the exogenous processes driving the model. The rationale for this grouping is that it is relatively straightforward to design proposal distributions for the statistical parameters. However, the grouping is unlikely to be optimal, because, for instance, economic parameters related to the persistence generated by the internal propagation mechanism of a DSGE model may be highly correlated with the parameters of the exogenous processes. Chib and Ramamurthy (2010) propose grouping parameters randomly. Essentially, the user specifies how many blocks to partition the parameter vector into and every iteration a new set of blocks is constructed. While there will be correlated blocks sometimes, the randomization ensures that this feature does not persist. Key to the algorithm is that the block configuration is independent of the Markov chain. This is crucial for ensuring the convergence of the chain. Otherwise, the chain is said to be adaptive and the asymptotic theory is substantially more complicated. Herbst (2011) constructs a Block MH algorithm in which the blocking is explicitly based on the posterior correlation structure which is approximated based on draws from a burn-in period. He provides evidence that the distributional blocking procedure outperforms the random blocking.

In the remainder of this book we will use random-block MH algorithms of the following form:

Algorithm 7 (Random-Block MH Algorithm)

1. *Generate a sequence of random partitions $\{B^i\}_{i=1}^{N}$ of the parameter vector θ into N_{blocks} equally sized blocks, denoted by θ_b, $b = 1, \ldots, N_{blocks}$ as follows:*

    (a) *assign an $iidU[0,1]$ draw to each element of θ;*

    (b) *sort the parameters according to the assigned random number;*

    (c) *let the b'th block consist of parameters $(b-1)N_{blocks}$, $\ldots, bN_{blocks}$.*[1]

2. *Execute Algorithm 6.*

In order to tailor the block-specific proposal distributions, Chib and Ramamurthy (2010) advocate using an optimization routine—specifically, simulated annealing—to find the mode of the conditional posterior distribution. As in the RWMH-V algorithm, the variance of the proposal distribution is based on the inverse Hessian of the conditional log posterior density evaluated at the mode. This algorithm is called Tailorized Random Block MH (TaRBMH) algorithm. While the TaRBMH algorithm is very successful in reducing the persistence of the Markov chain relative to the benchmark RWMH-V algorithm, the downside is that the algorithm is very slow due to the likelihood evaluations required to execute the simulated annealing step and the computation of the Hessian.

4.4.2 Metropolis-Adjusted Langevin Algorithm

A natural evolution from the RWMH, which uses only the level of the (unnormalized) posterior, is the Metropolis-Adjusted Langevin (MAL) algorithm, which also incorporates information from the slope of the posterior. The MAL algorithm has a long history, dating back to Roberts and Tweedie (1992) and Phillips and Smith (1994). The location vector of the proposal distribution (4.1) is given by

$$\mu(\theta^i) = \theta^{i-1} + \frac{c_1}{2} \frac{\partial}{\partial \theta} \ln p(\theta^{i-1}|Y)\bigg|_{\theta=\theta^{i-1}}, \qquad (4.6)$$

that is θ^{i-1} is adjusted by a step in the direction of the gradient of the log posterior density function. Roberts and Rosenthal (1998) show that the optimal rate of acceptance is 57% in

---

[1]If the number of parameters is not divisible by N_{blocks}, then the size of a subset of the blocks has to be adjusted.

the special case when the elements of θ are uncorrelated. The higher acceptance rate suggests improved statistical performance relative to the RWMH algorithm. Intuitively, the MAL algorithm pushes the chain toward regions of higher probability density, where most of the draws should lie. A benchmark choice for the scale matrix is $\Sigma(\theta^{i-1}) = c_2^2 I$. Thus, the algorithm has two tuning parameters, c_1 and c_2, in addition to the degrees of freedom of the t distribution, ν.

Unfortunately, in a multidimensional setting it becomes difficult to scale step size c_1 as parameters tend to have different magnitudes. Moreover, simply using the gradient ignores any potential relationship between the parameters, the knowledge of which is informative in any MCMC algorithm. It turns out (see, for example, Roberts and Stramer (2002)) that it is extremely helpful to adjust (or *precondition*) the proposal distribution as follows:

$$\mu(\theta^{i-1}) = \theta^{i-1} + \frac{c_1}{2} M_1 \frac{\partial}{\partial \theta} \ln p(\theta^{i-1}|Y)\Big|_{\theta=\theta^{i-1}}, \quad (4.7)$$

$$\Sigma(\theta_{t-1}) = c_2^2 M_2.$$

One standard practice is to set $M_1 = M_2 = M$, with

$$M = -\left[\frac{\partial}{\partial\theta\partial\theta'} \ln p(\theta|Y)\Big|_{\theta=\hat{\theta}}\right]^{-1}, \quad (4.8)$$

where $\hat{\theta}$ is the mode of the posterior distribution obtained using a numerical optimization routine. The use of the Hessian at the mode in a sense accounts for the "average" relationships between the parameters. The mean $\mu(\theta^i)$ takes (approximately) the form of a Newton step in a numerical optimization routine. If the log posterior density has an elliptical shape, then the preconditioned MAL (p-MAL) algorithm can be quite efficient. When examining the effectiveness of this algorithm below, we abstract from the difference between the Hessian and the posterior covariance, $\mathbb{V}_\pi[\theta]$, and simply use the latter:

$$\text{MAL}: M_1 = M_2 = \mathbb{V}_\pi[\theta].$$

4.4.3 Newton MH Algorithm

The connection between posterior simulation and Newtonian optimization is more closely exploited by Qi and Minka (2002) in an algorithm called Newton MH algorithm. Their algorithm replaces the Hessian evaluated at the posterior mode $\hat{\theta}$ by the Hessian evaluated at θ^{i-1}. Using the general form of the proposal density in (4.1) the location vector and scale matrix are given by

$$
\begin{aligned}
\mu(\theta^{i-1}) &= \theta^{i-1} - s \left[\frac{\partial}{\partial\theta\partial\theta'} \ln p(\theta|Y) \Big|_{\theta=\theta^{i-1}} \right]^{-1} \quad (4.9) \\
&\quad \times \frac{\partial}{\partial\theta} \ln p(\theta^{i-1}|Y) \Big|_{\theta=\theta^{i-1}} \\
\hat{\Sigma}(\theta^{i-1}) &= -c_2^2 \left[\frac{\partial}{\partial\theta\partial\theta'} \ln p(\theta|Y) \Big|_{\theta=\theta^{i-1}} \right]^{-1}.
\end{aligned}
$$

The constant s can be interpreted as the size of the Newton step. If the log posterior is quadratic, i.e., the posterior distribution is normal, the posterior mode can be reached in one step by setting $s = 1$. Thus, for $i > 2$ the mean of the proposal distribution is equal to the mean of the target distribution and the algorithm turns into an independence MH algorithm.

In DSGE model applications the posterior distribution is non-Gaussian and the mean $\mu(\theta^{i-1})$ differs from the posterior mode and varies with i. In this case, it is useful to let s, sometimes called the learning rate, be stochastic (independently of θ^{i-1}):

$$
c_1 = 2s, \quad s \sim iidU[0, \bar{s}],
$$

where $\bar{s}$ is a tuning parameter.[2] This means that average step-size is $\bar{s}/2$. For our simulations below, we will set the hyper-parameters of the algorithm

$$
\text{Newton MH}: \bar{s} = 2, c_2 = 1.
$$

---

[2]As long as s and θ^{i-1} are independent, the Markov transition implied will still preserve the posterior as its invariant distribution. This can seen by thinking of an augmented posterior $p(s, \theta|Y)$ and casting the algorithm as the so-called Metropolis-within-Gibbs.

While the RWMH algorithm blindly searches through the parameter space looking for areas of high posterior density, the proposal densities of the MAL algorithm and the Newton MH algorithm explicitly account for the slope and the curvature of the log posterior density. This leads to a reduction in the persistence of the Markov chain and, for a given number of draws, to more accurate Monte Carlo approximations of posterior moments. Unfortunately, there is a significant computational cost associated with evaluating the first and second derivatives of the log posterior. For DSGE models, these derivatives cannot be obtained analytically. Herbst (2011) uses matrix calculus to derive an efficient algorithm for computing these objects for linearized DSGE models. In some applications, even brute-force numerical differentiation can produce reasonably sized chains without taking too much time.

It should be noted that the we could potentially extend the set of algorithms even further. For example, Hamiltonian Monte Carlo (HMC)—see Neal (2010)—uses the gradient to generate proposals in a form suggested by Hamiltonian dynamics. Girolami and Calderhead (2011) extend both MAL and HMC to explicitly account for the Riemann geometric structure of the posterior. Preliminary trials with both of these algorithms suggested, that, yes, they represented a statistical improvement from the algorithms presented above. However, the computational burden associated with them outweighed any gains. For example, computing the information matrix—a requirement for the Riemann-based method—of a DSGE is still too cumbersome to be used within an MH algorithm. Computational gains in these kinds of calculations, a subject of on-going research, might make them more feasible and, thus, preferred.

4.5 Comparing the Accuracy of MH Algorithms

We now compare the accuracy of the MH samplers discussed in the preceding sections. As a measure of accuracy we consider the small-sample inefficiency factor InEff_N computed based on $N_{run} = 50$ independent runs (initialized based on draws from the posterior distribution of θ) of each MCMC algorithm considered. We also compare the small-sample variance of $\bar{\theta}$ across the runs to Newey-West HAC$[\bar{\theta}]$ estimates computed from each of the chains. The set of algorithms includes the benchmark 1-Block RWMH-V algorithm; a 1-Block RWMH-I algorithm in which the scale matrix of the proposal distribution is set to the identity matrix, i.e., $\hat{\Sigma} = I$; 3-Block RWMH-V and RWMH-I algorithms; a 3-Block MAL algorithm; and a 3-Block Newton MH algorithm.

The RWMH-I algorithms do not require any specific knowledge of the posterior distribution, which is attractive because it is easy to implement. In particular, this choice does not require a preliminary numerical maximization of the posterior, which may be difficult to execute if the posterior is very non-elliptical. The downside of choosing the identity matrix is that it ignores the scaling of the parameters and the orientation of the posterior contours. If the prior distribution is proper and the marginal distributions are appropriately scaled, then the identity matrix could be replaced by a diagonal matrix with the prior variances on the diagonal.

The multi-block algorithms all use the random blocking procedure of Algorithm 6. With the exception of the RWMH-I algorithm, we use the posterior covariance matrix associated with the parameters of each block to specify the scale matrix of the proposal distribution. For each algorithm we select the tuning constants to achieve an acceptance rate between 30% and 50%. For each run of the six algorithms we generate $N = 100,000$ draws from the posterior distribution. The first $N_0 = 50,000$ draws are discarded and the remaining 50,000 draws are used to compute Monte Carlo averages. We subsequently present results for the risk-aversion parameter τ. Results for the other parameters are qualitatively similar.

The fastest run time [hh:mm:ss], the average acceptance rate, and the tuning constants for each algorithm are reported in Table 4.2. The 1-Block RWMH algorithms are the fastest because they only require one likelihood evaluation per draw. The 3-Block RWMH-I and RWMH-V algorithms are approximately three times slower than their 1-block counterparts because they require three likelihood evaluations and some additional time to assign parameters to blocks. MAL and New-

Table 4.2: Run Times and Tuning Constants

Algorithm	Run Time [hh:mm:ss]	Acceptance Rate	Tuning Constants
1-Block RWMH-I	00:01:13	0.28	$c = 0.015$
1-Block RWMH-V	00:01:13	0.37	$c = 0.400$
3-Block RWMH-I	00:03:38	0.40	$c = 0.070$
3-Block RWMH-V	00:03:36	0.43	$c = 1.200$
3-Block MAL	00:54:12	0.43	$c_1 = 0.400$
			$c_2 = 0.750$
3-Block Newton MH	03:01:40	0.53	$\bar{s} = 0.700$
			$c_2 = 0.600$

Notes: In each run we generate $N = 100,000$ draws. We report the fastest run time and the average acceptance rate across $N_{run} = 50$ independent Markov chains.

ton MH are computationally the most demanding algorithms because they rely on the evaluation of the Hessian associated with the log posterior density.

Before examining the accuracy of the Monte Carlo approximations, we will take a look at the persistence of the Markov chains generated by the six algorithms. For each algorithm, the top panel of Figure 4.7 depicts the autocorrelation function up to lag $l = 40$. Each autocorrelation function is computed based on the sequence of draws $\{\tau^i\}_{i=N_0+1}^{N}$ from a single chain. The choice of proposal distribution for the MH algorithm has a profound effect on the persistence of the chain. The comparison between the 1-Block RWMH-I and the 1-Block RWMH-V algorithms highlights that aligning the contours of the proposal distribution with the contours of the posterior distribution (at the mode) leads to a drastic reduction in the persistence. While the chain generated by the 1-Block RWMH-I algorithm is nearly perfectly correlated even at a displacement of 40, the autocorrelation of the RWMH-V chain drops below 0.5 after about 28 iterations of the algorithm.

Once the number of blocks is increased from one to three

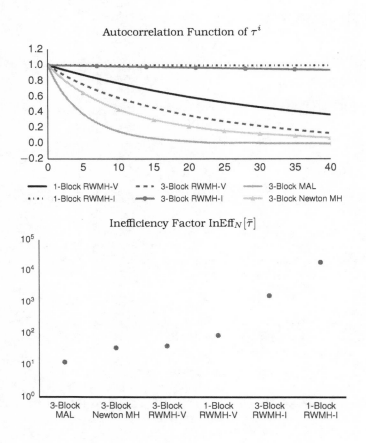

Figure 4.7: Autocorrelation Functions and Inefficiency Factors. The autocorrelation functions in the top panel are computed based on a single run of each algorithm. The small-sample inefficiency factors in the bottom panel are computed based on $N_{run} = 50$ independent runs of each algorithm.

the persistence of the Markov chains generated by the RWMH-I and RWMH-V algorithms drops noticeably. Thus, blocking indeed has the desired effect. The 3-Block RWMH-I algorithm, however, still performs worse than the 1-Block RWMH-V algorithm, highlighting the importance of well-tailored proposal densities. The autocorrelation of the 3-Block RWMH-V algorithm falls below 0.5 after about thirteen iterations. Finally, the MAL and Newton MH algorithms yield very low serial correlation but are also quite costly computationally, as the run times in Table 4.2 indicate.

The second panel of Figure 4.7 shows an estimate of the small-sample inefficiency factor InEff$_N$ of each sampler, again for the relative risk aversion parameter. Recall that this inefficiency factor is computed as $\mathbb{V}[\bar{\tau}]/(\mathbb{V}_\pi[\tau]/N)$. The numerator is the small-sample variance of $\bar{\tau}$ across chains and the denominator is the Monte Carlo variance associated with the (infeasible) direct sampling from the posterior. The inefficiency measures are qualitatively consistent with the autocorrelation plot in the top panel of the figure. The inefficiency factor for the 1-Block RWMH-I algorithm is about 18,500, meaning that the 100,000 draws that we generated deliver a Monte Carlo approximation that is about as accurate as an approximation obtained from 5.5 iid draws. The 1-Block RWMH-V algorithm has an inefficiency factor of 88 and blocking reduces it to 41. Thus, the 100,000 draws obtained from the 3-Block RWMH-V algorithm are equivalent to 2,440 iid draws.

Based on the total number of draws, the run time of the algorithm, and the inefficiency factor InEff$_N$ which measures the Monte Carlo variance associated with the MH algorithm relative to the Monte Carlo variance associated with iid sampling, we can determine how many iid-equivalent draws the algorithm produces per unit of time:

$$iid\text{-equivalent draws per second}$$
$$= \frac{N}{\text{Run Time [seconds]}} \cdot \frac{1}{\text{InEff}_N}.$$

Accounting for the run time, the 3-Block RWMH-V algorithm generates about 5.65 iid-equivalent draws from the posterior distribution of τ per second, whereas the 1-Block RWMH-V algorithm produces 7.76 iid-equivalent draws per second. Thus, while blocking reduces the persistence in the chain, there is also a computational cost associated with the additional likelihood evaluations. On balance, in this particular application the one-block algorithm is marginally more effective in generating iid-equivalent draws per second than

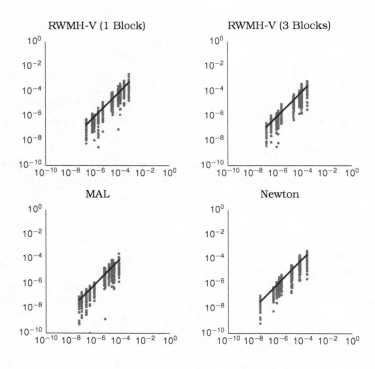

Figure 4.8: Small-Sample Variance versus HAC Estimates. Each panel contains scatter plots of the small-sample variance $\mathbb{V}[\bar{\theta}]$ computed across multiple chains (x-axis) vs. the $\text{HAC}[\bar{h}]$ estimates of $\Omega(\theta)/N$ (y-axis) computed for each chain based on (3.72) with $L = 10,000$. The solid line plots the 45 degree line.

the three-block algorithm. The MAL and Newton MH algorithms have low inefficiency ratios of 12 and 36, respectively, which translate into 1.24 and 0.13 iid-equivalent draws per second due to the large run times of these two algorithms. Thus, in terms of iid-equivalent draws per second, the benchmark 1-Block RWMH-V algorithm is in fact the most efficient. However, in our experience, in applications with a high-dimensional parameter space, blocking is advantageous.

Finally, in Figure 4.8 we compare the small-sample variance $\mathbb{V}(\bar{\tau})$ computed as the sample variance of $\bar{\tau}$ across multiple chains to the HAC estimates $\text{HAC}[\bar{\tau}]$ computed for each chain based on (3.72) with $L = 10,000$. If the chains have converged and the central limit theorem is operational, then the HAC estimates should be very close to the small-sample variance of $\bar{\tau}$. It turns out that this is indeed the case for the small-scale New Keynesian DSGE model: by and large the estimates line up along the 45-degree line. The variation in the vertical dimension reflects the variability of the HAC estimates across the independent chains. On average, the HAC estimates slightly underestimate the variability of the Monte Carlo approximation.

4.6 Evaluation of the Marginal Data Density

As discussed in Chapter 3, marginal data densities play an important role in Bayesian model selection and averaging. The marginal data density of a model M is defined as

$$p(Y|M) = \int p(Y|\theta, M)p(\theta|M)d\theta \qquad (4.10)$$

and it is used to turn prior model probabilities into posterior model probabilities; see Equation (3.31). In general, the evaluation of the marginal data density involves a high-dimensional integral. Numerical approximations can be obtained by post-processing the output of MH samplers. In this section we will review the approximations proposed by Geweke (1999), Sims, Waggoner, and Zha (2008), and Chib and Jeliazkov (2001) and assess their accuracy in the context of the small-scale New Keynesian DSGE models. Additional algorithms to approximate marginal data densities and numerical illustrations are provided in Ardia, Bastürk, Hoogerheide, and van Dijk (2012). To simplify the notation we will omit the model indicator M from now on from the conditioning set.

4.6.1 *Harmonic Mean Estimators*

Starting point for the harmonic mean estimator of $p(Y)$ (or reciprocal importance sampling) is the slightly rewritten version of Bayes Theorem

$$\frac{1}{p(Y)} = \frac{1}{p(Y|\theta)p(\theta)}p(\theta|Y). \tag{4.11}$$

We assume that the dimension of the parameter vector is d. Note that we can multiply both sides of this equation by a function $f(\theta)$ with the property that $\int f(\theta)d\theta = 1$. After integrating the left-hand side and the right-hand side with respect to θ we obtain

$$\frac{1}{p(Y)} = \int \frac{f(\theta)}{p(Y|\theta)p(\theta)}p(\theta|Y)d\theta. \tag{4.12}$$

Recall that the MH samplers deliver a sequence of draws $\{\theta^i\}_{i=1}^N$ from the posterior distribution $p(\theta|Y)$. This suggests that a Monte Carlo approximation of the marginal data density can be obtained as

$$p(Y) \approx \left[\frac{1}{N - N_0} \sum_{i=N_0+1}^{N} \frac{f(\theta^i)}{p(Y|\theta^i)p(\theta^i)} \right]^{-1}, \tag{4.13}$$

where N_0 is the size of the discarded burn-in sample. The convergence of the Monte Carlo average depends on the existence of the moments of the ratio of $f(\theta^i)/[p(Y|\theta^i)p(\theta^i)]$. Draws of θ^i associated with a low likelihood value can generate large outliers and invalidate the convergence of the Monte Carlo average. We will now discuss two specific choices of $f(\theta)$. The general idea is to construct a function that approximates the choice of the posterior distribution and is equal to zero for parameters that are associated with a very low posterior density.

Geweke's Choice of $f(\cdot)$. If the posterior distribution is unimodal and the contours are elliptical, then the density of a truncated normal distribution can serve as $f(\cdot)$. Geweke (1999) proposes to proceed as follows. Let $\bar{\theta}$ and $\bar{V}_\theta$ be numerical approximations of the posterior mean and covariance matrix of θ computed from the output of the posterior sampler. Now define $f(\theta)$ as

$$\begin{aligned} f(\theta) &= \tau^{-1}(2\pi)^{-d/2}|\bar{V}_\theta|^{-1/2} \exp\left[-0.5(\theta - \bar{\theta})'\bar{V}_\theta^{-1}(\theta - \bar{\theta})\right] \\ &\quad \times \mathbb{I}\left\{(\theta - \bar{\theta})'\bar{V}_\theta^{-1}(\theta - \bar{\theta}) \leq F_{\chi_d^2}^{-1}(\tau)\right\}, \tag{4.14} \end{aligned}$$

where $\mathbb{I}\{x \leq a\}$ is the indicator function that equals one if $x \leq a$ and is zero otherwise and $F_{\chi_d^2}^{-1}(\tau)$ is the inverse cdf of a χ^2 random variable with d degrees of freedom.

The threshold τ is a tuning parameter. A low value for τ eliminates θ^is which lie in tails of the posterior. On the one hand, this truncation reduces the influence that outliers can have on the average and thereby lowers the variability of the estimator. On the other hand, the more draws that are excluded (i.e., $f(\theta^i) = 0$) in (4.13), the higher the variability the estimator owing to the smaller sample used. In situations where the posterior is approximately normal, it is better to use a higher τ. Usually, when the posterior has already been sampled, the associated posterior kernel $\{p(Y|\theta^i)p(\theta^i)\}_{i=1}^N$ has already been stored, making the evaluation of (4.13) straightforward. For applications it is recommended to try different values of τ, to assess the stability of the estimator.

Sims, Waggoner, and Zha's Choice of $f(\cdot)$. If the posterior is non-elliptical, the ratio $f(\theta)/[p(Y|\theta)p(\theta)]$ can vary substantially across the parameter space, leading to poor estimates from a multivariate Gaussian $f(\cdot)$. Sims, Waggoner, and Zha (2008), hereafter SWZ, propose an alternative function $f(\cdot)$. Instead of centering the function at the mean of the posterior distribution, SWZ center their $f(\cdot)$ at a (or the) mode $\hat{\theta}$. If a distribution is multimodal, the posterior mean may be located in an area of very low density, leading to a severe mismatch between $f(\cdot)$ and the posterior. Using draws from the posterior, construct the scale matrix

$$\hat{V}_\theta = \frac{1}{N} \sum_{i=1}^N (\theta^i - \hat{\theta})(\theta^i - \hat{\theta})', \tag{4.15}$$

define the distance

$$r(\theta) = \sqrt{(\theta - \hat{\theta})' \hat{V}_\theta^{-1} (\theta - \hat{\theta})}, \tag{4.16}$$

and let $r^i = r(\theta^i)$. The function $f(\cdot)$ is constructed in four steps.

First, SWZ construct a heavy-tailed univariate density, $g(\cdot)$, to match the behavior of the posterior:

$$g(r) = \begin{cases} \frac{\nu r^{\nu-1}}{b^\nu - a^\nu} & \text{if } r \in [a, b] \\ 0 & \text{otherwise} \end{cases}. \qquad (4.17)$$

Letting c_1, c_{10}, and c_{90} be the first, 10th and 90th percentiles of the empirical distribution of $\{r^i\}_{i=1}^N$, respectively, the hyperparameters of $g(r)$ are chosen as follows:

$$\nu = \frac{\ln(0.1/0.9)}{\ln(c_{10}/c_{90})}, \quad a = c_1, \quad \text{and } b = \frac{c_{90}}{0.9^{1/\nu}}.$$

The choice of ν and b implies that the 10th and 90th percentiles of $g(\cdot)$ are identical to the corresponding percentiles of the empirical distribution of $\{r^i\}_{i=1}^N$ if $a = 0$. Because c_1 is non-zero, albeit potentially small, these percentiles will not match perfectly.

Second, SWZ define the density $\tilde{f}(r)$ as

$$\tilde{f}(r) = \frac{\Gamma(d/2)}{2\pi^{d/2}|V_{\hat\theta}|^{1/2}} \frac{g(r)}{r^{d-1}}, \qquad (4.18)$$

where $\Gamma(x)$ is the Gamma function and d the dimension of the parameter vector θ. Third, because potential multimodality implies that $p(Y|\theta)p(\theta)$ can be very small in regions of the parameter space where $\tilde{f}(\cdot)$ is relatively high, the lowest $1 - q$ proportion of draws are excluded from the evaluation of (4.13). Denote the associated cutoff value for the log posterior density kernel by L_{1-q}. Recall that the function $g(r)$ was truncated at the boundary of the interval $[a, b]$ Thus, the overall truncation is

$$\mathcal{I}(\theta) = \mathbb{I}\{\ln p(Y|\theta)p(\theta) > L_{1-q}\} \times \mathbb{I}\{r(\theta) \in [a, b]\}. \qquad (4.19)$$

Unlike Geweke's estimator, the probability that $\mathcal{I}(\theta)$ equals one can only be computed through simulation, because it relies on information from the posterior and not only on the properties $\tilde{f}(\cdot)$ per se. An estimate can be obtained by:

$$\hat{\tau} = \hat{\mathbb{P}}\{\mathcal{I}(\theta) = 1\} = \frac{1}{J}\sum_{j=1}^{J} \mathcal{I}(\theta^j), \quad \theta^j \sim iid\ \tilde{f}(\theta).$$

Fourth, combining $\tilde{f}(r)$ and $\mathcal{I}(\theta)$, we obtain the approximating function

$$f_{SWZ}(\theta) = \hat{\tau}^{-1}\tilde{f}\left(\sqrt{(\theta - \hat{\theta})'\hat{V}_{\theta}^{-1}(\theta - \hat{\theta})}\right)\mathcal{I}(\theta). \qquad (4.20)$$

There are two drawbacks associated with $f_{SWZ}(\theta)$. First, it can be quite noisy, requiring a large J to achieve a stable estimate $\hat{\tau}$. Second, computationally it can be quite costly to compute $\hat{\tau}$ because this requires the evaluation of the log-likelihood function of the DSGE model. Still, if the posterior exhibits multimodality and/or fat tails, the SWZ estimator can be much more reliable than Geweke's estimator.

4.6.2 Chib and Jeliazkov's Estimator

While Geweke's (1999) and SWZ's (2008) harmonic mean estimators could be computed for the output of any posterior simulator, the following method proposed by Chib and Jeliazkov (2001) is closely tied to the MH algorithm (Algorithm 5). We start by rewriting Bayes Theorem as follows:

$$p(Y) = \frac{p(Y|\tilde{\theta})p(\tilde{\theta})}{p(\tilde{\theta}|Y)}. \qquad (4.21)$$

Note that this relationship holds for any parameter value $\tilde{\theta}$. We will take $\tilde{\theta}$ to be a parameter value that is associated with a high posterior density, e.g., the posterior mode. In order to make the formula operational, we need to numerically approximate the value of the posterior density $p(\tilde{\theta}|Y)$.

Using the notation introduced in Section 3.5, the proposal density for a transition from θ to $\tilde{\theta}$ is given by $q(\tilde{\theta}|\theta)$. Moreover, the probability of accepting the proposed draw is

$$\alpha(\tilde{\theta}|\theta) = \min\left\{1, \frac{p(\tilde{\theta}|Y)q(\theta|\tilde{\theta})}{p(\theta|Y)q(\tilde{\theta}|\theta)}\right\}. \qquad (4.22)$$

Using the definition of $\alpha(\tilde{\theta}|\theta)$ we can express the marginal density of an accepted draw as[3]

$$\int \alpha(\tilde{\theta}|\theta)q(\tilde{\theta}|\theta)p(\theta|Y)d\theta \tag{4.23}$$

$$= \int \min\left\{1, \frac{p(\tilde{\theta}|Y)q(\theta|\tilde{\theta})}{p(\theta|Y)q(\tilde{\theta}|\theta)}\right\} q(\tilde{\theta}|\theta)p(\theta|Y)d\theta$$

$$= p(\tilde{\theta}|Y)\int q(\theta|\tilde{\theta})\min\left\{\frac{p(\theta|Y)q(\tilde{\theta}|\theta)}{p(\tilde{\theta}|Y)q(\theta|\tilde{\theta})}, 1\right\} d\theta$$

$$= p(\tilde{\theta}|Y)\int q(\theta|\tilde{\theta})\alpha(\theta|\tilde{\theta})d\theta.$$

In turn, the posterior density at $\tilde{\theta}$ can be approximated as

$$\hat{p}(\tilde{\theta}|Y) = \frac{\frac{1}{N}\sum_{i=1}^{N} \alpha(\tilde{\theta}|\theta^i)q(\tilde{\theta}|\theta^i)}{\frac{1}{J}\sum_{j=1}^{J} \alpha(\theta^j|\tilde{\theta})}. \tag{4.24}$$

Here $\{\theta^i\}_{i=1}^N$ is the sequence of draws generated with the MH algorithm and $\{\theta^j\}_{j=1}^J$ are draws from $q(\theta|\tilde{\theta})$ that can be generated by direct sampling. The final approximation of the marginal data density is given by

$$\hat{p}_{CS}(Y) = \frac{p(Y|\tilde{\theta})p(\tilde{\theta})}{\hat{p}(\tilde{\theta}|Y)}. \tag{4.25}$$

Just as the SWZ modified harmonic mean estimator, the CS estimator also requires the user evaluate the log posterior kernel J additional times, which can be expensive for large models.

4.6.3 Numerical Illustration

We estimate log marginal data density of the small-scale New Keynesian DSGE model using $50,000$ draws from the posterior from $N_{run} = 50$ separate runs of the RWMH-V algorithm (we set $N = 100,000$ and discard the first $N_0 = 50,000$

---

[3]Recall that for the RWMH algorithm $q(\tilde{\theta}|\theta) = q(\theta|\tilde{\theta})$ and the formulas simplify considerably.

Table 4.3: MH-Based Marginal Data Density Estimates

Model	Mean($\ln \hat{p}(Y)$)	Std. Dev.($\ln \hat{p}(Y)$)
Geweke ($\tau = 0.5$)	-346.17	0.03
Geweke ($\tau = 0.9$)	-346.10	0.04
SWZ ($q = 0.5$)	-346.29	0.03
SWZ ($q = 0.9$)	-346.31	0.02
Chib and Jeliazkov	-346.20	0.40

Notes: Table shows mean and standard deviation of log marginal data density estimators, computed over $N_{run} = 50$ runs of the RWMH-V sampler using $N = 100,000$ draws, discarding a burn-in sample of $N_0 = 50,000$ draws. The SWZ estimator uses $J = 100,000$ draws to compute $\hat{\tau}$, while the CJ estimators uses $J = 100,000$ to compute the denominator of $\hat{p}(\tilde{\theta}|Y)$.

draws). Table 4.3 displays the mean and standard deviation across the fifty runs for each log MDD approximation. For the harmonic mean estimators we use two different truncation probabilities. All the algorithms give roughly the same answer, although the Chib and Jeliazkov approximation is much more variable. Moving to the modified harmonic mean estimators, the SWZ estimate is essentially robust to the choice of truncation. The mean of Geweke's estimator slightly changes with truncation τ, consistent with the observation that the DSGE posterior has slightly fatter tails than a multivariate normal, which the SWZ is less affected by. Overall the SWZ harmonic mean estimator has the smallest standard deviation, albeit at a higher computational cost than Geweke's estimator.

Chapter 5

Sequential Monte Carlo Methods

Importance sampling has been rarely used in DSGE model applications. A key difficulty with Algorithm 4, in particular in high-dimensional parameter spaces, is to find a good proposal density. In this chapter, we will explore methods in which proposal densities are constructed sequentially. Suppose ϕ_n, $n = 1, \ldots, N_\phi$, is a sequence that slowly increases from zero to one. We can define a sequence of tempered posteriors as

$$\pi_n(\theta) = \frac{[p(Y|\theta)]^{\phi_n} p(\theta)}{\int [p(Y|\theta)]^{\phi_n} p(\theta) d\theta} \quad n = 0, \ldots, N_\phi, \quad \phi_n \uparrow 1. \quad (5.1)$$

Provided that ϕ_1 is close to zero, the prior density $p(\theta)$ may serve as an efficient proposal density for $\pi_1(\theta)$. Likewise, the density $\pi_n(\theta)$ may be a good proposal density for $\pi_{n+1}(\theta)$. Sequential Monte Carlo (SMC) algorithms try to exploit this insight efficiently.

SMC algorithms were initially developed to solve filtering problems that arise in nonlinear state-space models. We will consider such filtering applications in detail in Chapter 8. Chopin (2002) showed how to adapt the particle filtering techniques to conduct posterior inference for a static parameter vector. Textbook treatments of SMC algorithms can be found, for instance, in Liu (2001) and Cappé, Moulines, and Ryden (2005). The volume by Doucet, de Freitas, and Gordon (2001) discusses many applications and practical aspects of SMC. Creal (2012) provides a recent survey focusing on SMC applications in econometrics.

The first paper that applied SMC techniques to posterior inference in DSGE models is Creal (2007). He presents a basic SMC algorithm and uses it for posterior inference in a small-scale DSGE model that is similar to the model in Section 1.1. Herbst and Schorfheide (2014) developed the algorithm further, provided some convergence results for an adaptive version of the algorithm building on the theoretical analysis of Chopin (2004), and showed that a properly tailored SMC algorithm delivers more reliable posterior inference for large-scale DSGE models with multimodal posteriors than the widely used RMWH-V algorithm. Much of the exposition in this chapter borrows from Herbst and Schorfheide (2014). An additional advantage of the SMC algorithms over MCMC algorithms, on the computational front, highlighted by Durham and Geweke (2014), is that SMC is much more amenable to parallelization. Durham and Geweke (2014) show how to implement an SMC algorithm on a graphical processing unit (GPU), facilitating massive speed gains in estimations. While the evaluation of DSGE likelihoods is not (yet) amenable to GPU calculation, we will show how to exploit the parallel structure of the algorithm.

We present a generic SMC algorithm in Section 5.1. Further details on the implementation of the algorithm, the adaptive choice of tuning constants, and the convergence of the Monte Carlo approximations constructed from the output of the algorithm are provided in Section 5.2. Finally, we apply the algorithm to the small-scale New Keynesian DSGE model in Section 5.3. Because we will generate draws of θ sequentially, from a sequence of posterior distributions $\{\pi_n(\theta)\}_{n=1}^{N_\phi}$, it is useful to equip the parameter vector with a subscript n. Thus, θ_n is associated with the density $\pi_n(\cdot)$.

5.1 A Generic SMC Algorithm

Just like the basic importance sampling algorithm, SMC algorithms generate weighted draws from the sequence of posteriors $\{\pi_n\}_{n=1}^{N_\phi}$ in (5.1). The weighted draws are called particles. We denote the overall number of particles by N. At any stage the posterior distribution $\pi_n(\theta)$ is represented by a swarm of particles $\{\theta_n^i, W_n^i\}_{i=1}^N$ in the sense that the Monte Carlo average

$$\bar{h}_{n,N} = \frac{1}{N} \sum_{i=1}^{N} W_n^i h(\theta^i) \xrightarrow{a.s.} \mathbb{E}_{\pi}[h(\theta_n)]. \qquad (5.2)$$

Starting from stage $n-1$ particles $\{\theta_{n-1}^i, W_{n-1}^i\}_{i=1}^N$ the algorithm proceeds in three steps, using Chopin (2004)'s terminology: *correction*, that is, reweighting the stage $n-1$ particles to reflect the density in iteration n; *selection*, that is, eliminating a highly uneven distribution of particle weights (degeneracy) by resampling the particles; and *mutation*, that is, propagating the particles forward using a Markov transition kernel to adapt the particle values to the stage n bridge density.

The sequence of posteriors in (5.1) was obtained by tempering the likelihood function, that is, we replaced $p(Y|\theta)$ by $[p(Y|\theta)]^{\phi_n}$. Alternatively, one could construct the sequence of posteriors by sequentially adding observations to the likelihood function, that is, $\pi_n(\theta)$ is based on $p(Y_{1:\lfloor \phi_n T \rfloor}|\theta)$:

$$\pi_n^{(D)}(\theta) = \frac{p(Y_{1:\lfloor \phi_n T \rfloor})p(\theta)}{\int p(Y_{1:\lfloor \phi_n T \rfloor})p(\theta)d\theta}, \qquad (5.3)$$

where $\lfloor x \rfloor$ is the largest integer that is less than or equal to x. This data tempering is particularly attractive in sequential applications. Because individual observations are not divisible, the data tempering approach is slightly less flexible. This may matter for the early stages of the SMC sampler in which it may be advantageous to add information in very small increments. The subsequent algorithm is presented in terms of likelihood tempering. However, we also discuss the necessary adjustments for data tempering.

The SMC algorithm provided below relies on sequences of tuning parameters. To make the exposition more transparent, we begin by assuming that these sequences are provided *ex ante*. Let $\{\rho_n\}_{n=1}^{N_\phi}$ be a sequence of zeros and ones that determine whether the particles are resampled in the selection step and let $\{\zeta_n\}_{n=1}^{N_\phi}$ of tuning parameters for the Markov transition density in the mutation step. The adaptive choice of these tuning parameters will be discussed in Section 5.2.2.

Algorithm 8 (Generic SMC with Likelihood Tempering)

1. **Initialization.** ($\phi_0 = 0$). Draw the initial particles from the prior: $\theta_1^i \overset{iid}{\sim} p(\theta)$ and $W_1^i = 1$, $i = 1, \ldots, N$.

2. **Recursion.** For $n = 1, \ldots, N_\phi$,

   (a) **Correction.** Reweight the particles from stage $n-1$ by defining the incremental weights

   $$\tilde{w}_n^i = [p(Y|\theta_{n-1}^i)]^{\phi_n - \phi_{n-1}} \qquad (5.4)$$

   and the normalized weights

   $$\tilde{W}_n^i = \frac{\tilde{w}_n^i W_{n-1}^i}{\frac{1}{N} \sum_{i=1}^N \tilde{w}_n^i W_{n-1}^i}, \quad i = 1, \ldots, N. \qquad (5.5)$$

   An approximation of $\mathbb{E}_{\pi_n}[h(\theta)]$ is given by

   $$\tilde{h}_{n,N} = \frac{1}{N} \sum_{i=1}^N \tilde{W}_n^i h(\theta_{n-1}^i). \qquad (5.6)$$

   (b) **Selection.**
   Case (i): If $\rho_n = 1$, resample the particles via multinomial resampling. Let $\{\hat{\theta}\}_{i=1}^N$ denote N iid draws from a multinomial distribution characterized by support points and weights $\{\theta_{n-1}^i, \tilde{W}_n^i\}_{i=1}^N$ and set $W_n^i = 1$.
   Case (ii): If $\rho_n = 0$, let $\hat{\theta}_n^i = \theta_{n-1}^i$ and $W_n^i = \tilde{W}_n^i$, $i = 1, \ldots, N$. An approximation of $\mathbb{E}_{\pi_n}[h(\theta)]$ is given by

   $$\hat{h}_{n,N} = \frac{1}{N} \sum_{i=1}^N W_n^i h(\hat{\theta}_n^i). \qquad (5.7)$$

   (c) **Mutation.** Propagate the particles $\{\hat{\theta}_i, W_n^i\}$ via N_{MH} steps of a MH algorithm with transition density $\theta_n^i \sim K_n(\theta_n|\hat{\theta}_n^i; \zeta_n)$ and stationary distribution $\pi_n(\theta)$ (see Algorithm 9 below for details). An approximation of $\mathbb{E}_{\pi_n}[h(\theta)]$ is given by

   $$\bar{h}_{n,N} = \frac{1}{N} \sum_{i=1}^N h(\theta_n^i) W_n^i. \qquad (5.8)$$

3. *For $n = N_\phi$ ($\phi_{N_\phi} = 1$) the final importance sampling approximation of $\mathbb{E}_\pi[h(\theta)]$ is given by:*

$$\bar{h}_{N_\phi, N} = \sum_{i=1}^{N} h(\theta_{N_\phi}^i) W_{N_\phi}^i. \qquad (5.9)$$

5.1.1 Three-Step Particle Propagation

A stylized representation of the propagation of the particles is depicted in Figure 5.1. Each dot corresponds to a particle and its size indicates the weight. At stage $n = 0$, $N = 21$ draws are generated from a $U[-10, 10]$ distribution and each particle receives the weight $W_0^i = 1$. At stage $n = 1$ the particles are reweighted during the correction step (the size of the dots is no longer uniform) and the particle values are modified during the mutation step (the location of the dots shifted). The bottom of the figure depicts the target posterior density. As n and ϕ_n increase, the target distribution becomes more concentrated. The concentration is mainly reflected in the increased weight of the particles with values between -3 and 3. The figure is generated under the assumption that ρ_n equals one for $n = 3$ and zero otherwise. Thus, in iteration $n = 3$ the resampling step is executed and the uneven particle weights are equalized. While the selection step generates twenty-one particles with equal weights, there are only six distinct particle values, four of which have multiple copies. The subsequent mutation step restores the diversity in particle values.

5.1.2 A Closer Look at the Algorithm

Algorithm 8 is initialized for $n = 0$ by generating *iid* draws from the prior distribution. This initialization works well as long as the prior is sufficiently diffuse to assign non-trivial probability mass to the area of the parameter space in which the likelihood function peaks. There do exist papers in the DSGE model estimation literature in which the *posterior mean* of some parameters is several *prior* standard deviations away from the *prior mean*. For such applications it might be necessary to choose $\phi_0 > 0$ and to use an initial distribution that is also informed by the tempered likelihood function $[p(Y|\theta)]^{\phi_0}$.

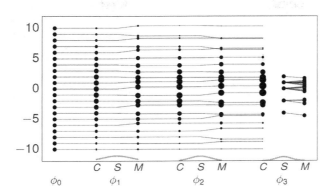

Figure 5.1: SMC Evolution of Particles. The vertical location of each dot represents the particle value and the diameter of the dot represents its weight. The densities at the bottom represent the tempered target posterior $\pi_n(\cdot)$. C is Correction; S is Selection; and M is Mutation.

If the particles are initialized based on a more general distribution with density $g(\theta)$, then for $n = 1$ the incremental weights have to be corrected by the ratio $p(\theta)/g(\theta)$.

The correction step reweights the stage $n - 1$ particles to generate an importance sampling approximation of π_n. Because the parameter value θ^i does not change in this step, no further evaluation of the likelihood function is required. The likelihood value $p(Y|\theta_{n-1}^i)$ was computed as a by-product of the mutation step in iteration $n - 1$. As discussed in Section 3.4, the accuracy of the importance sampling approximation depends on the distribution of the particle weights $\tilde{W}_n^i$. The more uniformly the weights are distributed, the more accurate the approximation. If likelihood tempering is replaced by data tempering, then the incremental weights $\tilde{w}_n^i$ in (5.4) have to be defined as

$$\tilde{w}_n^{i(D)} = p(Y_{(\lfloor \phi_n T \rfloor + 1):\lfloor \phi_n T \rfloor}|\theta). \tag{5.10}$$

The correction steps deliver a numerical approximation of the marginal data density as a by-product. Using arguments that we will present in more detail in Section 5.2.4 below, it can be verified that the unnormalized particle weights converge under suitable regularity conditions as follows:

$$\frac{1}{N}\sum_{i=1}^{N}\tilde{w}_n^i W_{n-1}^i \tag{5.11}$$

$$\xrightarrow{a.s.} \int [p(Y|\theta)]^{\phi_n-\phi_{n-1}} \frac{[p(Y|\theta)]^{\phi_{n-1}}p(\theta)}{\int [p(Y|\theta)]^{\phi_{n-1}}p(\theta)d\theta} d\theta$$

$$= \frac{\int [p(Y|\theta)]^{\phi_n}p(\theta)d\theta}{\int [p(Y|\theta)]^{\phi_{n-1}}p(\theta)d\theta}.$$

Thus, the data density approximation is given by

$$\hat{p}_{SMC}(Y) = \prod_{n=1}^{N_\phi} \left(\frac{1}{N}\sum_{i=1}^{N}\tilde{w}_n^i W_{n-1}^i \right). \tag{5.12}$$

Computing this approximation does not require any additional likelihood evaluations. The selection step equalizes the particle weights if its distribution becomes very uneven. In Algorithm 8 the particles are resampled whenever the indicator ρ_n is equal to one. On the one hand, resampling introduces noise in the Monte Carlo approximation, which makes it undesirable. On the other hand, resampling equalizes the particle weights and therefore increases the accuracy of the correction step in the subsequent iteration. In Algorithm 8 we use multinomial resampling. Alternative resampling algorithms are discussed in Section 5.2.3 below. The mutation step changes the values of the particles from θ_{n-1}^i to θ_n^i. To understand the importance of the mutation step, consider what would happen without this step. For simplicity, suppose also that $\rho_n = 0$ for all n. In this case the particle values would never change, that is, $\theta_n^i = \theta_1^i$ for all n. Thus, we would be using the prior as importance sampling distribution and reweight the draws from the prior by the tempered likelihood function $[p(Y|\theta_1^i)]^{\phi_n}$. Given the information contents in a typical DSGE model likelihood function, this procedure would lead to a degenerate distribution of particles, in which in the last stage N_ϕ the weight is concentrated on a very small number of particles and the importance sampling approximation is very inaccurate. Thus, the goal of the mutation step is to adapt the values of the stage n particles to $\pi_n(\theta)$. This is achieved by using steps of an MH algorithm with a transition density that satisfies the invariance property

$$\int K_n(\theta_n|\hat{\theta}_n^i)\pi_n(\hat{\theta}_n^i)d\hat{\theta}_n^i = \pi_n(\theta_n).$$

The execution of the MH steps during the particle mutation phase requires at least one, but possibly multiple, evaluations of the likelihood function for each particle i. To the extent that the likelihood function is recursively evaluated with a filter, data tempering has a computational advantage over likelihood tempering, because the former only requires $\lfloor \phi_n T \rfloor \leq T$ iterations of the filter, whereas the latter requires T iterations. The particle mutation is ideally suited for parallelization, because the MH steps are independent across particles and do not require any communication across processors. For DSGE models, the evaluation of the likelihood function is computationally very costly because it requires running a model solution procedure as well as a filtering algorithm. Thus, gains from parallelization are potentially quite large.

5.1.3 A Numerical Illustration

We provide a first numerical illustration of the SMC algorithm in the context of the stylized state-space model introduced in Section 4.3. Recall that the model is given by

$$
\begin{aligned}
y_t &= [1\ 1]s_t, \\
s_t &= \begin{bmatrix} \theta_1^2 & 0 \\ (1-\theta_1^2)-\theta_1\theta_2 & (1-\theta_1^2) \end{bmatrix} s_{t-1} + \begin{bmatrix} 1 \\ 0 \end{bmatrix} \epsilon_t,
\end{aligned}
$$

where $\epsilon_t \sim iidN(0,1)$. We simulate $T = 200$ observations given $\theta = [0.45, 0.45]'$, which is observationally equivalent to $\theta = [0.89, 0.22]'$, and use a prior distribution that is uniform on the square $0 \leq \theta_1 \leq 1$ and $0 \leq \theta_2 \leq 1$. Because the state-space model has only two parameters and the model used for posterior inference is correctly specified, the SMC algorithm works extremely well. It is configured as follows. We use $N = 1,024$ particles, $N_\phi = 50$ stages, and a linear

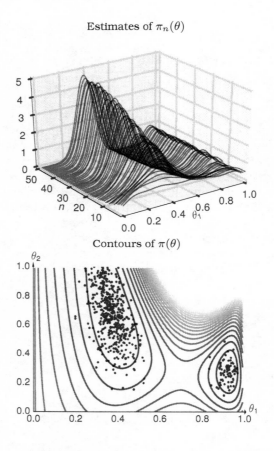

Figure 5.2: SMC Posterior Approximation. The top panel depicts kernel density estimates of the sequence $\pi_n(\theta)$, $n = 0, \ldots, 50$, for stylized state-space model. The bottom panel depicts the contours of the posterior $\pi(\theta)$ as well as draws from $\pi(\theta)$.

tempering schedule that sets $\phi_n = n/50$. The transition kernel for the mutation step is generated by a single step of the RWMH-V algorithm.

Some of the output of the SMC algorithm is depicted in Figure 5.2. The left panel displays the sequence of tempered (marginal) posterior distributions $\pi_n(\theta_1)$. It clearly shows that the tempering dampens the posterior density. While the posterior is still unimodal during the first few stages of the algorithm, a clear bimodal shape has emerged for $n = 10$. As ϕ_n approaches one, the bimodality of the posterior becomes more pronounced. The left panel also suggests that the stage $n = N_\phi - 1$ tempered posterior provides a much better importance sampling distribution for the overall posterior $\pi(\cdot)$ than the stage $n = 1$ (prior) distribution. The right panel shows a contour plot of the joint posterior density of θ_1 and θ_2 as well as the draws from the posterior $\pi(\theta) = \pi_{N_\phi}(\theta)$ obtained in the last stage of Algorithm 8. The algorithm successfully generates draws from the two high-posterior-density regions.

5.2 Further Details of the SMC Algorithm

Our initial description of the SMC algorithm left out some details that are important for the successful implementation of the algorithm. Section 5.2.1 discusses the choice of the transition kernel in the mutation step. Section 5.2.2 considers the adaptive choice of various tuning parameters of the algorithm. The resampling step is discussed in more detail in Section 5.2.3. Finally, 5.2.4 outlines some convergence results for Monte Carlo approximations constructed from the output of the SMC sampler.

5.2.1 The Transition Kernel for the Mutation Step

The transition kernel $K_n(\theta_n | \hat{\theta}_n; \zeta_n)$ in the particle mutation phase is generated through a sequence of MH steps. The kernel is indexed by a vector of tuning parameters ζ_n, which may be different at every stage n. In our subsequent DSGE model applications we will use M steps of a Block RWMH-V algorithm to transform the particle values $\hat{\theta}_n^i$ into θ_n^i. Under a Gaussian proposal density, this algorithm requires a covariance matrix Σ_n^*, which can be partitioned into submatrices for the various parameter blocks, as well as a scaling constant c_n. In principle, this scaling constant could be different for each block, but in our experience with DSGE models the gain from using block-specific scaling is small. Let

$$\zeta_n = \left[c_n, \, vech(\Sigma_n^*)'\right]'. \tag{5.13}$$

The transition kernel is constructed such that for each ζ_n the posterior $\pi_n(\theta)$ is an invariant distribution. The MH steps are summarized in the following algorithm.

Algorithm 9 (Particle Mutation)
Prior to executing Algorithm 8:

>   0. *Generate a sequence of random partitions* $\{B_n\}_{n=2}^{N_\phi}$ *of the parameter vector* θ_n *into* N_{blocks} *equally sized blocks, denoted by* $\theta_{n,b}$, $b = 1, \ldots, N_{blocks}$ *(see Algorithm 7.) Let* $\Sigma_{n,b}^*$ *be the partitions of* Σ_n^* *that correspond to the sub-vector* $\theta_{n,b}$.

In Step 2(c) in iteration n of Algorithm 8:

>   1. *For each particle* i, *run* N_{MH} *steps of the Block MH Algorithm 6 using a RWMH-V proposal density of the form*
>
> $$\vartheta_{n,b}^{i,m} | \zeta_n \sim N\left(\theta_{n,b}^{i,m-1}, c_n^2 \Sigma_{n,b}^*\right). \tag{5.14}$$

For expository purposes, the sequence of blocks $\{B_n\}$ in Algorithm 9 is generated prior to running the SMC algorithm. This is of no practical consequences. One can also generate B_n as part of Step 2(c) in iteration n of Algorithm 8. The Block RWMH-V could be replaced by some of the alternative MH samplers discussed in Chapter 4. However, in our experience the most important consideration for the performance of the SMC algorithm is parameter blocking and the careful tailoring of the scaling constant c_n and the covariance matrix Σ_n^*. As stated, the matrix $\Sigma_{n,b}^*$ refers to the covariance matrix associated with the marginal distribution of $\theta_{n,b}$. Alternatively, one could also use the covariance matrix associated with the conditional distribution of $\theta_{n,b} | (\theta_{n,<b}, \theta_{n,>b})$. The larger the number of MH steps, N_{MH}, the higher the probability that the particle value mutates (which tends to increase the accuracy of the SMC approximations) and the larger the required number of likelihood evaluations (which decreases the speed of the algorithm). We will explore this trade-off more carefully in the context of the DSGE model application in Section 5.3.

5.2.2 Tuning and Adaption of the Algorithm

The SMC algorithm involves several tuning parameters. Some of these tuning parameters are chosen *ex ante*, whereas others are determined adaptively, based on the output of the algorithm in earlier stages. This section provides a broad overview of the tuning parameters. Their effect on the performance of the algorithm will be studied in Section 5.3 below.

Number of Particles, Number of Stages, Tempering Schedule. In our implementation of Algorithm 8 the tuning parameters N, N_ϕ, λ, and N_{MH} are chosen *ex ante* based on some preliminary experiments. The number of particles N scales the overall accuracy of the Monte Carlo approximation. Because most of the computational burden arises in the mutation step, the computing time increases approximately linearly in N. Under suitable regularity conditions $\bar{h}_{N_\phi,N}$ is $\sqrt{N}$ consistent and satisfies a CLT. N_ϕ determines the number of stages $\pi_n(\cdot)$ used to approximate the posterior distribution $\pi(\cdot)$. Increasing the number of stages, N_ϕ, will decrease the distance between bridge distributions and thus make it easier to maintain particle weights that are close to being uniform. The cost of increasing N_ϕ is that each stage requires additional likelihood evaluations.

The user also has to determine the tempering schedule $\{\phi_n\}_{n=0}^{N_\phi}$. To control its shape we introduce a parameter λ and let

$$\phi_n = \left(\frac{n}{N_\phi}\right)^\lambda. \qquad (5.15)$$

A large value of λ implies that the bridge distributions will be very similar (and close to the prior) for small values of n and very different as n approaches N_ϕ. In the DSGE model applications we found a value of $\lambda = 2$ to be very useful because for smaller values the information from the likelihood function will dominate the priors too quickly and only a few particles will survive the correction and selection steps. Conversely, if λ is much larger than 2, it makes some of the bridge distributions essentially redundant and leads to unnecessary computations in the early iterations of the algorithm. The choice of λ does not affect the overall number of likelihood evaluations.

Resampling. Resampling becomes necessary when the distribution of particles degenerates. As discussed in Section 3.4, the larger the variance of the particle weights, the more inefficient the importance sampling approximation: $\text{InEff}_\infty \approx 1 + \mathbb{V}_g[\pi/g]$. Thus, $N/(1 + \mathbb{V}_g[\pi/g])$ could be interpreted as effective sample size. To monitor the particle degeneracy in the SMC algorithm, one can compute the the reciprocal of the uncentered variance of the particles weights in the selection step of Algorithm 8:

$$\widehat{ESS}_n = N / \left(\frac{1}{N} \sum_{i=1}^{N} (\tilde{W}_i^n)^2 \right). \tag{5.16}$$

If all particles receive equal weights, then $\widehat{ESS}_n = N$. Using this degeneracy measure, we can now replace the resampling ρ_n by the adaptive indicator

$$\hat{\rho}_n = \mathbb{I}\{\widehat{ESS}_n < N/2\}, \tag{5.17}$$

where $\mathbb{I}\{x < a\}$ is the indicator function that is equal to one if $x < a$ and equal to zero otherwise. The threshold value $N/2$ is a rule-of-thumb and could be lowered or raised in any particular application.

It is important to note that $\widehat{ESS}_n$ for $n = N_\phi$ should not be interpreted as the number of *iid*-equivalent draws from the posterior distribution $\pi(\theta)$ produced by the SMC algorithm. However, the sequence $\widehat{ESS}_n$ is very useful for monitoring and tuning the performance of the algorithm. If in the early stages of the SMC $\widehat{ESS}_n$ drops into the single digits, the algorithm needs to be re-tuned. For instance, one could increase the number of stages N_ϕ or raise the value of λ to reduce the gap between the bridge distributions during the initial iterations.

Mutation Step. The number of MH steps in the mutation phase of the SMC algorithm affects the likelihood with which a particle mutation occurs. The larger N_{MH}, the higher the probability that during the N_{MH} steps at least one of the proposed draws is accepted and the particle value changes. However, each additional MH step also requires additional likelihood evaluations. As we have seen in Chapter 4, increasing the number of blocks N_{blocks} generally reduces the persistence of the MH chain, which increases the probability of a significant change in the particle value.

We choose the sequence of tuning parameters ζ_n defined in (5.13) for the proposal distribution of the Block RWMH-V algorithm adaptively. First, we replace Σ_n^* by the importance sampling approximation of $\mathbb{V}_{\pi_n}[\theta]$. Second, we adjust the scaling factor c_n to ensure that the acceptance rate in the MH step is approximately 25%, which according to the bottom panel of Figure 4.3 delivers a high degree of accuracy. At each iteration n we then replace ζ_n in (5.13) with[1]

$$\hat{\zeta}_n = \left[\hat{c}_n, vech(\tilde{\Sigma}_n)'\right]'. \tag{5.18}$$

The following algorithm describes how $\hat{\zeta}_n$ is constructed at each iteration n.

Algorithm 10 (SMC with Adaptive Particle Mutation)
For $n \geq 1$, prior to Step 1 of Algorithm 9:

1. *Compute an importance sampling approximation $\tilde{\Sigma}_n$ of $\mathbb{V}_{\pi_n}[\theta]$ based on the particles $\{\theta_{n-1}^i, \tilde{W}_n^i\}_{i=1}^N$.*

2. *Compute the average empirical rejection rate $\hat{R}_{n-1}(\hat{\zeta}_{n-1})$, based on the Mutation step in iteration $n-1$. The average is computed across the N_{blocks} blocks.*

3. *Let $\hat{c}_1 = c^*$ and for $n > 2$ adjust the scaling factor according to*

$$\hat{c}_n = \hat{c}_{n-1} f\left(1 - \hat{R}_{n-1}(\hat{\zeta}_{n-1})\right),$$

   where
$$f(x) = 0.95 + 0.10 \frac{e^{16(x-0.25)}}{1 + e^{16(x-0.25)}}.$$

---

[1]We use "tilde" instead of "hat" for θ and Σ because the approximations are based on the correction step in Algorithm 8.

4. *Execute Algorithm 9 by replacing ζ_n with*
   $\hat{\zeta}_n = \left[\hat{c}_n, vech(\tilde{\Sigma}_n)'\right]'$.

Note that $f(0.25) = 1$, which means that the scaling factor stays constant whenever the target acceptance rate is achieved. If the acceptance rate is below (above) 25% the scaling factor is decreased (increased). The range of the adjustment is determined by the factor 0.1 and the sensitivity to the deviation of the actual from the targeted acceptance rate is determined by the factor 16 in the expression for $f(x)$. We found that these particular constants in the definition of $f(x)$ worked well in our applications.

Figure 5.3 illustrates the adaptive choice of the scaling constant c in the RWMH-V mutation step in the context of the stylized state-space model of Section 5.1.3. We use Algorithm 10 which is configured to target the acceptance rate of 25%. The initial value of the scaling constant is 0.5, which leads to an acceptance rate of more than 70% in the first few steps of the algorithm. Gradually, the scaling constant is lowered according to Algorithm 10. In stage $n = 30$ we are reaching the desired acceptance rate. The acceptance rate subsequently drops slightly below 25% which triggers a small drop in c. Starting from a value close to 1,000, the effective sample size $\widehat{ESS}_n$ slowly decreases and at $n = 41$ falls below the threshold of $N/2$. This triggers the resampling of particles and in turn $\widehat{ESS}_n$ jumps up toward about 1,000. Thus, qualitatively, the adaption of the algorithm works as desired: the scaling constant c in the RWMH-V algorithm is adjusted to achieve the desired acceptance rate and the particles are resampled if the distribution of weights becomes uneven.

5.2.3 Beyond Multinomial Resampling

The resampling step in Algorithm 8 is based on multinomial resampling. While the use of multinomial resampling facilitates the theoretical analysis of the algorithm, in particular the derivation of a CLT, it is not the most efficient resampling algorithm. We will provide some discussion of the implementation of multinomial resampling and a brief overview of alternative resampling algorithms, including stratified re-

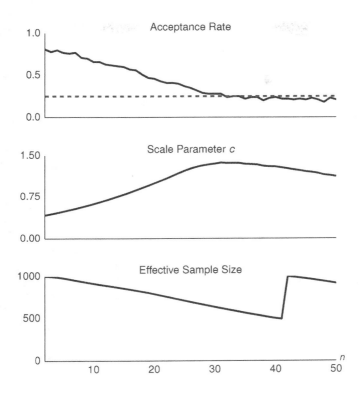

Figure 5.3: Adaption of SMC Algorithm for Stylized State-Space Model. The dashed line in the top panel indicates the target acceptance rate of 0.25.

sampling, systematic resampling, and residual resampling. We refer the reader for more detailed treatments to the books by Liu (2001) or Cappé, Moulines, and Ryden (2005) (and references cited therein) as well as Murray, Lee, and Jacob (2014) for a discussion of parallelization of these algorithms.

Resampling algorithms take as input the collection of particle weights $\{\tilde{W}_n^i\}_{i=1}^N$ and produce as output either an ancestry vector or a vector that contains the number of offsprings for each particle. An ancestry vector A_n has elements A_n^i such that $A_n^i = j$ if and only if particle j is the ancestor of resam-

Table 5.1: Resampling: Ancestors and Offsprings

i	θ_{n-1}^i	$\hat{\theta}_n^i$	A_n^i	O_n^i
1	1/2	2/5	4	1
2	3/5	2/5	4	3
3	0	3/5	2	0
4	2/5	3/5	2	2
5	2/3	3/5	2	0
6	1/3	1/2	1	0

pled particle i, that is, $\hat{\theta}_n^i = \theta_{n-1}^j$. For instance, suppose that during the resampling step particle $i = 1$ was assigned the value θ_{n-1}^4, then $A_n^1 = 4$. Alternatively, the offspring vector O_n with elements O_n^i would contain the number of offsprings for each particle θ_{n-1}^i. Both A_n and O_n contain the same information and each one can be transformed into the other. An illustration of ancestors and offsprings is provided in Table 5.1.

The multinomial resampling step of Algorithm 8 can be implemented by generating an ancestry vector as follows. Compute the standardized cumulative weights $\tilde{W}_n^{c,i} = \sum_{j=1}^i \tilde{W}_n^j$ for $i = 1, \ldots, N$ and draw N iid $U[0, N]$ random numbers u^i. Define the element A_n^i as

$$A_n^i = LB\big(\{\tilde{W}_n^{c,i}\}_{i=1}^N, u^i\big),$$

where the function $LB(W, u)$ returns the smallest integer i such that the scalar u can be inserted into position i of a vector W, sorted in ascending order, while maintaining the sorting. Suppose that $W = [1, 3, 4, 6]$ and $u = 3.7$. Then one could replace either element 2 or element 3 of the vector W without affecting the sorting. The function LB returns the value 2.

The variance of multinomial resampling can be reduced by stratification. The stratified resampling algorithm can be implemented as follows. Divide the interval $[0, N]$ into N strata of the form $\mathcal{U}^i = ((i-1), i]$, $i = 1, \ldots, N$, and for each stratum generate a uniform random number $u^i \sim U\big((i-1), i\big]$. Then, define the ancestor vector A_n^i as $LB\big(\{\tilde{W}_n^{c,i}\}_{i=1}^N, u^i\big)$. To show that stratification can lead to variance reduction, we compute the distribution of the offspring vector for the case $N = 2$ and $\tilde{W}_n^1 \leq 1$. For particle $i = 1$, $u^1 \sim U(0,1]$, which means that with probability $\tilde{W}_n^1$ the value θ_{n-1}^1 is selected and with probability $1 - \tilde{W}_n^1$ the value θ_{n-1}^2 is chosen. For particle $i = 2$, one always chooses θ_{n-1}^2 because $u^2 \sim U(1,2]$ which implies that $u^2 \geq 1 \geq \tilde{W}_n^1$. The distribution of offsprings takes the form

$$\text{Stratified:} \quad O_n^1 = \begin{cases} 0 & \text{w.p. } 1 - \tilde{W}_n^1 \\ 1 & \text{w.p. } \tilde{W}_n^1 \\ 2 & \text{w.p. } 0 \end{cases},$$

$$O_n^2 = \begin{cases} 0 & \text{w.p. } 0 \\ 1 & \text{w.p. } \tilde{W}_n^1 \\ 2 & \text{w.p. } 1 - \tilde{W}_n^1 \end{cases}.$$

For the regular multinomial resampling described above, the distribution of offsprings is

$$\text{Multinominal:} \quad O_n^1 = \begin{cases} 0 & \text{w.p. } (1 - \tilde{W}_n^1/2)^2 \\ 1 & \text{w.p. } 2(1 - \tilde{W}_n^1/2)(\tilde{W}_n^1/2) \\ 2 & \text{w.p. } (\tilde{W}_n^1/2)^2 \end{cases},$$

$$O_n^2 = \begin{cases} 0 & \text{w.p. } (\tilde{W}_n^1/2)^2 \\ 1 & \text{w.p. } 2(1 - \tilde{W}_n^1/2)(\tilde{W}_n^1/2) \\ 2 & \text{w.p. } (1 - \tilde{W}_n^1/2)^2 \end{cases}.$$

Both resampling schemes are unbiased, meaning that $\mathbb{E}[O_n^i] = \tilde{W}_n^i$, but the offspring vector generated by the stratified resampler has a lower variance. The variance reduction extends to $N > 2$ (see, e.g., Cappé, Moulines, and Ryden (2005)). A stratified resampling algorithm to efficiently compute the cumulative offspring function is provided in Murray, Lee, and Jacob (2014).

Stratified resampling aims to reduce the discrepancy between the empirical distribution of the generated draws and the uniform distribution. This is achieved by defining $u^i = (i-1) + \xi^i$ where $\xi^i \sim iidU[0,1]$. Alternatively, one could consider the sequence $u^i = (i-1) + \xi$ where $\xi \sim U[0,1]$, that is, the random term ξ is common for all i. This method is known as systematic resampling. The theoretical properties of systematic resampling algorithms are more difficult to establish because the draws u^i, $i = 1, \ldots, N$, are perfectly correlated. In sequential Monte Carlo applications, this generates cross-sectional dependence of particles.

Let $\lfloor x \rfloor$ denote the floor operator, i.e., the largest integer that is less than or equal to $x \geq 0$. The residual resampling algorithm initially assigns $\lfloor \tilde{W}_n^i \rfloor$ offsprings to each particle and then determines the remaining offsprings randomly:

$$O_n^i = \lfloor \tilde{W}_n^i \rfloor + \hat{O}_n^i. \tag{5.19}$$

Now only $N - \sum_{i=1}^{N} \lfloor \tilde{W}_n^i \rfloor$ draws are required and the probability associated with particle i is proportional to $\tilde{W}_n^i - \lfloor \tilde{W}_n^i \rfloor$. The residuals $\hat{O}_n^i$ can be generated with one of the algorithms described above. None of the algorithms discussed thus far is well suited for parallelization because it is necessary to compute the sum of the particle weights (the summation step appears as the last operation of the correction step in Algorithm 8). The Metropolis resampling algorithm and the rejection resampling algorithm discussed in Murray, Lee, and Jacob (2014) are designed to avoid collective operations over the weights.

5.2.4 Asymptotic Properties of SMC Algorithms

Under suitable regularity conditions the Monte Carlo approximations of posterior means obtained from the output of Algorithm 8 satisfy a SLLN and a CLT as the number of particles tends to infinity: $N \longrightarrow \infty$. A careful statement of these regularity conditions and a rigorous large sample analysis of Monte Carlo averages is provided by Chopin (2004). Herbst and Schorfheide (2014) adapt the proofs of the SLLN and CLT in Chopin (2004) to cover the SMC Algorithm 10 with adaptive particle mutation.[2] The SLLN and CLT can be elegantly proved recursively, that is, by showing that the convergence of $\bar{h}_{n-1,N}$ implies the convergence of $\bar{h}_{n,N}$. In the remainder of

---

[2] A more general mathematical treatment of SMC algorithms based on mean field simulation theory is provided by Del Moral (2013).

this subsection we outline the derivation of the limit distribution of the Monte Carlo approximations for the non-adaptive version of the SMC algorithm (Algorithm 8), meaning we assume that the sequence $\{\rho_n, B_n, \zeta_n\}_{n=1}^{N_\phi}$ is predetermined.

The subsequent exposition abstracts from many of the technical details for which we refer the interested reader to the abovementioned references. Our goal is to convey the basic recursive structure of the convergence proof and to gain some insights into the accuracy of the Monte Carlo approximations from the asymptotic variance formulas. While the recursive form of the asymptotic variance formulas renders them unusable for the computation of numerical standard errors, their general structure sheds some light on how the various tuning parameters of the algorithm affect its accuracy.

Assumptions. The SLLN and CLT rely on three types of assumptions. (i) We assume that the prior is proper, the likelihood function is uniformly bounded, and that the tempered marginal likelihood of the data in stage $n = 1$ is non-zero:

$$\int p(\theta)d\theta < \infty, \ \sup_{\theta \in \Theta} p(Y|\theta) < M < \infty, \\ \int [p(Y|\theta)]^{\phi_2} p(\theta)d\theta > 0 \qquad (5.20)$$

(ii) We require the existence of moments by considering functions $h(\theta)$ that belong to the classes $\mathcal{H}_j$ defined as

$$\mathcal{H}_j = \left\{ h(\theta) \mid \exists \delta > 0 \text{ s.t. } \int |h(\theta)|^{j+\delta} p(\theta)d\theta < \infty \right\}, \qquad (5.21)$$

for $j = 1, 2$. Because the likelihood is assumed to be bounded, we can immediately deduce the existence of $j + \delta$ moments of the tempered posterior distributions $\pi_n(\theta)$, $n = 2, \ldots, N_\phi$, for functions in $\mathcal{H}_j$. The existence of these moments is necessary for obtaining a SLLN ($h \in \mathcal{H}_1$) and a CLT ($h \in \mathcal{H}_2$).

(iii) We assume that

$$\bar{h}_{n-1,N} \xrightarrow{a.s.} \mathbb{E}_{\pi_{n-1}}[h], \qquad (5.22)$$

$$\sqrt{N}(\bar{h}_{n-1,N} - \mathbb{E}_{\pi_{n-1}}[h]) \implies N(0, \Omega_{n-1}(h))$$

as the number of particles $N \longrightarrow \infty$. Recall that in stage $n = 0$ we directly sample from the prior distribution. Thus, the moment bounds in (5.21) suffices to ensure that $\bar{h}_{0,N}$ satisfies the conditions in (5.22). The subsequent proof proceeds recursively. We show that if $\bar{h}_{n-1,N}$ satisfies a SLLN and CLT, then $\bar{h}_{n,N}$ also converges almost surely and in distribution.

Correction Step. Let $Z_n = \int [p(Y|\theta)]^{\phi_n} p(\theta) d\theta$ be the (generally unknown) normalization constant of the stage n posterior $\pi_n(\theta)$ defined in (5.1). For the subsequent calculations, it is convenient to normalize the incremental weight $\tilde{w}_n^i$ as follows:

$$v_n(\theta) = \frac{Z_{n-1}}{Z_n} \tilde{w}_n^i = \frac{Z_{n-1}}{Z_n} [p(Y|\theta)]^{\phi_n - \phi_{n-1}}. \qquad (5.23)$$

Because the normalization factor Z_{n-1}/Z_n does not depend on θ, we can write the Monte Carlo approximation in the correction step in terms of the normalized incremental weights:

$$\tilde{h}_{n,N} = \frac{1}{N} \sum_{i=1}^{N} \tilde{W}_n^i h(\theta_{n-1}^i) \qquad (5.24)$$

$$= \frac{\frac{1}{N} \sum_{i=1}^{N} h(\theta_{n-1}^i) v_n(\theta_{n-1}^i) W_{n-1}^i}{\frac{1}{N} \sum_{i=1}^{N} v_n(\theta_{n-1}^i) W_{n-1}^i}.$$

The normalized incremental weights have the following useful property:

$$\int h(\theta) v_n(\theta) \pi_{n-1}(\theta) d\theta \qquad (5.25)$$

$$= \int \frac{Z_{n-1}}{Z_n} [p(Y|\theta)]^{\phi_n - \phi_{n-1}} \frac{[p(Y|\theta)]^{\phi_{n-1}} p(\theta)}{Z_{n-1}} d\theta$$

$$= \int h(\theta) \pi_n(\theta) d\theta,$$

which implies for $h(\theta) = 1$ that $\int v_n(\theta) \pi_n(\theta) d\theta = 1$.

A SLLN and a CLT for $\tilde{h}_{n,N}$ can now be obtained from Assumption (iii) in (5.22) and the property of the normalized incremental weights in (5.25). As the number of particles $N \longrightarrow \infty$, the Monte Carlo approximation $\tilde{h}_{n,N}$ converges as follows:

$$\tilde{h}_{n,N} \xrightarrow{a.s.} \int h(\theta_n) \pi_n(\theta_n) d\theta_n = \mathbb{E}_{\pi_n}[h]$$

$$\sqrt{N}(\tilde{h}_{n,N} - \mathbb{E}_{\pi_n}[h]) \implies N(0, \tilde{\Omega}_n(h)), \qquad (5.26)$$

where

$$\tilde{\Omega}_n(h) = \Omega_{n-1}\big(v_n(\theta)(h(\theta) - \mathbb{E}_{\pi_n}[h])\big).$$

The asymptotic covariance matrix associated with $\tilde{h}_{n,N}$ has the same form as the asymptotic covariance matrix $\Omega(h)$ in (3.52) associated with the importance sampler. In particular, the larger the variance of the incremental particle weights $v_n(\theta)$, the less accurate the Monte Carlo approximation in the selection step. Therefore, the adaptive version of the algorithm described in Section 5.2.2 monitors the variance of the particle weights, transformed into $\widehat{ESS}_n$. If the distribution of particle weights is very uneven, then the particles are resampled.

Selection Step. In the non-adaptive version of the algorithm resampling occurs whenever $\rho_n = 1$. To examine the effect of resampling on the accuracy of the Monte Carlo approximation, recall that we denoted the resampled particles by $\hat{\theta}_n^i$. Let $\mathcal{F}_{n-1,N}$ be the σ-algebra generated by $\{\theta_{n-1}^i, \tilde{W}_n^i\}$, where $\tilde{W}_n^i$ are the normalized particle weights computed in the correction step (see (5.24)). Under multinomial resampling, the expected value of functions of resampled particles is given by

$$\mathbb{E}[h(\hat{\theta})|\mathcal{F}_{n-1,N}] = \frac{1}{N}\sum_{i=1}^{N} h(\theta_{n-1}^i)\tilde{W}_n^i = \tilde{h}_{n,N}. \tag{5.27}$$

Using this equality, we can decompose

$$
\begin{aligned}
\hat{h}_{n,N} - \mathbb{E}_{\pi_n}[h] &= \big(\tilde{h}_{n,N} - \mathbb{E}_{\pi_n}[h]\big) \tag{5.28}\\
&\quad + \frac{1}{N}\sum_{i=1}^{N}\big(h(\hat{\theta}_n^i) - \mathbb{E}[h(\hat{\theta})|\mathcal{F}_{n-1,N}]\big)\\
&= I + II,
\end{aligned}
$$

say. The large sample behavior of I follows directly from (5.26). For term II, note that conditional on $\mathcal{F}_{n-1,N}$ the $h(\hat{\theta}_n^i)$ form a triangular array of (discrete) random variables that are iid within each row with mean $\mathbb{E}[h(\hat{\theta})|\mathcal{F}_{n-1,N}]$. Using a SLLN and a CLT for triangular arrays of iid random variables, it can be shown that

$$\hat{h}_{n,N} \xrightarrow{a.s.} \int h(\theta_n)\pi_n(\theta_n)d\theta_n \qquad (5.29)$$

$$\sqrt{N}\big(\hat{h}_{n,N} - \mathbb{E}_{\pi_n}[h]\big) \implies N\big(0, \hat{\Omega}_n(h)\big),$$

$$\hat{\Omega}_n(h) = \tilde{\Omega}_n(h) + \mathbb{V}_{\pi_n}[h].$$

The second term in asymptotic variance $\hat{\Omega}_n(h)$ indicates that resampling increases the variance of the Monte Carlo approximation. However, it also equalizes the particle weights which tends to lower the approximation errors in the subsequent iteration of the algorithm.

Mutation Step. Let the conditional mean and variance of the transition kernel $K_n(\theta|\hat{\theta}; \zeta_n)$ be $\mathbb{E}_{K_n(\cdot|\hat{\theta};\zeta_n)}[\cdot]$ and $\mathbb{V}_{K_n(\cdot|\hat{\theta};\zeta_n)}[\cdot]$. Because π_n is the invariant distribution associated with the transition kernel K_n, note that if $\hat{\theta} \sim \pi_n$, then

$$\int_{\hat{\theta}} \mathbb{E}_{K_n(\cdot|\hat{\theta};\zeta_n)}[h]\pi_n(\hat{\theta})d\hat{\theta} \qquad (5.30)$$

$$= \int_{\hat{\theta}} \int_{\theta} h(\theta)K_n(\theta|\hat{\theta};\zeta_n)d\theta\pi_n(\hat{\theta})d\hat{\theta}$$

$$= \int_{\theta} h(\theta) \int_{\hat{\theta}} K_n(\theta|\hat{\theta};\zeta_n)\pi_n(\hat{\theta})d\hat{\theta}d\theta$$

$$= \int_{\theta} h(\theta)\pi_n(\theta)d\theta = \mathbb{E}_{\pi_n}[h].$$

Using the fact that $\frac{1}{N}\sum_{i=1}^{N} W_n^i = 1$ we can write

$$\bar{h}_{n,N} - \mathbb{E}_{\pi_n}[h] \qquad (5.31)$$

$$= \frac{1}{N}\sum_{i=1}^{N} \big(h(\theta_n^i) - \mathbb{E}_{K_n(\cdot|\hat{\theta}_n^i;\zeta_n)}[h]\big)W_n^i$$

$$+ \frac{1}{N}\sum_{i=1}^{N} \big(\mathbb{E}_{K_n(\cdot|\hat{\theta}_n^i;\zeta_n)}[h] - \mathbb{E}_{\pi_n}[h]\big)W_n^i$$

$$= I + II,$$

say. While term I captures deviations of $h(\theta_n^i)$ from its conditional mean $\mathbb{E}_{K_n(\cdot|\hat{\theta}_n^i;\zeta_n)}[h]$, the second term captures deviations from the conditional mean of $\mathbb{E}_{K_n(\cdot|\hat{\theta}_n^i;\zeta_n)}[h]$ from the tempered posterior $\mathbb{E}_{\pi_n}[h]$.

The large sample behavior of the Monte Carlo approximation in the mutation step, $\bar{h}_{n,N}$, depends on the particle weights W_n^i, which in turn depends on how many iterations ago the resampling step was executed. To simplify the exposition, we assume that $\rho_n = 1$, which implies that $W_n^i = 1$. Let $\hat{\mathcal{F}}_{n,N}$ be the σ-algebra generated by $\{\hat{\theta}_n^i, W_n^i\}_{i=1}^N$. Notice that conditional on $\hat{\mathcal{F}}_{n,N}$ the weights W_n^i are known and the summands in term I form a triangular array of mean-zero random variables that within each row are independently but not identically distributed because the (conditional) variance and higher-order moments of $h(\theta_n^i)$ may depend on $\hat{\theta}_n^i$. In turn, we can deduce that I satisfies a SLLN and a CLT. The convergence of II is a consequence of (5.29). It can be shown that

$$\bar{h}_{n,N} \xrightarrow{a.s.} \int h(\theta_n)\pi_n(\theta_n)d\theta_n \quad (5.32)$$

$$\sqrt{N}\big(\hat{h}_{n,N} - \mathbb{E}_{\pi_n}[h]\big) \implies N\big(0, \Omega_n(h)\big),$$

where

$$\Omega_n(h) = \mathbb{E}_{\pi_n}\big[\mathbb{V}_{K_n(\cdot|\hat{\theta};\zeta_n)}[h]\big] + \hat{\Omega}_n\big(\mathbb{E}_{K_n(\cdot|\hat{\theta};\zeta_n)}[h]\big).$$

To establish the convergence results (5.26), (5.29), and (5.32) in a rigorous manner mainly requires the verification of moment bounds for the various random variables that are being averaged in the Monte Carlo approximations. Herbst and Schorfheide (2014) provide some high-level assumptions that ensure that choosing the tuning sequences adaptively according to $\{\hat{\rho}_n, \hat{\zeta}_n\}$ does not affect the asymptotic covariance matrices.

The recursive form of the asymptotic covariances makes them difficult to use the results in practice. Durham and Geweke (2014) propose to collect the particles into G groups of size N/G. When running the algorithm, each group of particles is treated independently such that the scaled variance of Monte Carlo approximations across groups provides instantaneous estimates of the covariance matrices $\tilde{\Omega}_n$, $\hat{\Omega}_n$, and Ω_n. The CLT ensures that these across-group variance estimates

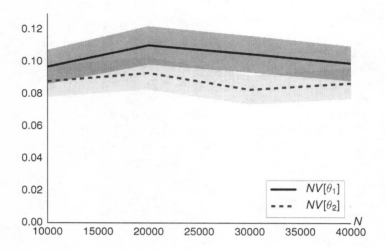

Figure 5.4: Convergence of SMC Approximation for Stylized State-Space Model. The figure shows $N\mathbb{V}[\bar\theta_j]$ for each parameter as a function of the number of particles N. $\mathbb{V}[\bar\theta_j]$ is computed based on $N_{run} = 1,000$ runs of the SMC algorithm with $N_\phi = 100$. The width of the bands is $(2 \cdot 1.96)\sqrt{3/N_{run}}(N\mathbb{V}[\bar\theta_j])$.

provide a reliable measure of accuracy. We adopt a similar strategy in the subsequent numerical illustrations. However, rather than assigning the particles to independent groups, we simply run the SMC algorithm independently multiple times and construct estimates of the final-stage covariance matrix $\Omega_{N_\phi}(h)$.

Figure 5.4 illustrates the CLT in the context of the stylized state-space model considered in Section 5.1.3. We run the SMC algorithm $N_{run} = 1,000$ times and compute the small-sample variances $\mathbb{V}[\bar\theta_1]$ and $\mathbb{V}[\bar\theta_2]$ of the Monte Carlo approximations of $\mathbb{E}_\pi[\theta_1]$ and $\mathbb{E}_\pi[\theta_2]$ as a function of N. We use $N_\phi = 100$ stages and a linear tempering schedule. The figure depicts $N\mathbb{V}[\bar\theta_j]$ as a function of N, which approximately equals the asymptotic variance $\Omega_{N_\phi}(\theta_j)$ if the CLT is operational. The standardized small-sample variances of the Monte Carlo approximations are fairly flat as a function of N. The variability that is visible in the plots is consistent with the fact that $\mathbb{V}[\bar{\theta}_j]$ is computed based on 1,000 runs of the SMC. Suppose that $Z_r \sim iidN(0, v)$. Then the standard deviation of $\frac{1}{N_{run}} \sum_{r=1}^{N_{run}} (Z_r^2 - v)$ is given by $\sqrt{3/N_{run}} v$. Accordingly, we plot $+/- 1.96\sqrt{3/N_{run}}(N\mathbb{V}[\bar{\theta}_j])$ bands around $N\mathbb{V}[\bar{\theta}_j]$ in Figure 5.4.

5.3 SMC for the Small-Scale DSGE Model

We now apply Algorithm 10 to conduct posterior inference for the three-equation New Keynesian model. We use the same prior specification and the same data set as in Section 4.2. We illustrate how the accuracy of the SMC approximation changes as we vary the choice of tuning parameters for the algorithm. We run each configuration of the algorithm $N_{run} = 50$ times and compute the cross-sectional variance of the Monte Carlo approximations $\mathbb{V}[\bar{\theta}]$. Throughout this section we fix the number of MH steps in the mutation step to be equal to $N_{MH} = 1$.

Figure 5.5 explores the connection between accuracy, measured through $\text{InEff}_N[\bar{\theta}]$ and the tempering schedule ϕ_n, controlled by the tuning parameter λ. Each "hair" in the figure corresponds to a specific DSGE model parameter. The results are based on $N = 1,000$, $N_\phi = 100$, and $N_{blocks} = 1$. For $\lambda = 1$ this schedule is linear in n and for $\lambda > 1$ it is convex. A convex tempering schedule implies that we add very little information in the initial stages of the SMC algorithm to ensure that the particles adapt well to the bridge distribution. As n increases, the incremental amount of likelihood information added in each stage also increases. The linear schedule performs relatively poorly. A choice of λ in the range of 1.5 to 2 yields the most accurate approximations for the posterior means of the DSGE model parameters. Beyond $\lambda = 2$ the accuracy slowly deteriorates and for $\lambda \geq 4$, the convex tempering schedule is worse than the linear tempering schedule. Note that the choice of λ has essentially no effect on the number of likelihood evaluations and on the computational time (except that poor choices of λ may require additional resampling steps). In the subsequent experiments we let $\lambda = 2$.

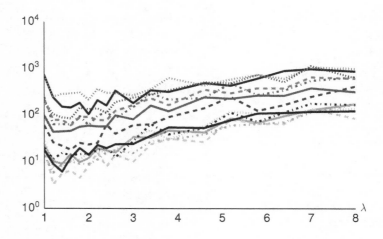

Figure 5.5: Effect of λ on Inefficiency Factors $\text{InEff}_N[\bar{\theta}]$. The figure depicts hairs of $\text{InEff}_N[\bar{\theta}]$ as function of λ. The inefficiency factors are computed based on $N_{run} = 50$ runs of the SMC algorithm. Each hair corresponds to a DSGE model parameter.

Figure 5.6 explores the trade-offs between number of particles N, number of stages N_ϕ, and number of blocks N_{blocks} in the mutation step. Because the number of particles differs across experiments, we report the ratio $\mathbb{V}[\bar{\theta}]/\mathbb{V}_\pi[\theta]$ instead of the inefficiency factor $\text{InEff}_N[\bar{\theta}]$. The experiments are designed such that we keep the number of likelihood evaluations constant.

The top panel indicates that a large number of particles, e.g., $N = 4,000$, combined with a moderate number of stages, e.g., $N_\phi = 25$, delivers a less accurate approximation than a small number of particles, e.g., $N = 250$ or $N = 500$, and a large number of stages, e.g., $N_\phi = 400$ or $N_\phi = 200$. Of course, if we were to increase the number of stages even more drastically and reduce the number of particles further, the accuracy would at some point deteriorate. If the number of stages is too large, then a lot of computational resources are allocated to approximating very similar bridge distributions. If the number of stages is too small, then the stage $n - 1$

Number of Stages N_ϕ vs. Number of Particles N

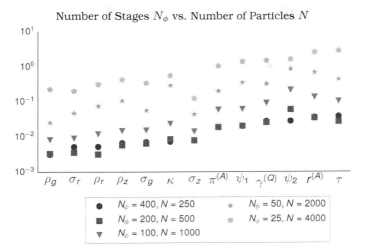

Number of blocks N_{blocks} in Mutation Step vs. Number of Particles N

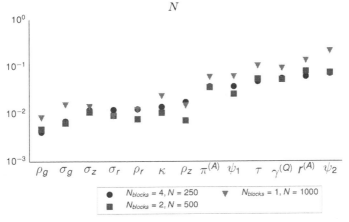

Figure 5.6: Effect of Tuning on Inaccuracy $\mathbb{V}[\bar\theta]/\mathbb{V}_\pi[\theta]$. Each panel shows plots of $\mathbb{V}[\bar\theta]/\mathbb{V}_\pi[\theta]$ for a specific configuration of the SMC algorithm. The inefficiency factors are computed based on $N_{run} = 50$ runs of the SMC algorithm. Top panel: $N_{blocks} = 1$, $\lambda = 2$, $N_{MH} = 1$. Bottom panel: $N_\phi = 100$, $\lambda = 2$, $N_{MH} = 1$.

Table 5.2: SMC-Based Marginal Data Density Estimates

| | $N_\phi = 100$ | | $N_\phi = 400$ | |
N	Mean	StdD	Mean	StdD
500	-352.19	(3.18)	-346.12	(0.20)
1,000	-349.19	(1.98)	-346.17	(0.14)
2,000	-348.57	(1.65)	-346.16	(0.12)
4,000	-347.74	(0.92)	-346.16	(0.07)

Notes: Table shows mean and standard deviation of log marginal data density estimates $\ln \hat{p}(Y)$ as a function of the number of particles N computed over $N_{run} = 50$ runs of the SMC sampler with $N_{blocks} = 4$, $\lambda = 2$, and $N_{MH} = 1$.

posterior is poor proposal density in the correction step of iteration n.

The bottom panel of Figure 5.6 depicts the effect of blocking. Blocking tends to reduce the persistence of MH chains and in the context of the SMC algorithm increases the probability that the particle values change in the mutation step, at least for a subvector of θ. In the small-scale model, using $N_{blocks} = 2$ blocks in combination with $N = 500$ appears to be the preferred choice. It dominates the $N_{blocks} = 1$ and $N = 1,000$ configuration for all parameters and is preferred to the $N_{blocks} = 4$ and $N = 250$ configuration for all but three parameters.

Finally, Table 5.2 presents estimates of the log marginal data density of the small-scale New Keynesian DSGE model based on $N_{run} = 50$ runs of the SMC algorithm. The marginal data densities are computed according to (5.12). The accuracy of the approximation increases, as evidenced by the decreasing standard deviation across the 50 runs, as the number of particles increases. For $N_\phi = 100$ stages the approximation is fairly inaccurate, also in comparison to the MCMC approximations reported in Table 4.3. The estimate of the log density appears to be downward biased, which is consistent with Jensen's inequality and the estimate of the marginal data density (before taking the log transformation) being unbiased. If the number of stages is increased to $N_\phi = 400$ the standard deviation of the Monte Carlo approximations drops by a factor of more than 10.

Chapter 6

Three Applications

After having applied the MH and SMC algorithms to the small-scale New Keynesian model we now consider three applications to larger DSGE models. We modify the baseline DSGE model in three dimensions. In Section 6.1 we replace the AR(1) processes for technology growth and government spending by a VAR(1) process, that is, we are generalizing the law of motion of the exogenous shocks to make the DSGE model specification more flexible and improve its fit. In Section 6.2 we add capital as a factor of production to the baseline New Keynesian DSGE model and include nominal wage stickiness as well as other forms of rigidities. This leads us to the Smets and Wouters (2007) model. The estimation of the SW model is more challenging than the estimation of the small-scale New Keynesian model because it has more state variables, many more parameters, and it is used to track seven instead of only three macroeconomic time series. We estimate the SW model under a more diffuse prior distribution than Smets and Wouters (2007) to highlight important non-elliptical features of the likelihood function. Finally, in Section 6.3 we consider a DSGE model that is designed to analyze fiscal as opposed to monetary policy. This model abstracts from nominal rigidities and instead focuses on fiscal policy rules that determine the level of government spending and taxation as a function of the state of the economy.

The applications in this chapter are chosen because on the one hand they feature important extensions of the model studied in Chapters 4 and 5. On the other hand, the applications are selected because they lead to posterior distributions with strong non-elliptical features that lead to challenges for posterior simulators. The resulting posterior distributions are multimodal and the widely used single block RWMH algorithm works relatively poorly because it has difficulties generating draws from the multiple high-posterior density regions in the correct proportion. The SMC algorithm, on the other hand, produces much more accurate and stable approximations of the posterior. While the applications are to some extent chosen to highlight the strength of the SMC approach, we think that the posteriors arising in these three applications are representative of the posteriors that arise in many other DSGE model applications as well.

6.1 A New Keynesian Model with Correlated Shocks

The fit of DSGE models can be improved either by enriching the endogenous propagation mechanism of the model or by generalizing the law of motion for the exogenous shocks. Most of the DSGE model literature has focused on augmenting the basic neoclassical stochastic growth model with more sophisticated economic mechanism, e.g., frictions in the adjustment of labor and capital inputs, costs of changing nominal prices and wages, or information imperfections. The effects of monetary and fiscal policy depend crucially on the endogenous propagation mechanisms built into a DSGE model. For instance, in the absence of nominal rigidities, changes in the monetary policy rule or unanticipated deviations from the monetary policy rule have no effects on real output, consumption, and investment.

In this section we follow the second route and generalize the law of motion of the exogenous shocks in the small-scale New Keynesian DSGE model. In most DSGE models the exogenous shocks are assumed to follow independent AR(1) processes. However, *a priori* it is not unreasonable to assume that the exogenous shocks follow richer ARMA(p, q) processes. Moreover, *a priori* there is nothing that rules out correlations between exogenous shocks. For instance, the SW model features some generalizations of the widely used AR(1) law of motion for exogenous shocks: price and wage mark-up shocks follow ARMA$(1,1)$ processes and the innovations to technology and government spending are allowed to be correlated.

The reason that most researchers prefer a simple specification for the exogenous processes is that one of the goals of the DSGE research program is to develop economic mechanisms that can generate the observed comovements and persistence of macroeconomic time series *endogenously* from a set of uncorrelated exogenous shocks. Nonetheless, in environments in which model fit is important, e.g., central bank forecasting with DSGE models, the generalization of the law of motion of exogenous shocks is a plausible modeling strategy.

The subsequent application is inspired by Curdia and Reis (2010) who consider a fairly general vector-autoregressive law of motion for the exogenous processes of a small-scale DSGE model. While this modeling strategy is helpful in overcoming DSGE model misspecification, it also introduces potential identification problems. The more flexible and densely parameterized the law of motion of the exogenous shocks, the more difficult it becomes to identify the shock parameters and the parameters associated with the endogenous propagation mechanism jointly. From a computational perspective, this may introduce multimodal posterior distributions, which are the focus of the remainder of this section.

6.1.1 Model Specification

In the small-scale DSGE model of Section 1.1 the technology growth shock $\hat{z}_t$ and the government spending shock $\hat{g}_t$ evolve according to independent AR(1) processes:

$$
\begin{aligned}
\hat{z}_t &= \rho_z \hat{z}_{t-1} + \epsilon_{z,t}, \quad \epsilon_{z,t} \sim N(0, \sigma_z^2), \\
\hat{g}_t &= \rho_g \hat{g}_{t-1} + \epsilon_{g,t}, \quad \epsilon_{z,t} \sim N(0, \sigma_g^2).
\end{aligned}
$$

We now replace the two AR(1) processes by the following VAR process:

$$
\begin{bmatrix} \hat{z}_t \\ \hat{g}_t \end{bmatrix} = \begin{bmatrix} \rho_z & \rho_{zg} \\ \rho_{gz} & \rho_g \end{bmatrix} \begin{bmatrix} \hat{z}_{t-1} \\ \hat{g}_{t-1} \end{bmatrix} + \begin{bmatrix} \epsilon_{z,t} \\ \epsilon_{g,t} \end{bmatrix}, \quad (6.1)
$$

$$
\begin{bmatrix} \epsilon_{z,t} \\ \epsilon_{g,t} \end{bmatrix} \sim N \left(\begin{bmatrix} 0 \\ 0 \end{bmatrix}, \begin{bmatrix} \sigma_z^2 & 0 \\ 0 & \sigma_g^2 \end{bmatrix} \right).
$$

This VAR process is combined with the log-linearized consumption Euler equation, the New Keynesian Phillips curve, and the monetary policy in (2.1), which we reproduce for convenience:

$$
\begin{aligned}
\hat{y}_t &= \mathbb{E}_t[\hat{y}_{t+1}] - \frac{1}{\tau}\left(\hat{R}_t - \mathbb{E}_t[\hat{\pi}_{t+1}] - \mathbb{E}_t[\hat{z}_{t+1}]\right) \\
&\quad +\hat{g}_t - \mathbb{E}_t[\hat{g}_{t+1}], \\
\hat{\pi}_t &= \beta\mathbb{E}_t[\hat{\pi}_{t+1}] + \kappa(\hat{y}_t - \hat{g}_t), \\
\hat{R}_t &= \rho_R\hat{R}_{t-1} + (1 - \rho_R)\psi_1\hat{\pi}_t \\
&\quad +(1 - \rho_R)\psi_2\left(\hat{y}_t - \hat{g}_t\right) + \epsilon_{R,t}.
\end{aligned}
$$

While we maintain the assumption that the innovations of the exogenous processes are uncorrelated, we let the technology growth process be affected by the lagged government spending process and vice versa. This adds two parameters, ρ_{zg} and ρ_{gz}, to the vector θ. A non-zero coefficient ρ_{gz} could be interpreted as a reduced-form fiscal policy rule in which government spending is increased if the supply conditions are poor. Likewise, a positive coefficient ρ_{zg} could potentially capture productivity enhancing public infrastructure investments. While these interpretations suggest that $\rho_{gz} < 0$ and $\rho_{zg} > 0$, we use more agnostic priors of the form

$$
\rho_g, \rho_z \sim U[0, 1], \quad \rho_{gz}, \rho_{zg} \sim U[-1, 1]. \tag{6.2}
$$

The marginal prior distributions for the remaining parameters are identical to those in Table 2.2. The joint prior distribution is truncated to ensure stationarity of $\hat{z}_t$ and $\hat{g}_t$ and determinacy of the overall system.

6.1.2 Estimation Results from a Highly Accurate SMC Run

The modified small-scale DSGE model is estimated using the same data as in Sections 4.2 and 5.3. We begin the numerical analysis by examining the posterior distribution based on a highly accurate run of the SMC algorithm, meaning that the number of particles is sufficiently large such that the variance of the Monte Carlo approximations is negligible. Figure 6.1 depicts the marginal prior and posterior distributions of ρ_{gz} and ρ_{zg}. The marginal prior distributions are represented by the gray shaded histograms. After the truncation induced by the

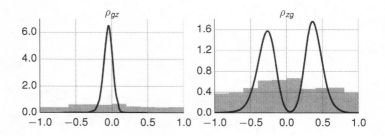

Figure 6.1: Correlated Shocks: Priors and Posteriors of ρ_{gz} and ρ_{zg}. The two panels depict histograms of prior distributions (shaded area) and kernel density estimates of the posterior densities (solid lines).

stationarity restriction the marginal prior distributions of the two parameters are no longer uniform, but they are unimodal and spread out across the unit interval. The posterior distributions are represented by kernel density estimates. The most striking feature of the posterior is that the distribution of ρ_{zg} is bimodal with peaks at approximately -0.3 and 0.3, respectively. The posterior density of ρ_{gz}, on the other hand, is unimodal and sharply peaks around zero.

IRFs associated with the parameter estimates are plotted in Figures 6.2 and 6.3. Each panel in the two figures shows three types of IRFs: responses associated with $\rho_{zg} = 0$, $\rho_{zg} < 0$, and $\rho_{zg} > 0$. The $\rho_{zg} = 0$ IRFs serve as a benchmark and are identical to the posterior mean responses of the small-scale New Keynesian DSGE model with uncorrelated exogenous shocks reported in Section 4.2 (see Figures 4.4 and 4.5). The other two IRFs are motivated by the bimodal posterior distribution of ρ_{zg}, which is almost symmetric around zero, and are computed from the conditional posterior distributions $\theta|(Y, \rho_{gz} > 0)$ and $\theta|(Y, \rho_{gz} < 0)$. Formally, the figures depict $\mathbb{E}[IRF|Y, \rho_{gz} > 0]$ and $\mathbb{E}[IRF|Y, \rho_{gz} < 0]$, respectively. These posterior means can be easily approximated by discarding the posterior draws θ^i that do not satisfy the desired restriction on ρ_{zg}.

Figure 6.2 shows the responses of the exogenous processes to government spending and technology growth shock in-

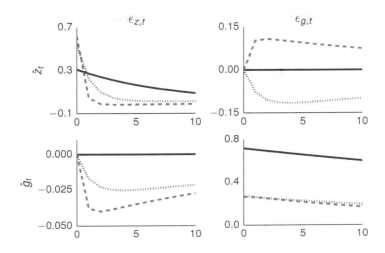

Figure 6.2: Correlated Shocks: Impulse Responses (Part 1). The graphs depict posterior mean IRFs based on the conditional posteriors $\theta|(Y, \rho_{gz} > 0)$ (dashed), and $\theta|(Y, \rho_{gz} < 0)$ (dotted). For comparison, the graph also shows IRFs (solid) from the small-scale DSGE model with uncorrelated shocks (see Section 4.2).

novations. Under the benchmark specification of the DSGE model ($\rho_{zg} = \rho_{gz} = 0$), the exogenous shocks are independent of each other, which means that the demand shifter processes $\hat{g}_t$ does not respond to the technology shock innovation $\epsilon_{z,t}$ and vice versa. In the DSGE model with correlated exogenous shocks, on the other hand, there are spillovers. The government spending process drops slightly (2 to 4 basis points) in response to a 50 to 60 basis points increase in $\epsilon_{z,t}$. The response is qualitatively very similar for the two modes of the posterior, which is consistent with the unimodal shape of the marginal posterior of ρ_{gz}. More interesting is the response of technology growth to a government spending (or general demand) shock innovation. The impulse responses in the bottom left panel of Figure 6.2 reflect the bimodal shape of the ρ_{zg} posterior. If $\rho_{zg} > 0$ ($\rho_{zg} < 0$) then technology growth increases (decreases) by about 10 basis points in response to

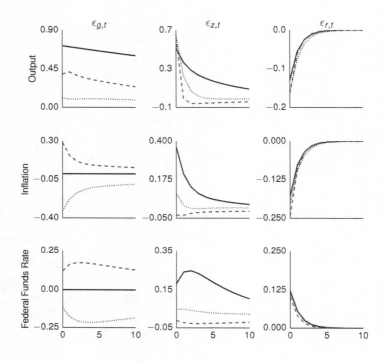

Figure 6.3: Correlated Shocks: Impulse Responses (Part 2). The graphs depict posterior mean IRFs based on the conditional posteriors $\theta|(Y, \rho_{gz} > 0)$ (dashed), and $\theta|(Y, \rho_{gz} < 0)$ (dotted). For comparison, the graph also shows IRFs (solid) from the small-scale DSGE model with uncorrelated shocks (see Section 4.2).

a 25 basis point $\epsilon_{g,t}$ shock.

Figure 6.3 depicts the impulse responses of output, inflation, and interest rates. The effect of a monetary policy shock is approximately the same for the two modes of the model with correlated shocks. The monetary policy responses closely resemble the IRFs obtained from the benchmark version of the small-scale DSGE model with uncorrelated shocks. The IRFs for the government spending and the technology growth shock, on the other hand, are markedly different for the two modes of the correlated shocks model and the benchmark model.

In the benchmark model, neither inflation nor interest rates respond to a change in government spending. In the correlated shocks model, on the other hand, a rise in government spending also triggers a change in technology. We saw in Figure 6.2 that depending on the sign of ρ_{zg}, technology growth either rises or falls in response to a positive $\epsilon_{g,t}$ innovation. As a consequence, depending on the sign of the spillover, inflation and interest rates may either rise or fall in response to a positive demand shock. Moreover, because a drop in technology growth is associated with lower output, the magnitude of the output response also differs significantly. The IRFs of inflation and interest rates to a technology growth shock are generally more muted under the correlated shocks specification than under the baseline specification. Conditional on $\rho_{zg} > 0$ these responses are slightly positive, whereas for $\rho_{zg} < 0$ they are slightly negative.

6.1.3 Comparison of RWMH-V and SMC Performance

The small-scale New Keynesian DSGE model places strong restrictions on the autocovariance function of output growth, inflation, and interest rates and the generalization of the law of motion of the exogenous shocks relaxes these restrictions somewhat, pointing toward an omitted endogenous propagation mechanism. Given the stylized nature of this model, we do not offer a detailed economic interpretation of the bimodal posterior distribution. However, multimodal posterior distribution can also arise in more elaborate DSGE models, e.g., the SW model with a diffuse prior distribution and the news shock model of Schmitt-Grohé and Uribe (2012), as illustrated in Herbst and Schorfheide (2014). The remainder of this section focuses on the computational challenges created by the bimodal posterior and compares the accuracy of the standard RWMH-V algorithm to the SMC algorithm.

Accuracy Assessment and Tuning of Algorithms. To compare the performance of the widely used 1-Block RWMH-V algorithm to an SMC algorithm, we run each of these algorithms $N_{run} = 50$ times and evaluate the posterior probabil-

Table 6.1: Correlated Shocks: Algorithm Configuration

RWMH-V	SMC
$N = 100,000$	$N = 4,800$
$N_{burn} = 50,000$	$N_\phi = 500$
$N_{blocks} = 1$	$N_{blocks} = 6, N_{MH} = 1$
$c = 0.125$	$\lambda = 2$
Run Time: 00:28 (1 core)	Run Time: 05:52 (12 cores)

Note: We run each algorithm $N_{run} = 50$ times. Run time is reported as mm:ss.

ity that $\rho_{zg} > 0$ and the probability that inflation increases in response to a government spending shock. The 1-Block RWMH-V algorithm is initialized with a random draw from the posterior distribution of the DSGE model parameters and it runs for about 1 minute on a single processor. The SMC algorithm uses $N = 4,800$ particles, $N_{blocks} = 6$ blocks, $N_\phi = 500$ stages, and $\lambda = 2$. The run time of the SMC algorithm is about 6 minutes on 12 processors. Allocating more computational resources to the RWMH algorithm did not change the basic result that the RWMH algorithm is unable to generate draws from the two high-posterior density regions in the correct proportion. A summary of our choice of tuning parameters for the posterior samplers is provided in Table 6.1.

Results. The two panels of Figure 6.4 show estimates of posterior probability that $\rho_{zg} > 0$ and inflation responds positively to an expansionary government spending shock. The bimodal posterior density depicted in Figure 6.1 in conjunction with the IRF plots in Figure 6.3 imply that these posterior probabilities should be around 50%. In order to correctly estimate these probabilities the posterior sampler has to generate draws from the two high-posterior-density areas in the correct proportion.

The Monte Carlo approximations of the posterior probabilities obtained from the SMC algorithm are very stable and close to 50% in all $N_{run} = 50$ runs. The RWMH algorithm, on the other hand, generates estimates that essentially switch

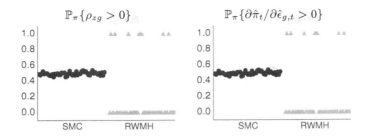

Figure 6.4: Correlated Shocks: Posterior Probability Approximations. Each symbol (50 in total) corresponds to one run of the SMC algorithm (dot) or the RWMH algorithm (triangle).

between zero and one across runs, depending on whether the sampler gets stuck near the $\rho_{zg} > 0$ mode or the $\rho_{zg} < 0$ mode. In other words, the RWMH sampler does not travel frequently enough between the two modes to generate draws from the two high-posterior-probabilities areas of the parameter space in the correct proportion. Increasing the number of draws from 100,000 to 1,000,000 did not correct the problem, and the inspection of the output from a single chain does not flag the convergence problem if the sampler never visits the second high-posterior-density area.

Estimates of the marginal data density associated with the generalized shock model are depicted in Figure 6.5. The Monte Carlo approximation generated by the SMC algorithm is very stable, whereas the approximation obtained with the modified harmonic mean estimator described in Section 4.6 appears to be downward biased (as it misses a high-likelihood region of the parameter space) and highly variable.

Allowing for correlated technology and demand shocks is important for model fit. Table 6.2 displays estimates of the log marginal data density for the benchmark specification of the small-scale DSGE model with uncorrelated shocks and the alternative specification in which the technology growth and government spending shocks follow a VAR(1). In both cases we use the output from the SMC sampler because it is more accurate. The benchmark specification with uncorre-

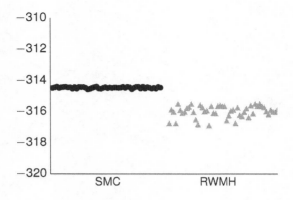

Figure 6.5: Correlated Shocks: Marginal Data Density Approximations. Each symbol (50 in total) corresponds to one run of the SMC
algorithm (dots) or the RWMH algorithm (triangles). The SMC algorithm automatically generates an estimate of the MDD; for the
RWMH algorithm we use Geweke's modified harmonic mean estimator.

Table 6.2: Correlated Shocks: Marginal Data Density

Model	Mean(ln $\hat{p}(Y)$)	Std. Dev.(ln $\hat{p}(Y)$)
AR(1) Shocks	−346.16	(0.07)
VAR(1) Shocks	−314.45	(0.05)

Notes: Table shows mean and standard deviation of SMC-based estimate of the log marginal data density, computed over $N_{run} = 50$
runs of the SMC sampler under each prior. The hyperparameters
used for the SMC algorithm are given in Table 6.1.

lated shocks has a log marginal data density of −346.2, over
30 points below that of the model with a VAR(1) shock process.
Under the calculus of probabilities associated with Bayesian
model comparison, the marginal data densities place overwhelming odds on the diffuse prior model, indicating that the
$AR(1)$ restrictions are severe.

6.2 The Smets-Wouters Model with a Diffuse Prior

We now turn to the estimation of the SW model, which, given the current state of the DSGE model literature, is considered to be a medium-scale DSGE model. It is significantly larger, both in terms of state variables as well as in terms of parameters to be estimated, than the small-scale New Keynesian model considered thus far. The SW model forms the core of many DSGE models that are used in central banks to generate DSGE model-based forecasts and to conduct monetary policy analysis.

The subsequent empirical illustration is an extension of one of the applications in Herbst and Schorfheide (2014). Instead of considering the accuracy of posterior mean approximations, we subsequently focus on the accuracy of posterior quantiles which are frequently used to construct equal-tail-probability credible sets.

6.2.1 Model Specification

Our version of the SW model is identical to the version presented in Smets and Wouters (2007). The log-linearized equilibrium conditions, steady states, and measurement equations are reproduced in Appendix A.1. The model is estimated using the growth rates of GDP, aggregate consumption, and investment; the log level of hours worked; and price inflation, wage inflation, and the federal funds rate. The estimation sample ranges from 1966:Q1 to 2004:Q4.

Our estimation differs from Smets and Wouters (2007) in that we are using a more diffuse prior distribution. This prior is obtained as follows. Our starting point is the original SW prior. For parameters on the unit interval we replace Beta distributions by uniform distributions. Moreover, we scale the prior standard deviations of the other parameters by a factor of three—with the exception that we leave the priors for the shock standard deviations unchanged. The specifications of our modified prior as well as SW's original prior distribution are also provided in Appendix A.1.

Some researchers have argued that the prior distribution originally used by SW is implausibly tight, in the sense that it seems hard to rationalize based on information independent of the information in the estimation sample. For instance, under the original prior the quarterly steady state inflation rate follows a Gamma distribution with mean 0.62 and standard deviation 0.1. Approximately, this prior translates into a 95% credible interval ranging from 1.7% to 3.3% for average annual inflation. Given the history of inflation prior to 1966 in the United States, this prior distribution is unlikely to reflect *a priori* beliefs of someone who has seen macroeconomic data only from the 1950s and 1960s. The prior distribution seems to reflect the low inflation rates in the United States after Alan Greenspan became chairman of the Federal Reserve Board in 1987.

It turns out that the tight prior for the steady state inflation rate has a strong influence on the forecasting performance of the SW model. Under a more diffuse prior the posterior mean estimate of steady state inflation would be close to 4% because of the high inflation rates in the 1970s. Given the mean reverting features of the DSGE model, an estimated average inflation rate of 4% yields poor medium- and long-run inflation forecasts in the 2000s when inflation rates fluctuated around 2.5%. This is documented in more detail in Del Negro and Schorfheide (2013). Under our alternative prior we increase the standard deviation for the quarterly steady state inflation rate to 0.3, which translates into a 95% credible interval ranging from approximately 0.1% to 5% annual inflation.

The effect of monetary policy in the SW model is closely tied to the magnitude of the price and wage rigidity parameters ξ_p and ξ_w. In the SW model nominal rigidities are generated through the so-called *Calvo* mechanism. The ξ parameters correspond to the probability that price- and wage setters are unable to re-optimize their nominal prices. The closer the ζ's are to one the larger the nominal rigidity, the flatter the implied New Keynesian Phillips curve, and the larger the effect of unanticipated changes in monetary policy on real activity.

Empirical evidence that the estimates of these key parameters are very sensitive to the prior distribution is provided in Del Negro and Schorfheide (2008) and Müller (2011). The former paper estimates a DSGE model similar to the SW model under different prior distributions for ξ_p and ξ_w, whereas the latter derives an analytical approximation for the sensitivity of posterior means to shifts in prior means that does not require the DSGE model to be re-estimated.

A numerical side benefit of using tight prior distributions for the Bayesian estimation of DSGE models is that such priors tend to smooth out the posterior surface by down-weighting areas of the parameter space that exhibit local peaks in the likelihood function but are deemed unlikely under the prior distribution. Moreover, if the likelihood function contains hardly any information about certain parameters and is essentially flat with respect to these parameters, tight priors induce curvature in the posterior. In both cases the prior information stabilizes the posterior computations. For posterior simulators such as the RWMH this is crucial, as they work best when the posterior has a fairly regular elliptical shape.

6.2.2 Estimation Results from a Highly Accurate SMC Run

Table 6.3 summarizes the estimates of the quantiles of the marginal posterior distribution for each DSGE model parameter. These quantiles can be used to construct equal-tail-probability credible intervals. While these intervals are typically not the shortest intervals that have a pre-specified posterior coverage probability, they are easier to compute than highest-posterior-density intervals and frequently reported in practice. The quantile estimates are obtained from the output of a run of the SMC algorithm in which the number of particles is chosen to be large enough such that the numerical standard errors are negligible.

Quantile estimates can be computed in two different ways. First, they can be obtained as order statistics by sorting the posterior draws $\{\theta_j^i\}_{i=1}^N$ for each element j of the parameter vector θ and selecting the $\lfloor \tau N \rfloor$'th element (of course, one could also use the $\lceil \tau N \rceil$ element or the average of the two) from the vector of sorted draws. Second, sample quantiles can

Table 6.3: SW Model: Posterior Quantiles

	Quantile τ [%]				
	2.5	5.0	50	95	97.5
$100(\beta^{-1}-1)$	0.00	0.00	0.03	0.15	0.18
π	0.42	0.50	0.87	1.17	1.23
l	-2.22	-1.81	0.27	2.58	3.09
α	0.13	0.14	0.17	0.21	0.21
σ_c	1.31	1.36	1.64	2.00	2.08
Φ	1.46	1.50	1.70	1.92	1.97
φ	3.65	4.24	7.77	12.46	13.49
h	0.56	0.60	0.70	0.78	0.79
ξ_w	0.77	0.80	0.96	0.99	1.00
σ_l	1.18	1.39	2.93	5.33	5.88
ξ_p	0.59	0.62	0.74	0.83	0.84
ι_w	0.30	0.37	0.72	0.96	0.98
ι_p	0.00	0.01	0.09	0.29	0.33
ψ	0.39	0.43	0.68	0.93	0.96
r_π	1.99	2.09	2.72	3.48	3.64
ρ	0.83	0.84	0.88	0.92	0.92
r_y	0.08	0.09	0.15	0.24	0.27
$r_{\Delta y}$	0.20	0.21	0.27	0.34	0.35

	Quantile τ [%]				
	2.5	5.0	50	95	97.5
ρ_a	0.95	0.96	0.97	0.98	0.98
ρ_b	0.01	0.03	0.16	0.43	0.55
ρ_g	0.96	0.97	0.98	0.99	0.99
ρ_i	0.59	0.61	0.71	0.82	0.84
ρ_r	0.00	0.00	0.05	0.15	0.17
ρ_p	0.80	0.83	0.93	0.99	1.00
ρ_w	0.17	0.23	0.78	0.99	0.99
ρ_{ga}	0.25	0.28	0.46	0.62	0.66
μ_p	0.45	0.52	0.81	0.99	1.00
μ_w	0.06	0.11	0.74	0.97	0.97
σ_a	0.40	0.41	0.46	0.51	0.52
σ_b	0.17	0.19	0.25	0.29	0.30
σ_g	0.48	0.49	0.54	0.60	0.61
σ_i	0.37	0.39	0.46	0.55	0.57
σ_r	0.21	0.21	0.24	0.26	0.27
σ_p	0.09	0.09	0.13	0.24	0.25
σ_w	0.21	0.21	0.25	0.29	0.30

be computed by solving the following minimization problem:

$$
\hat{q}_\tau(\theta_j) = \text{argmin}_q \left[(1 - \tau) \frac{1}{N} \sum_{i:\, \theta_j^i < q} (\theta_j^i - q) \right.
$$

$$
\left. + \tau \frac{1}{N} \sum_{i:\, \theta_j^i \geq q} (\theta_j^i - q) \right].
$$

(6.3)

This is a special case of a quantile regression (see Koenker and Bassett (1978) or, for a textbook treatment, Koenker (2005)) in which the regressor is simply a constant term. The computations can be easily adjusted to account for particle weights.

According to Table 6.3, the posterior median estimates of the price and wage rigidity parameters ξ_p and ξ_w are 0.74 and 0.96, respectively, indicating that nominal wages are more rigid than nominal prices. The equal-tail-probability 90% credible intervals range from 0.63 to 0.80 and 0.77 to 0.99, respectively. The posterior median of the annualized steady state inflation rate is about 3.5% and lies outside of the 95% prior credible set under the original SW prior.

6.2.3 Comparison of RWMH-V and SMC Performance

In the remainder of this section we compare the accuracy of the quantile estimates obtained from the RWMH-V and the SMC algorithm. For the posterior mean approximations we computed finite sample inefficiency factors by dividing the small-sample variance of the mean approximations by the variance that could be achieved if *iid* sampling were feasible. For the posterior mean this benchmark variance simply is $\mathbb{V}_\pi[\theta]/N$. The corresponding variance for the quantile estimate is more complicated. Under (the infeasible) direct *iid* sampling from the posterior distribution, the accuracy of the quantile estimates is given by the following CLT:

$$
\sqrt{N}(\hat{q}_\tau - q_\tau) \Longrightarrow N\left(0, \frac{\tau(1 - \tau)}{\pi^2(q_\tau)}\right),
$$

(6.4)

where $\pi(\theta)$ is the posterior density.[1] Generally speaking, the further the quantile in the tails of the posterior distribution, the less precise its estimate. We will use an estimate of the asymptotic variance in (6.4) to standardize the Monte Carlo variance of the posterior samplers below. In particular, we now define the finite sample inefficiency factor as

$$\text{InEff}_N = \frac{\mathbb{V}[\hat{q}_\tau]}{\tau(1-\tau)/(N\pi^2(q_\tau))}, \tag{6.5}$$

where $\mathbb{V}[\hat{q}_\tau]$ is an estimate of the variability of the posterior quantiles based on multiple runs of the sampler and the posterior density $\pi(q_\tau)$ can be replaced by a kernel density estimate based on the output of the posterior simulator.

Accuracy Assessment and Tuning of Algorithms. The computations are executed exactly as described in Herbst and Schorfheide (2014). For convenience, we reproduce the most important details. To assess the precision of the Monte Carlo approximations, we run both algorithms $N_{run} = 50$ times and compute standard deviations of quantile estimates across runs. We constrained the processing time to be roughly the same across algorithms. The SMC algorithm runs about 2 hours and 32 minutes using 24 processors in parallel. In principle, we could instead run 24 copies of the RWMH on separate processor cores and merge the results afterwards. This may reduce sampling variance if each of the RWMH chains has reliably converged to the posterior distribution. However, if there is a bias in the chains—because of, say, the failure to mix on a mode in a multimodal posterior or simply a slowly converging chain—then merging chains will not eliminate that bias.

To facilitate the comparison among the MCMC and the SMC algorithm we use a poor-man's parallelization of the RWMH algorithm. It is possible to parallelize MH algorithms via pre-fetching, as discussed in Strid (2010). Pre-fetching

---

[1]If the posterior distribution of θ_j is $N(\bar{\theta}_j, \bar{V}_{\theta_j})$ then $q_\tau(\theta_j) = \bar{\theta}_j + \Phi_N^{-1}(\tau)\sqrt{\bar{V}_{\theta_j}}$, where $\Phi_N(\cdot)$ is the cdf of a $N(0,1)$. In turn, $\pi(q_\tau) = \phi_N(\Phi_N^{-1}(\tau))/\sqrt{V_{\theta_h}}$.

Table 6.4: SW Model: Algorithm Configuration

RWMH-V	SMC
$N = 10,000,000$	$N = 12,000$
$N_{burn} = 5,000,000$	$N_\phi = 500$
$N_{blocks} = 1$	$N_{blocks} = 6$, $N_{MH} = 1$
$c = 0.08$	$\lambda = 2.1$
Run Time: 14:06 (1 core)	Run Time: 02:32 (24 cores)

Note: We run each algorithm $N_{run} = 50$ times. Run time is reported as hh:mm.

tries to anticipate the points in the parameter space that the MH algorithm is likely to visit in the next k iterations and executes the likelihood evaluation for these parameter values in parallel. Once the likelihood values have been computed one can quickly determine the next k draws. While coding the parallel RWMH algorithm efficiently is quite difficult, the simulation results reported in Strid (2010) suggest that a parallelization using 24 processors would lead to a speedup factor of eight at best. Thus, in our poor-man's parallelization, we simply increase the run time of the RWMH algorithm on a single CPU by a factor of approximately six. This results in approximately 10 million draws.

The hyperparameters of the SMC algorithm are $N = 12,000$, $N_\phi = 500$, $\lambda = 2.1$, and $N_{blocks} = 6$, $N_{MH} = 1$. In this application we follow Herbst and Schorfheide (2014) and use a mixture proposal distribution in the mutation step of the SMC algorithm:

$$\vartheta_b | (\theta^i_{n,b,m-1}, \theta^i_{n,-b,m}, \theta^*_{n,b}, \Sigma^*_{n,b}) \qquad (6.6)$$

$$\sim \quad \omega N\left(\theta^i_{n,b,m-1}, c_n^2 \Sigma^*_{n,b}\right)$$

$$+ \frac{1-\omega}{2} N\left(\theta^i_{n,b,m-1}, c_n^2 diag(\Sigma^*_{n,b})\right)$$

$$+ \frac{1-\omega}{2} N\left(\theta^*_{n,b}, c_n^2 \Sigma^*_{n,b}\right).$$

The choice of this mixture proposal is based on ideas in Kohn,

Giordani, and Strid (2010) on how to improve MH algorithms for DSGE models. The first part corresponds to the standard random walk proposal, the second part sets the off-diagonal elements to zero, and the third part is an independence MH proposal. In the implementation of the algorithm the vector of means θ_n^* and the the covariance matrix Σ_n^* are replaced by SMC approximations constructed after the correction step. We set the weight on the mixture components to $\omega = 0.1$. The choice of $N_\phi = 500$ ensured that the bridge distributions were never too "different."

The parameter λ was calibrated by examining the correction step at $n = 1$. Essentially, we increased λ until the effective sample size after adding the first piece of information from the likelihood was at least $10,000$; roughly speaking, 80% of the initial particles retained substantial weight. We settled on the number of blocks by examining the behavior of the adaptive scaling parameter c in a preliminary run. Setting $N_{blocks} = 6$ ensured that the proposal variances were never scaled down too much for sufficient mutation. For the RWMH algorithm, we scale the proposal covariance to achieve an acceptance rate of approximately 30% over 5 million draws after a burn-in period of 5 million. Each RWMH chain was initialized with a draw from the prior distribution. A summary of the configuration of the algorithms is provided in Table 6.4.

Results. Figure 6.6 depicts estimates of marginal posterior densities for four parameters: the capital share parameter α, the policy rule coefficient on output growth $r_{\delta y}$, the wage stickiness parameter ζ_w, and the degree of wage indexation to lagged inflation and productivity growth ι_w. These parameters were chosen based on the shapes of the marginal posterior distributions. The posterior of α is fairly symmetric around its mean/mode, the posterior of $r_{\Delta y}$ is skewed toward the right, the posterior of ξ_w is bimodal, and the posterior of ι_w has a long left tail.

The multimodal features of the posterior distribution are discussed in detail in Herbst and Schorfheide (2014). At one of the modes the values of the wage stickiness parameter, ξ_w, and wage indexation parameter, ι_w, are relatively low, while

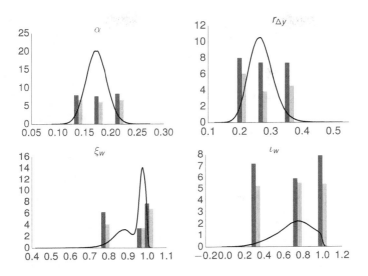

Figure 6.6: SW Model: Precision of Quantile Approximations (Part 1). Each panel depicts a Kernel estimate of the posterior density (solid) and $\ln(N_{eff}) = \ln(N/\text{InEff}_N)$ (light gray bars correspond to RWMH and dark gray bars correspond to SMC) for τ equal to 0.025, 0.5, and 0.975.

the parameters governing the exogenous wage markup process imply a lot of persistence. At the other mode, the relative importance of endogenous and exogenous propagation is reversed. The persistence of measured wages is captured by ξ_w and ι_w that are close to one. The multimodality of the joint posterior translates into a bimodal marginal posterior density of the wage stickiness parameter ζ_w, which peaks around 0.87 and 0.97, respectively.

In addition to the posterior densities Figure 6.6 also shows an approximation of the number of *iid* draws that one has to generate from the posterior distribution to achieve a quantile approximation that is as accurate as the approximation obtained from the posterior simulators:

$$N_{eff} = \frac{N}{\text{InEff}_N}. \tag{6.7}$$

The SMC approximations of the quantiles are generally more accurate than the MCMC approximations from the RWMH-V algorithm. This difference is most pronounced for the monetary policy rule parameter $r_{\Delta y}$ and the wage stickiness parameter ζ_w. For the labor share parameter α, which has an approximately Gaussian shape, the measure N_{eff} does not vary much as a function of the quantile τ. For the parameters ξ_w and ι_w the efficiency measure is larger for the 0.95 and 0.975 quantiles, which may be due to the fact that we are using a kernel density estimator to obtain $\hat{\pi}(\hat{q}_\tau)$ that does not account for the upper bound of one for these two parameters.

The precision of the quantile approximations for all of the estimated DSGE model parameters is summarized in Figure 6.7. Each panel corresponds to a particular quantile and the bottom right panel contains results for the posterior mean. Each dot in the scatter plots depicts N_{eff} for the RWMH-V and the SMC approximation of the posterior quantile of a particular parameter. Essentially all dots lie above the 45-degree line, indicating that the SMC algorithm provides more accurate approximations than the RWMH algorithm. For most parameters the gain in accuracy from using the SMC algorithm exceeds a factor of five. As with the quantile estimates for the parameters, the SMC estimate of the marginal data density is also more accurate. Herbst and Schorfheide (2014) report that the standard deviation of the estimate of the log marginal data density is five times larger under 50 simulations from the RWMH-V than it is under the SMC sampler, owing the poor performance of both the posterior simulator and modified harmonic mean estimators on multi-modal models. The log marginal likelihood estimates also imply that making the prior distribution more diffuse improves the fit of the SW model.

6.3 The Leeper-Plante-Traum Fiscal Policy Model

In the third application we revisit the estimation of a DSGE model developed by Leeper, Plante, and Traum (2010), hereafter LPT, to analyze the effect of fiscal policy interventions. The model is based on a real business cycle model with habit formation in consumption, investment adjustment costs, and

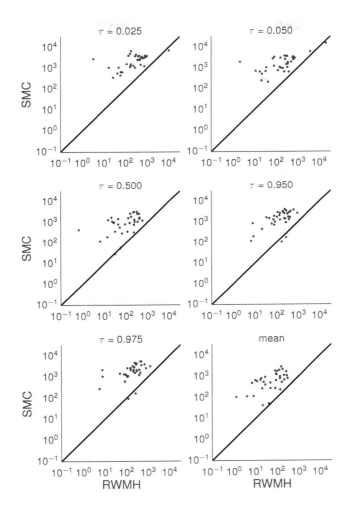

Figure 6.7: SW Model: Precision of Quantile Approximations (Part 2). N_{eff} for the RWMH-V and SMC quantile approximations. Each dot corresponds to one parameter. The 45-degree line appears in solid.

variable capital utilization. Most importantly, the model includes a detailed description of fiscal policy. LPT estimate their model with Bayesian techniques and use it to track the dynamics of fiscal financing and to assess the role of debt in the determination of spending, taxes, and transfers. Here we present only the portion of the model relevant to the fiscal sector. The full set of log-linearized equations can be found in Section A.2 of the Appendix.

There are three sources of time-varying distortionary taxes in the model, represented by the tax rates τ_t^c, τ_t^k, and τ_t^l. These taxes are levied on consumption, capital, and labor income, respectively. Households allocate their income between consumption, c_t (taxed at rate τ_t^c); government bonds, b_t; and capital investment, i_t. Household income is composed of labor income ($w_t l_t$, taxed at rate τ_t^l), utilized-capital income ($R_t^k u_t k_{t-1}$, taxed at rate τ_t^k), income from the sale of riskless government bonds ($R_{t-1} b_{t-1}$), and transfers z_t. The (flow) budget constraint of the households can be written as:

$$(1 + \tau_t^c)c_t + i_t + b_t \tag{6.8}$$
$$= (1 - \tau_t^l)w_t l_t + (1 - \tau_t^k)R_t^k u_t k_{t-1} + R_{t-1} b_{t-1} + z_t.$$

The government uses the income from these taxes to finance government spending, G_t. The budget constraint for the government, using capital letters to denote aggregate quantities, is:

$$B_t + \tau_t^k R_t^k u_t K_{t-1} + \tau_t^l w_t L_t + \tau_t^c C_t = R_{t-1}B_{t-1} + G_t + Z_t. \tag{6.9}$$

The tax rates are assumed to be functions of the state of the economy and some exogenous shocks. These functions are called fiscal policy rules, because they in part describe the reaction of the fiscal authority to the level of output and debt in the economy. Letting $\hat{x}_t$ denote the log deviation from steady state of x_t, the fiscal policy rules take the form:

$$\hat{\tau}_t^k = \varphi_k \hat{Y}_t + \gamma_k \hat{B}_{t-1} + \phi_{kl}\hat{u}_t^l + \phi_{kc}\hat{u}_t^c + \hat{u}_t^k, \tag{6.10}$$

$$\hat{\tau}_t^l = \varphi_l \hat{Y}_t + \gamma_l \hat{B}_{t-1} + \phi_{lk}\hat{u}_t^k + \phi_{lc}\hat{u}_t^c + \hat{u}_t^l, \tag{6.11}$$

$$\hat{\tau}_t^c = \phi_{ck}\hat{u}_t^k + \phi_{cl}\hat{u}_t^l + \hat{u}_t^c. \tag{6.12}$$

Capital and labor taxes respond to output, $\hat{Y}_t$, capturing the effects of automatic stabilizers via parameters φ_k and φ_l, and the level of debt, $\hat{B}_{t-1}$, via parameters γ_k and γ_l for capital and labor, respectively. The processes u_t^c, u_t^k, and u_t^l capture exogenous movements in tax and transfer rates. Exogenous movements of one tax category can contemporaneously affect the other tax rates. The degree of comovement is controlled by the parameters ϕ_{kl}, ϕ_{kc}, and ϕ_{lc}. The exogenous movements in taxes follow AR(1) processes:

$$\hat{u}_t^k = \rho_k \hat{u}_{t-1}^k + \sigma_k \epsilon_t^k, \quad \epsilon_t^k \sim N(0,1), \qquad (6.13)$$

$$\hat{u}_t^l = \rho_l \hat{u}_{t-1}^l + \sigma_l \epsilon_t^l, \quad \epsilon_t^l \sim N(0,1), \qquad (6.14)$$

$$\hat{u}_t^c = \rho_c \hat{u}_{t-1}^c + \sigma_c \epsilon_t^c, \quad \epsilon_t^c \sim N(0,1). \qquad (6.15)$$

On the outlays side, the fiscal rule for government spending, $\hat{G}_t$, is a function of current output and the previous period's debt, controlled by the parameters, φ_g and γ_g, respectively. Spending is also affected by an exogenous, $AR(1)$ process, u_t^g. In log deviations from steady state, the government spending rule is given by:

$$\hat{G}_t = -\varphi_g \hat{Y}_t - \gamma_g \hat{B}_{t-1} + \hat{u}_t^g, \qquad (6.16)$$

$$\hat{u}_t^g = \rho_g \hat{u}_{t-1}^g + \sigma_g \epsilon_t^g, \quad \epsilon_t^g \sim N(0,1). \qquad (6.17)$$

The fiscal authority also facilitates lump-sum transfers to the households, $\hat{Z}_t$, according to a rule that again responds to output (via parameter φ_Z) and debt (via parameter γ_z). Moreover, transfers are affected by the exogenous $AR(1)$ shock u_t^z. Expressed in log deviations from steady state, the transfer rule is given by:

$$\hat{Z}_t = -\varphi_z \hat{Y}_t - \gamma_z \hat{B}_{t-1} + \hat{u}_t^z, \qquad (6.18)$$

$$\hat{u}_t^z = \rho_z \hat{u}_{t-1}^z + \sigma_z \epsilon_t^z, \quad \epsilon_t^z \sim N(0,1). \qquad (6.19)$$

The level of debt adjusts to ensure that the government budget constraint is satisfied.

Prior Specifications. We will subsequently compare estimation results obtained based on two different prior distributions. The first prior distribution is the original one used by LPT. The second prior distribution is obtained by increasing the prior variance of some of the fiscal policy parameters and by removing some of the constraints on the sign of these parameters. In general, LPT use tight but defensible priors for the fiscal parameters. Nonetheless, there is likely to be disagreement among analysts about these prior distributions and there are reasonable arguments for considering more diffuse distributions.

For example, in the original LPT prior, φ_g, the response of government spending to output is restricted to be greater than zero, implying counter-cyclical fiscal policy. There is room to relax the sign restriction because *a priori* it is plausible to allow for pro-cyclical government spending. Moreover, information on many of the tax comovement parameters, for example ϕ_{kc} and ϕ_{lc}, is difficult to elicit. Thus, it is plausible to assign a higher prior variance to these parameters than in the original estimation. Finally, estimation with diffuse priors allows us to parse the effects of the original LPT priors.

The LPT and our diffuse prior distributions for the fiscal policy parameters are displayed in Table 6.5. The prior distribution for the γ parameters, which determine the responses of spending, taxes, and transfers to movements in the lagged level of debt, are changed from gamma distributions centered tightly around 0.4 to uniform distributions on the interval $[0, 5]$. While the γ's are still restricted to be nonnegative, consistent with stable government debt dynamics, there is much more uncertainty about plausible values. Moreover, our modified prior is flat, denying the posterior a potential source of curvature.

The φ parameters control the extent to which current output affects spending, taxation, and transfers. The parametric assumption of Gamma distributions implies that spending and transfers are countercyclical, while capital and labor taxes are procyclical. These hard restrictions might seem undesirable, because there is substantial evidence that, for example, government spending is procyclical at times. Our diffuse priors on these parameters are centered at the same values as their original counterparts, but with substantially higher standard deviations (between a three- and ten-fold increase). Finally, we increase the prior standard deviations on the tax comovement parameters ϕ by a factor of 10. The priors for all other parameters are kept identical to the ones used by LPT, and are summarized in Table 6.6.

Table 6.5: LPT Model: Prior Distributions for Fiscal Rule Parameters

	LPT Prior			Diffuse Prior		
	Type	Para (1)	Para (2)	Type	Para (1)	Para (2)
Debt Response Parameters						
γ_g	G	0.4	0.2	U	0	5
γ_{tk}	G	0.4	0.2	U	0	5
γ_{tl}	G	0.4	0.2	U	0	5
γ_z	G	0.4	0.2	U	0	5
Output Response Parameters						
φ_{tk}	G	1.0	0.3	N	1.0	1
φ_{tl}	G	0.5	0.25	N	0.5	1
φ_g	G	0.07	0.05	N	0.07	1
φ_z	G	0.2	0.1	N	0.2	1
Exogenous Tax Comovement Parameters						
ϕ_{kl}	N	0.25	0.1	N	0.25	1
ϕ_{kc}	N	0.05	0.1	N	0.05	1
ϕ_{lc}	N	0.05	0.1	N	0.05	1

Notes: Para (1) and Para (2) correspond to the mean and standard deviation of the Beta (B), Gamma (G), and Normal (N) distributions and to the upper and lower bounds of the support for the Uniform (U) distribution. For the Inv. Gamma (IG) distribution, Para (1) and Para (2) refer to s and ν, where $p(\sigma|\nu, s) \propto \sigma^{-\nu-1} e^{-\nu s^2/2\sigma^2}$.

Data and Tuning of Algorithm. LPT use U.S. data from 1960:Q1 to 2008:Q1 on nine series to estimate the model: the deviations of log real per capita consumption, investment, hours, government debt, government spending, capital tax revenues, labor tax revenues, consumption tax revenues, and government transfers from independent linear trends. Details on the construction of the data set are available in the Appendix of LPT. Under the diffuse prior the posterior distribution is multimodal. Because we already highlighted the difficulty of the RWMH-V algorithm with multimodal posterior surfaces above, we focus on the substantive results obtained from a single run of the SMC algorithm. The configuration of the algorithm is summarized in Table 6.7.

Table 6.6: LPT Model: Common Prior Distributions

	Type	Para (1)	Para (2)		Type	Para (1)	Para (2)
Endogenous Propagation Parameters							
γ	G	1.75	0.5	s''	G	5	0.5
κ	G	2.0	0.5	δ_2	G	0.7	0.5
h	B	0.5	0.2				
Exogenous Process Parameters							
ρ_a	B	0.7	0.2	σ_a	IG	1	4
ρ_b	B	0.7	0.2	σ_b	IG	1	4
ρ_l	B	0.7	0.2	σ_l	IG	1	4
ρ_i	B	0.7	0.2	σ_i	IG	1	4
ρ_g	B	0.7	0.2	σ_g	IG	1	4
ρ_{tk}	B	0.7	0.2	σ_{tk}	IG	1	4
ρ_{tl}	B	0.7	0.2	σ_{tl}	IG	1	4
ρ_{tc}	B	0.7	0.2	σ_{tc}	IG	1	4
ρ_z	B	0.7	0.2	σ_z	IG	1	4

Notes: Para (1) and Para (2) correspond to the mean and standard deviation of the Beta (B), Gamma (G), and Normal (N) distributions and to the upper and lower bounds of the support for the Uniform (U) distribution. For the Inv. Gamma (IG) distribution, Para (1) and Para (2) refer to s and ν, where $p(\sigma|\nu, s) \propto \sigma^{-\nu-1} e^{-\nu s^2/2\sigma^2}$.

Table 6.7: LPT Model: SMC Configuration

$N = 6,000$	$N_\phi = 500$
$N_{blocks} = 3$	$N_{MH} = 1$
$\lambda = 4.0$	
Run Time [mm:ss]: 48:00 (12 cores)	

Results. Table 6.8 summarizes the posterior distribution of the key parameters related to fiscal policy in the model.[2] The posterior means for the debt-response parameters are more or less that same across prior settings, indicating that the

---

[2]The posterior distribution of the other parameters is similar under the two priors and can be seen in Table A-3 in the Appendix.

Table 6.8: LPT Model: Posterior Moments (Part 1)

	Based on LPT Prior		Based on Diff. Prior	
	Mean	[5%, 95%] Int.	Mean	[5%, 95%] Int.
Debt Response Parameters				
γ_g	0.16	[0.07, 0.27]	0.10	[0.01, 0.23]
γ_{tk}	0.39	[0.22, 0.60]	0.38	[0.16, 0.62]
γ_{tl}	0.11	[0.04, 0.21]	0.04	[0.00, 0.11]
γ_z	0.32	[0.17, 0.47]	0.32	[0.14, 0.49]
Output Response Parameters				
φ_{tk}	1.67	[1.18, 2.18]	2.06	[1.44, 2.69]
φ_{tl}	0.29	[0.11, 0.53]	0.11	[-0.34, 0.58]
φ_g	0.06	[0.01, 0.13]	-0.43	[-0.87, 0.02]
φ_z	0.17	[0.06, 0.33]	-0.07	[-0.56, 0.41]
Exogenous Tax Comovement Parameters				
ϕ_{kl}	0.19	[0.14, 0.24]	1.57	[1.29, 1.87]
ϕ_{kc}	0.03	[-0.03, 0.08]	-0.33	[-2.84, 2.73]
ϕ_{lc}	-0.02	[-0.07, 0.04]	0.20	[-1.23, 1.40]
Innovations to Fiscal Rules				
σ_g	3.03	[2.79, 3.30]	2.91	[2.66, 3.19]
σ_{tk}	4.36	[4.01, 4.75]	1.26	[1.08, 1.46]
σ_{tl}	2.95	[2.71, 3.22]	2.00	[1.71, 2.33]
σ_{tc}	3.99	[3.67, 4.33]	1.14	[0.96, 1.35]
σ_z	3.34	[3.07, 3.63]	3.34	[3.07, 3.63]

prior is not substantially influencing the posterior. On the other hand, the posterior distribution of the elasticities of taxes, spending, and transfers with respect to output (the φ parameters) are substantially different under the two priors. In particular, the restriction that $\varphi_i > 0$ for $i \in \{tk, tl, g, z\}$, embodied in the LPT prior, is "binding" in the sense that the posterior under the diffuse prior has substantial density for φ_{tl}, φ_g, and $\varphi_z < 0$. Indeed, as shown in Figure 6.8, once this restriction is relaxed, the sign of the posterior for φ_g and φ_z switches.

Figure 6.9 depicts scatter plots of draws from bivariate posterior distributions in the off-diagonal panels and density

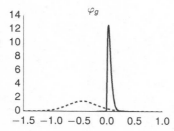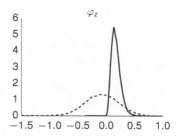

Figure 6.8: LPT Model: Posterior of Output Response Parameters. The figure depicts posterior densities under the LPT prior (solid) and the diffuse prior (dashed).

plots for univariate posteriors of the tax comovement parameters ϕ_{lc}, ϕ_{kc}, and ϕ_{kl}. Under the LPT prior distribution the posteriors appear to be unimodal and concentrated near zero. As the prior distribution is relaxed, the posterior distributions become multimodal. The marginal posterior of ϕ_{lc} has modes near -1 and 1, and the posterior of ϕ_{kc} has modes near -3 and 3. The posterior distributions are not symmetric. For ϕ_{lc} there is more mass in the positive region of the parameter space, whereas for ϕ_{kc} most of the posterior mass is in the negative region of the parameter space.

The multimodal posterior for the parameters translates into a multimodal posterior for impulse responses. The responses to a labor income tax shock ϵ_t^l are depicted in Figure 6.10. The figure depicts four types of posterior mean responses: the baseline responses obtained from the posterior distribution that is associated with the LPT prior; the unconditional posterior mean responses associated with the diffuse prior; posterior mean responses based on the diffuse prior that condition on $\phi_{lc} > 0, \phi_{kc} < 0$ or $\phi_{lc} < 0, \phi_{kc} > 0$, respectively. The lower right panel shows the response of the labor tax rate $\hat{\tau}_l$. To facilitate the comparison between the four sets of impulse responses, we normalize the labor tax innovation to one percent. If the steady state labor tax rate is 30% then a one percent increase raises the tax rate to 30.3%.

Under the diffuse prior distribution capital taxes increase

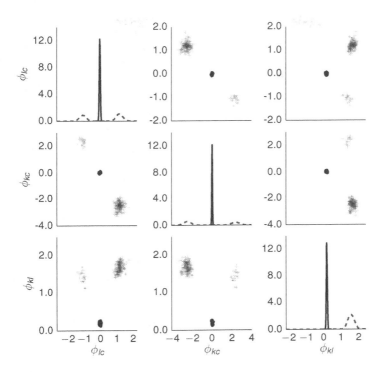

Figure 6.9: LPT Model: Posterior of Tax Comovement Parameters. The plots on the diagonal depict posterior densities under the LPT prior (solid) and the diffuse prior (dashed). The plots on the off-diagonals depict draws from the posterior distribution under the LPT prior (circles) and the diffuse prior (crosses).

in response to a labor tax shock, because τ_{kl} is unambiguously positive. Under the LPT prior the capital tax response is more muted and turns negative after one period. While the spillover from the labor tax innovation onto the consumption tax rate is roughly zero on average, under the diffuse prior the response is bimodal: conditional on the $\phi_{lc} > 0$ ($\phi_{lc} < 0$) there is a 1.2% rise (fall) in the consumption tax. In general, the increase in the labor tax lowers the labor supply, and the hours worked response is quite similar for all four cases. The

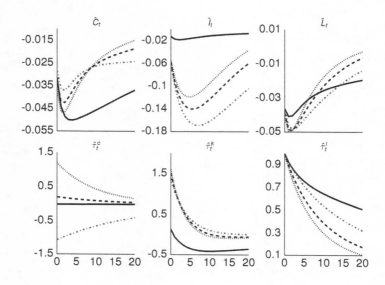

Figure 6.10: LPT Model: Impulse Response to a Labor Tax Innovation. The figure depicts posterior mean impulse responses under LPT prior (solid); diffuse prior (dashed); diffuse prior with $\phi_{lc} > 0$, $\phi_{kl} < 0$ (dotted); and diffuse prior with $\phi_{lc} < 0$, $\phi_{kl} > 0$ (dots and short dashes). $\hat{C}_t$, $\hat{I}_t$ and $\hat{L}_t$ are consumption, investment, and hours worked in deviation from steady state.

increase in capital taxes lowers investment conditional on the diffuse prior distribution. The drop in investment is amplified (dampened) if the consumption tax falls (rises) in response to the labor tax innovation, which creates a bimodal investment response. Falling (rising) consumption taxes create an incentive to allocate more (less) income to consumption and less (more) to investment. In turn, the consumption response is also bimodal.

Part III

Estimation of Nonlinear DSGE Models

Chapter 7

From Linear to Nonlinear DSGE Models

All of the DSGE models considered in this book are inherently nonlinear. Thus far, we considered *approximate* solutions to the equilibrium dynamics associated with these models that are linear (or log-linear) and we assumed that the innovations to the exogenous shock processes are Gaussian. This allowed us to use the Kalman filter to evaluate the DSGE model likelihood function and we could focus our attention on generating draws from the posterior distribution $p(\theta|Y) \propto p(Y|\theta)p(\theta)$. In the third part of the book, we will present computational techniques that can be used to estimate DSGE models that have been solved with nonlinear techniques such as higher-order perturbation methods or projection methods.

From the perspective of Bayesian estimation, the key difference between DSGE models that have been solved with a linearization technique and models that have been solved nonlinearly is that in the former case the resulting state-space representation is linear:

$$\begin{aligned} y_t &= \Psi_0(\theta) + \Psi_1(\theta)t + \Psi_2(\theta)s_t + u_t, & (7.1) \\ & u_t \sim N(0, \Sigma_u), \\ s_t &= \Phi_1(\theta)s_{t-1} + \Phi_\epsilon(\theta)\epsilon_t, \quad \epsilon_t \sim N(0, \Sigma_\epsilon) \end{aligned}$$

whereas in the latter case it takes the general nonlinear form

$$\begin{aligned} y_t &= \Psi(s_t, t; \theta) + u_t, \quad u_t \sim F_u(\cdot; \theta) & (7.2) \\ s_t &= \Phi(s_{t-1}, \epsilon_t; \theta), \quad \epsilon_t \sim F_\epsilon(\cdot; \theta). \end{aligned}$$

As in the linear case, the functions $\Psi(s_t; \theta)$ and $\Phi(s_{t-1}, \epsilon_t; \theta)$

are generated numerically by the solution method and u_t is an additive measurement error.

The remaining chapters of this book will focus on constructing sequential Monte Carlo approximations to the likelihood function associated with the nonlinear state-space model (7.2) and the consequences of using an approximate likelihood function for the accuracy of posterior simulations. Before delving into the Bayesian computations, we provide a brief discussion of nonlinear solution techniques for DSGE models in Section 7.1. Section 7.2 highlights some of the features that researchers have introduced into DSGE models to capture important nonlinearities in the data. Throughout this chapter, we use the small-scale New Keynesian DSGE model as illustrative example. This chapter is not meant to be a self-contained tutorial on nonlinear DSGE model solutions. Instead, its goal is to provide some context for the particle filtering techniques discussed in Chapter 8.

7.1 Nonlinear DSGE Model Solutions

When discussing nonlinear solutions to DSGE models, it is convenient to follow the convention in the dynamic programming literature and to distinguish between control and state variables.[1] In the small-scale DSGE model the control variables, which we denote in slight abuse of notation by c_t, are inflation, consumption, and output. The lagged interest rate is an endogenous state variable, which we denote by x_t, and the technology growth shock, the government spending shock, and the monetary policy shock are exogenous state variables, which we denote by z_t. The DSGE model solution will have the following structure:

$$c_t = \Phi_c(x_t, z_t), \; x_{t+1} = \Phi_x(x_t, z_t), \; z_{t+1} = \Phi_z(z_t, \epsilon_{t+1}). \quad (7.3)$$

The control variables depend on the current values of the endogenous and exogenous state variables. The function $\Phi_c(\cdot)$ summarizes the decision rules of the firms and households

---

[1] This distinction was not necessary to implement the solution algorithm for a linear rational expectations system discussed in Section 2.1.

that solve the underlying intertemporal optimization problems of the economic agents. In the context of the underlying dynamic programming problems, the decision rules are called policy functions. The functions $\Phi_x(\cdot)$ and $\Phi_z(\cdot)$ characterize the laws of motion of the state variables. The endogenous state variables in the subsequent period depend on the current values of the endogenous and exogenous state variables, and the exogenous state variables in period $t+1$ depend on the period t value and the period $t+1$ innovation.

For the sake of concreteness, we reproduce the equilibrium conditions for the small-scale DSGE model, written in terms of percentage deviations from steady state values (recall that $\hat{y}_t = \ln(y_t/y)$ and so forth):

$$1 = \beta \mathbb{E}_t \left[e^{-\tau \hat{c}_{t+1} + \tau \hat{c}_t + \hat{R}_t - \hat{z}_{t+1} - \hat{\pi}_{t+1}} \right] \tag{7.4}$$

$$0 = \left(e^{\hat{\pi}_t} - 1 \right) \left[\left(1 - \frac{1}{2\nu} \right) e^{\hat{\pi}_t} + \frac{1}{2\nu} \right] \tag{7.5}$$
$$- \beta \, \mathbb{E}_t \left[\left(e^{\hat{\pi}_{t+1}} - 1 \right) e^{-\tau \hat{c}_{t+1} + \tau \hat{c}_t + \hat{y}_{t+1} - \hat{y}_t + \hat{\pi}_{t+1}} \right]$$
$$+ \frac{1-\nu}{\nu \phi \pi^2} \left(1 - e^{\tau \hat{c}_t} \right)$$

$$e^{\hat{c}_t - \hat{y}_t} = e^{-\hat{g}_t} - \frac{\phi \pi^2 g}{2} \left(e^{\hat{\pi}_t} - 1 \right)^2 \tag{7.6}$$

$$\hat{R}_t = \rho_R \hat{R}_{t-1} + (1 - \rho_R)\psi_1 \hat{\pi}_t \tag{7.7}$$
$$+ (1 - \rho_R)\psi_2 \left(\hat{y}_t - \hat{g}_t \right) + \epsilon_{R,t}$$

$$\hat{g}_t = \rho_g \hat{g}_{t-1} + \epsilon_{g,t} \tag{7.8}$$

$$\hat{z}_t = \rho_z \hat{z}_{t-1} + \epsilon_{z,t}. \tag{7.9}$$

The vector of control variables is $c_t = [\hat{c}_t, \hat{y}_t, \hat{\pi}_t]'$. The endogenous state variable is $x_t = \hat{R}_{t-1}$ and the vector of exogenous state variables is $z_t = [\hat{z}_t, \hat{g}_t, \epsilon_{R,t}]'$. Finally, the innovation vector is given by $\epsilon_t = [\epsilon_{z,t}, \epsilon_{g,t}, \epsilon_{R,t}]'$. The law of motion $\Phi_z(\cdot)$ of the exogenous state variables is given by (7.8) and (7.9) as well as the trivial identity $\epsilon_{R,t+1} = \epsilon_{R,t+1}$. The key step of the nonlinear solution algorithm is to find decision rules $\Phi_{c,\hat{c}}(x_t, z_t)$ and $\Phi_{c,\hat{\pi}}(x_t, z_t)$ for consumption and inflation, respectively, such that the nonlinear rational expectations difference equations (7.4) to (7.9) and the model variables are non-explosive. Once the decision rules for consumption and inflation are determined, the decision rule $\Phi_{c,y}(x_t, z_t)$ for output can be directly obtained from the aggregate resource constraint (7.6). Finally, the law of motion of the endogenous state variable $\Phi_x(\cdot)$ is obtained by substituting $\Phi_{c,\hat{\pi}}(\cdot)$ and $\Phi_{c,y}(\cdot)$ into the monetary policy rule (7.7).

Nonlinear solution techniques for DSGE models can be broadly classified into global approximations and local perturbations. A global approximation method applied to the small-scale New Keynesian DSGE model would express the decision rules $\Phi_{c,\hat{c}}(x_t, z_t)$ and $\Phi_{c,\hat{\pi}}(x_t, z_t)$ as flexible functions, e.g., Chebyshev polynomials, indexed by coefficient vectors $\vartheta_{\hat{c}}$ and $\vartheta_{\hat{\pi}}$. The coefficient vectors are determined as follows: (i) specify a grid of points $\mathcal{G}$ in the model's state space; (ii) determine $\vartheta_{\hat{c}}$ and $\vartheta_{\hat{\pi}}$ by minimizing the discrepancy between the left-hand side and the right-hand side of (7.4) and (7.5), summed over all $(x_t, z_t) \in \mathcal{G}$. Note that the evaluation of the right-hand side of the intertemporal optimality conditions requires the numerical approximation of conditional expectations. A textbook treatment of global solution techniques is provided by Judd (1998).

The log-linear approximation of the DSGE model discussed in Section 2.1 is an example of a first-order perturbation approximation. Suppose that we pre-multiply the shock innovations $\epsilon_{z,t}$, $\epsilon_{g,t}$, and $\epsilon_{R,t}$ in (7.7) to (7.9) by a scaling constant σ. For $\sigma = 0$ the system is in its steady state, meaning that the model variables expressed in percentage deviations are equal to zero. The basic idea of a perturbation solution, say of order two, is to construct an approximation of the form

$$c_t = \Phi_c(x_t, z_t) = c^{(0)} + \sigma c_t^{(1)} + \sigma^2 c_t^{(2)} + \mathcal{O}_p(\sigma^3)$$
$$x_{t+1} = \Phi_x(x_t, z_t) = x^{(0)} + \sigma x_{t+1}^{(1)} + \sigma^2 x_{t+1}^{(2)} + \mathcal{O}_p(\sigma^3)$$

that satisfies the equilibrium conditions. The terms $c^{(0)}$ and $x^{(0)}$ correspond to steady states (or are equal to zero if the system is written in deviations from the steady state). The terms $c_t^{(1)}$ and $x_t^{(1)}$ are identical to the laws of motion that are implicitly obtained with the solution technique for linear rational expectations models discussed in Section 2.1. The terms $c_t^{(2)}$ and $x_{t+1}^{(2)}$ capture nonlinearities arising from quadratic terms of the form $x_{j,t}x_{k,t}$, $z_{j,t}z_{k,t}$, and $x_{j,t}z_{k,t}$. Finally, the remainder can be bounded by a term that converges to zero at least at the rate σ^3 as $\sigma \longrightarrow 0$. A second-order perturbation solution requires a second-order Taylor approximation of the equilibrium conditions. An introduction to perturbations methods is provided by Holmes (1995) and algorithms to compute second-order perturbation for DSGE models have been developed in Schmitt-Grohé and Uribe (2004) and Kim, Kim, Schaumburg, and Sims (2008). A comparison of linear and nonlinear solution techniques can be found in Aruoba, Fernández-Villaverde, and Rubio-Ramírez (2006).

7.2 Adding Nonlinear Features to DSGE Models

The nonlinearities that arise in the small-scale DSGE model under parameterizations that are consistent with U.S. data are fairly small. The decision rules are essentially linear in the neighborhood of the steady state. The model requires unrealistically volatile shocks or a large risk-aversion parameter τ to generate substantial nonlinearities. To capture the nonlinearities that are present in actual U.S. data, it is necessary to add some additional features to the small-scale DSGE model. We briefly discuss four such features in the remainder of this chapter.

Stochastic Volatility. One of the most striking features of postwar U.S. data is the reduction in the volatility of output growth and its components around 1984. This phenomenon has been termed the *Great Moderation* and was also observed for many other industrialized countries. To investigate the sources of this volatility reduction, Justiniano and Primiceri (2008) allow the volatility of structural shocks in an SW-style model to vary stochastically over time. In the context of our small-scale DSGE model the introduction of stochastic volatility would amount to assuming that the shock innovations are distributed according to

$$\epsilon_{j,t} \sim N(0, \sigma_j^2 v_{j,t}^2), \quad \ln v_{j,t} = \rho_{v,j} v_{j,t-1} + \eta_{j,t},$$
$$\eta_{j,t} \sim N(0, \omega_j^2), \quad j \in \{g, z, R\}. \tag{7.10}$$

Stochastic volatility is not just important to capture the Great

Moderation. It is also useful to capture increases in macroeconomic volatility during recessions as well as the time-varying volatility of financial data such as short-term interest rates, bond yields, and equity returns. Fernández-Villaverde and Rubio-Ramírez (2013) present empirical evidence for the importance of modeling macroeconomic volatility, show how nonlinear DSGE models with shocks that exhibit stochastic volatility along the lines of (7.10) can be estimated using particle filtering techniques, and provide some empirical illustrations.

Markov Switching. Hamilton (1989) developed a Markov-switching autoregressive model for U.S. output growth and showed that the regime switching process is able to capture recession and expansion periods. Markov-switching processes can also be incorporated into DSGE models. For instance, in the small-scale DSGE model we could replace the constant technology growth rate γ by a two-state Markov process, $\gamma(m_t)$, where m_t is either zero (say, expansion) or one (say, recession). The process m_t is described by the transition probabilities $\mathbb{P}\{m_t = l | m_{t-1} = k\} = \eta_{lk}$. This modification would be able to match the same features of output growth that Hamilton (1989) was able to match with his regime-switching model. Schorfheide (2005) replaced the constant target inflation rate π^* by a time-varying target inflation rate $\pi^*(m_t)$ that is assumed to follow a two-state Markov process, capturing shifts to a high target inflation rate in the 1970s and the reversion to a low target inflation rate in the early 1980s. Markov switching can also be introduced into parameters that are unrelated to exogenous processes, e.g., the monetary policy coefficients ψ_1 and ψ_2. Davig and Leeper (2007) and Bianchi (2013) use DSGE models with regime switching to study the interaction between U.S. monetary and fiscal policy. Solution methods for Markov-switching DSGE models are provided in Farmer, Waggoner, and Zha (2009) and Foerster, Rubio-Ramirez, Waggoner, and Zha (2014).

Asymmetric Adjustment Costs. The nonlinearity of DSGE models can also be enhanced by introducing asymmetric adjustment costs. For instance, it might be more costly for firms to lower nominal wages than to raise nominal wages. While wages in our small-scale model are flexible, we could make the price adjustment costs asymmetric by replacing

$$AC_t(j) = \frac{\phi}{2}\left(\frac{P_t(j)}{P_{t-1}(j)} - \pi\right)^2 Y_t(j),$$

with the linex function

$$\widetilde{AC}_t(j) = \phi\left(\frac{\exp\{-\zeta[P_t(j)/P_t(j-1) - \pi]\}}{\zeta^2}\right. \tag{7.11}$$
$$\left. + \frac{\zeta[P_t(j)/P_t(j-1) - \pi] - 1}{\zeta^2}\right)Y_t(j).$$

Here the additional parameter ζ controls the direction and the degree of asymmetry. Note that $\widetilde{AC}_t(j) \longrightarrow AC_t(j)$ as $\zeta \longrightarrow 0$. DSGE models with asymmetric adjustment costs have been analyzed, for instance, in Kim and Ruge-Murcia (2009) and Aruoba, Bocola, and Schorfheide (2013).

Occasionally Binding Constraints. Short-term interest rates in the United States have been essentially equal to zero in the United States since 2009. The availability of money as a non-interest-bearing asset effectively creates a zero lower bound (ZLB) for nominal interest rates. The baseline monetary policy rule in (7.7) ignores this ZLB and allows net interest rates to become negative. However, the ZLB can be easily imposed using a max operator as follows:

$$\hat{R}_t = \max\left\{-\ln(r\pi^*), \rho_R\hat{R}_{t-1} + (1-\rho_R)\psi_1\hat{\pi}_t\right.$$
$$\left. +(1-\rho_R)\psi_2\left(\hat{y}_t - \hat{g}_t\right) + \epsilon_{R,t}\right\}. \tag{7.12}$$

Because the interest rates are expressed in percentage deviations from the steady state $R = r\pi^*$, the ZLB translates into a lower bound of $-\ln(r\pi^*)$. The ZLB is an example of an occasionally binding constraint, in the sense that it only becomes binding if the economy is hit by adverse shocks that lead interest rates to fall to zero. Occasionally binding constraints often generate decision rules with kinks. Perturbation techniques, which rely on smoothness restrictions, are not well suited to solve such models. Papers by Fernández-Villaverde, Gordon, Guerrón-Quintana, and Rubio-Ramírez (2015); Gust, Lopez-Salido, and Smith (2012); Aruoba, Cuba-Borda, and Schorfheide (2014); and Maliar and Maliar (2015) all use global approximation methods to solve DSGE models with a ZLB constraint.

Chapter 8

Particle Filters

The key difficulty that arises when the Bayesian estimation of DSGE models is extended from linear to nonlinear models is the evaluation of the likelihood function. Throughout this book, we focus on the use of particle filters to accomplish this task. Our starting point is a state-space representation for the nonlinear DSGE model of the form

$$
\begin{aligned}
y_t &= \Psi(s_t, t; \theta) + u_t, \quad u_t \sim F_u(\cdot; \theta) \qquad (8.1) \\
s_t &= \Phi(s_{t-1}, \epsilon_t; \theta), \quad \epsilon_t \sim F_\epsilon(\cdot; \theta).
\end{aligned}
$$

As discussed in the previous chapter, the functions $\Psi(s_t, t; \theta)$ and $\Phi(s_{t-1}, \epsilon_t; \theta)$ are generated numerically by the solution method. For reasons that will become apparent below, we require that the measurement error u_t in the measurement equation is additively separable and that the probability density function $p(u_t|\theta)$ can be evaluated analytically. In many applications, $u_t \sim N(0, \Sigma_u)$. While the exposition of the algorithms in this chapter focuses on the nonlinear state-space model (8.1), the numerical illustrations and empirical applications are based on the linear Gaussian model

$$
\begin{aligned}
y_t &= \Psi_0(\theta) + \Psi_1(\theta)t + \Psi_2(\theta)s_t + u_t, \qquad (8.2) \\
&\quad u_t \sim N(0, \Sigma_u), \\
s_t &= \Phi_1(\theta)s_{t-1} + \Phi_\epsilon(\theta)\epsilon_t, \quad \epsilon_t \sim N(0, \Sigma_\epsilon)
\end{aligned}
$$

obtained by solving a log-linearized DSGE model. For model (8.2) the Kalman filter described in Table 2.1 delivers the exact distributions $p(y_t|Y_{1:t-1}, \theta)$ and $p(s_t|Y_{1:t}, \theta)$ against which the accuracy of the particle filter approximation can be evaluated.

There exists a large literature on particle filters. Surveys and tutorials can be found, for instance, in Arulampalam, Maskell, Gordon, and Clapp (2002), Cappé, Godsill, and Moulines (2007), Doucet and Johansen (2011), Creal (2012). Kantas, Doucet, Singh, Maciejowski, and Chopin (2014) discuss using particle filters in the context of estimating the parameters of state-space models. These papers provide detailed references to the literature. The basic bootstrap particle filtering algorithm is remarkably straightforward, but may perform quite poorly in practice. Thus, much of the literature focuses on refinements of the bootstrap filter that increases the efficiency of the algorithm; see, for instance, Doucet, de Freitas, and Gordon (2001). Textbook treatments of the statistical theory underlying particle filters can be found in Cappé, Moulines, and Ryden (2005), Liu (2001), and Del Moral (2013).

The remainder of this chapter is organized as follows. We introduce the bootstrap particle filter in Section 8.1. This filter is easy to implement and has been widely used in DSGE model applications. The bootstrap filter is a special case of a sequential importance sampling with resampling (SISR) algorithm. This more general algorithm is presented in Section 8.2. An important step in the generic particle filter algorithm is to generate draws that reflect the distribution of the states in period t conditional on the information $Y_{1:t}$. These draws are generated through an importance sampling step in which states are drawn from a proposal distribution and reweighted. For the bootstrap particle filter, this proposal distribution is based on the state transition equation. Unfortunately, the forward iteration of the state transition equation might produce draws that are associated with highly variable weights, which in turn leads to imprecise Monte Carlo approximations.

The accuracy of the particle filter can be improved by choosing other proposal distributions. We discuss in Section 8.3 how to construct more efficient proposal distributions. While the tailoring (or adaption) of the proposal distributions tends to require additional computations, the number of particles can often be reduced drastically, which leads to an improvement in efficiency. DSGE model-specific implementation issues of the particle filter are examined in Section 8.4. Finally, we present the auxiliary particle filter and a filter recently proposed by DeJong, Liesenfeld, Moura, Richard, and Dharmarajan (2013) in Section 8.5. Various versions of the particle filter are applied to the small-scale New Keynesian DSGE model and the SW model in Sections 8.6 and 8.7. We close this chapter with some computational considerations in Section 8.8. Throughout this chapter we condition on a fixed vector of parameter values θ and defer the topic of parameter estimation to Chapters 9 and 10.

8.1 The Bootstrap Particle Filter

We begin with a version of the particle filter in which the particles representing the hidden state vector s_t are propagated by iterating the state-transition equation in (8.1) forward. This version of the particle filter is due to Gordon, Salmond, and Smith (1993) and called bootstrap partical filter. As in Algorithm 8, we use the sequence $\{\rho_t\}_{t=1}^T$ to indicate whether the particles are resampled in period t. A resampling step is necessary to prevent the distribution of the particle weights from degenerating. We discuss the adaptive choice of ρ_t below. The function $h(\cdot)$ is used to denote transformations of interest of the state vector s_t. The particle filter algorithm closely follows the steps of the generic filter in Algorithm 1.

Algorithm 11 (Bootstrap Particle Filter)

1. **Initialization.** Draw the initial particles from the distribution $s_0^j \overset{iid}{\sim} p(s_0|\theta)$ and set $W_0^j = 1$, $j = 1, \ldots, M$.

2. **Recursion.** For $t = 1, \ldots, T$:

   (a) **Forecasting** s_t. Propagate the period $t-1$ particles $\{s_{t-1}^j, W_{t-1}^j\}$ by iterating the state-transition equation forward:

   $$\tilde{s}_t^j = \Phi(s_{t-1}^j, \epsilon_t^j; \theta), \quad \epsilon_t^j \sim F_\epsilon(\cdot; \theta). \tag{8.3}$$

   An approximation of $\mathbb{E}[h(s_t)|Y_{1:t-1}, \theta]$ is given by

   $$\hat{h}_{t,M} = \frac{1}{M} \sum_{j=1}^{M} h(\tilde{s}_t^j) W_{t-1}^j. \tag{8.4}$$

(b) **Forecasting** y_t. *Define the incremental weights*

$$\tilde{w}_t^j = p(y_t | \tilde{s}_t^j, \theta). \qquad (8.5)$$

The predictive density $p(y_t | Y_{1:t-1}, \theta)$ can be approximated by

$$\hat{p}(y_t | Y_{1:t-1}, \theta) = \frac{1}{M} \sum_{j=1}^{M} \tilde{w}_t^j W_{t-1}^j. \qquad (8.6)$$

If the measurement errors are $N(0, \Sigma_u)$ then the incremental weights take the form

$$\begin{aligned}
\tilde{w}_t^j &= (2\pi)^{-n/2} |\Sigma_u|^{-1/2} \qquad (8.7) \\
&\times \exp\left\{ -\frac{1}{2} \big(y_t - \Psi(\tilde{s}_t^j, t; \theta)\big)' \right. \\
&\left. \times \Sigma_u^{-1} \big(y_t - \Psi(\tilde{s}_t^j, t; \theta)\big) \right\},
\end{aligned}$$

where n here denotes the dimension of y_t.

(c) **Updating.** *Define the normalized weights*

$$\tilde{W}_t^j = \frac{\tilde{w}_t^j W_{t-1}^j}{\frac{1}{M} \sum_{j=1}^{M} \tilde{w}_t^j W_{t-1}^j}. \qquad (8.8)$$

An approximation of $\mathbb{E}[h(s_t) | Y_{1:t}, \theta]$ is given by

$$\tilde{h}_{t,M} = \frac{1}{M} \sum_{j=1}^{M} h(\tilde{s}_t^j) \tilde{W}_t^j. \qquad (8.9)$$

(d) **Selection.** *Case (i): If $\rho_t = 1$ resample the particles via multinomial resampling. Let $\{s_t^j\}_{j=1}^{M}$ denote M iid draws from a multinomial distribution characterized by support points and weights $\{\tilde{s}_t^j, \tilde{W}_t^j\}$ and set $W_t^j = 1$ for $j =, 1 \ldots, M$.*
Case (ii): If $\rho_t = 0$, let $s_t^j = \tilde{s}_t^j$ and $W_t^j = \tilde{W}_t^j$ for $j =, 1 \ldots, M$.
An approximation of $\mathbb{E}[h(s_t) | Y_{1:t}, \theta]$ is given by

$$\bar{h}_{t,M} = \frac{1}{M} \sum_{j=1}^{M} h(s_t^j) W_t^j. \qquad (8.10)$$

3. **Likelihood Approximation.** *The approximation of the log-likelihood function is given by*

$$\ln \hat{p}(Y_{1:T}|\theta) = \sum_{t=1}^{T} \ln \left(\frac{1}{M} \sum_{j=1}^{M} \tilde{w}_t^j W_{t-1}^j \right). \quad (8.11)$$

As for the SMC Algorithm 8, we can define an effective sample size (in terms of number of particles) as

$$\widehat{ESS}_t = M / \left(\frac{1}{M} \sum_{j=1}^{M} (\tilde{W}_t^j)^2 \right) \quad (8.12)$$

and replace the deterministic sequence $\{\rho_t\}_{t=1}^{T}$ by an adaptively chosen sequence $\{\hat{\rho}_t\}_{t=1}^{T}$, for which $\hat{\rho}_t = 1$ whenever $\widehat{ESS}_t$ falls below a threshold, say $M/2$. In the remainder of this section we discuss the asymptotic properties of the particle filters, letting the number of particles $M \longrightarrow \infty$, and the role of the measurement errors u_t in the bootstrap particle filter.

8.1.1 Asymptotic Properties

The convergence theory underlying the particle filter is similar to the theory sketched in Section 5.2.4 for the SMC sampler. As in our presentation of the SMC sampler, in the subsequent exposition we will abstract many of the technical details that underly the convergence theory for the SMC sampler. Our exposition will be mainly heuristic, meaning that we will present some basic convergence results and the key steps for their derivation. Rigorous derivations are provided in Chopin (2004). As in Section 5.2.4 the asymptotic variance formulas are represented in recursive form. While this renders them unusable for the computation of numerical standard errors, they do provide some qualitative insights into the accuracy of the Monte Carlo approximations generated by the particle filter.

To simplify the notation, we drop the parameter vector θ from the conditioning set. Starting point is the assumption that Monte Carlo averages constructed from the $t - 1$ particle swarm $\{s_{t-1}^j, W_{t-1}^j\}_{j=1}^M$ satisfy an SLLN and a CLT of the form

$$\bar{h}_{t-1,M} \xrightarrow{a.s.} \mathbb{E}[h(s_{t-1})|Y_{1:t-1}], \qquad (8.13)$$
$$\sqrt{M}\big(\bar{h}_{t-1,M} - \mathbb{E}[h(s_{t-1})|Y_{1:t-1}]\big)$$
$$\implies N\big(0, \Omega_{t-1}(h)\big).$$

Based on this assumption, we will show the convergence of $\hat{h}_{t,M}$, $\hat{p}(y_t|Y_{1:t-1})$, $\tilde{h}_{t,M}$, and $\bar{h}_{t,M}$. We write $\Omega_{t-1}(h)$ to indicate that the asymptotic covariance matrix depends on the function $h(s_t)$ for which the expected value is computed. The filter is typically initialized by directly sampling from the initial distribution $p(s_0)$, which immediately delivers the SLLN and CLT provided the required moments of $h(s_0)$ exist. We now sketch the convergence arguments for the Monte Carlo approximations in Steps 2(a) to 2(d) of Algorithm 11. A rigorous proof would involve verifying the existence of moments required by the SLLN and CLT and a careful characterization of the asymptotic covariance matrices.

Forecasting Steps. Forward iteration of the state-transition equation amounts to drawing s_t from a conditional density $g_t(s_t|s_{t-1}^j)$. In Algorithm 11 this density is given by

$$g_t(s_t|s_{t-1}^j) = p(s_t|s_{t-1}^j).$$

We denote expectations under this density as $\mathbb{E}_{p(\cdot|s_{t-1}^j)}[h]$ and decompose

$$\hat{h}_{t,M} - \mathbb{E}[h(s_t)|Y_{1:t-1}] \qquad (8.14)$$
$$= \frac{1}{M}\sum_{j=1}^M \Big(h(\tilde{s}_t^j) - \mathbb{E}_{p(\cdot|s_{t-1}^j)}[h]\Big) W_{t-1}^j$$
$$+ \frac{1}{M}\sum_{j=1}^M \Big(\mathbb{E}_{p(\cdot|s_{t-1}^j)}[h]W_{t-1}^j - \mathbb{E}[h(s_t)|Y_{1:t-1}]\Big)$$
$$= I + II,$$

say. This decomposition is similar to the decomposition (5.31) used in the analysis of the mutation step of the SMC algorithm.

Conditional on the particles $\{s_{t-1}^j, W_{t-1}^j\}_{i=1}^M$ the weights W_{t-1}^j are known and the summands in term I form a triangular array of mean-zero random variables that within each row are independently but not identically distributed. Provided the required moment bounds for $h(\tilde{s}_t^j)W_{t-1}^j$ are satisfied, I converges to zero almost surely and satisfies a CLT. Term II also converges to zero because

$$\frac{1}{M} \sum_{j=1}^M \mathbb{E}_{p(\cdot|s_{t-1}^j)}[h]W_{t-1}^j \tag{8.15}$$

$$\xrightarrow{a.s.} \mathbb{E}\big[\mathbb{E}_{p(\cdot|s_{t-1})}[h] \,\big|\, Y_{1:t-1}\big]$$

$$= \int \left[\int h(s_t)p(s_t|s_{t-1})ds_t\right] p(s_{t-1}|Y_{1:t-1})ds_{t-1}$$

$$= \mathbb{E}[h(s_t)|Y_{1:t-1}].$$

Thus, under suitable regularity conditions

$$\hat{h}_{t,M} \xrightarrow{a.s.} \mathbb{E}[h(s_t)|Y_{1:t-1}], \tag{8.16}$$

$$\sqrt{M}\big(\hat{h}_{t,M} - \mathbb{E}[h(s_t)|Y_{1:t-1}]\big)$$

$$\implies N\big(0, \hat{\Omega}_t(h)\big).$$

The asymptotic covariance matrix $\hat{\Omega}_t(h)$ is given by the sum of the asymptotic variances of the terms $\sqrt{M} \cdot I$ and $\sqrt{M} \cdot II$ in (8.14). The convergence of the predictive density approximation $\hat{p}(y_t|Y_{1:t-1})$ to $p(y_t|Y_{1:t-1})$ in Step 2(b) follows directly from (8.16) by setting $h(s_t) = p(y_t|s_t)$.

Updating and Selection Steps. The goal of the updating step is to approximate posterior expectations of the form

$$\mathbb{E}[h(s_t)|Y_{1:t}] = \frac{\int h(s_t)p(y_t|s_t)p(s_t|Y_{1:t-1})ds_t}{\int p(y_t|s_t)p(s_t|Y_{1:t-1})ds_t} \tag{8.17}$$

$$\approx \frac{\frac{1}{M}\sum_{j=1}^M h(\tilde{s}_t^j)\tilde{w}_t^j W_{t-1}^j}{\frac{1}{M}\sum_{j=1}^M \tilde{w}_t^j W_{t-1}^j} = \tilde{h}_{t,M}.$$

The Monte Carlo approximation of $\mathbb{E}[h(s_t)|Y_{1:t}]$ has the same form as the Monte Carlo approximation of $\tilde{h}_{n,M}$ in (5.24) in the correction step of the SMC Algorithm 8, and its convergence can be analyzed in a similar manner. Define the normalized incremental weights as

$$v_t(s_t) = \frac{p(y_t|s_t)}{\int p(y_t|s_t)p(s_t|Y_{1:t-1})ds_t}. \tag{8.18}$$

Then, under suitable regularity conditions, the Monte Carlo approximation satisfies a CLT of the form

$$\sqrt{M}\big(\tilde{h}_{t,M} - \mathbb{E}[h(s_t)|Y_{1:t}]\big) \Longrightarrow N\big(0, \tilde{\Omega}_t(h)\big), \tag{8.19}$$

where

$$\tilde{\Omega}_t(h) = \hat{\Omega}_t\big(v_t(s_t)(h(s_t) - \mathbb{E}[h(s_t)|Y_{1:t}])\big).$$

The expression for the asymptotic covariance matrix $\tilde{\Omega}_t(h)$ highlights that the accuracy depends on the distribution of the incremental weights. Roughly, the larger the variance of the particle weights, the less accurate the approximation.

Finally, the selection step in Algorithm 11 is identical to the selection step in Algorithm 8 and it adds some additional noise to the approximation. If $\rho_t = 1$, then under multinomial resampling

$$\sqrt{M}\big(\bar{h}_{t,M} - \mathbb{E}[h(s_t)|Y_{1:t}]\big) \Longrightarrow N\big(0, \Omega_t(h)\big), \tag{8.20}$$

where

$$\Omega_t(h) = \tilde{\Omega}_t(h) + \mathbb{V}[h(s_t)|Y_{1:t}].$$

As discussed in Section 5.2.3, the variance can be reduced by replacing the multinomial resampling with a more efficient resampling scheme.

8.1.2 Unbiasedness of the Likelihood Approximation

An important property of the particle filter is that it generates an unbiased approximation of the likelihood function. We will use this property subsequently when we embed the filter into posterior samplers for DSGE model parameters θ. At first glance, this unbiasedness property is surprising because importance sampling approximations are typically biased as they involve ratios of random variables. A general proof of the unbiasedness (as well as other properties of particle filter approximations) based on mean field theory was first provided by Del Moral (2004). Subsequently, Pitt, Silva, Giordani, and Kohn (2012) provided a proof that relies on less sophisticated mathematical tools and exploits the recursive structure of the algorithm. The exposition below closely follows Pitt, Silva, Giordani, and Kohn (2012).

The unbiasedness result can be formally stated as

$$\mathbb{E}\big[\hat{p}(Y_{1:T}|\theta)\big] = \mathbb{E}\left[\prod_{t=1}^{T}\left(\frac{1}{M}\sum_{j=1}^{M}\tilde{w}_t^j W_{t-1}^j\right)\right] \quad (8.21)$$

$$= p(Y_{1:T}|\theta).$$

The results can be proved by showing that for any h such that $0 \le h \le T-1$

$$\mathbb{E}\left[\hat{p}(Y_{T-h:T}|Y_{1:T-h-1},\theta)|\mathcal{F}_{T-h-1,M}\right] \quad (8.22)$$

$$= \frac{1}{M}\sum_{j=1}^{M} p(Y_{T-h:T}|s_{T-h-1}^j,\theta)W_{T-h-1}^j,$$

where the information set $\mathcal{F}_{t-1,M}$ consists of the particle system $\mathcal{F}_{t-1,M} = \left\{(s_0^j, W_0^j), \ldots, (s_{t-1}^j, W_{t-1}^j)\right\}_{j=1}^{M}$ and

$$\hat{p}(Y_{T-h:T}|Y_{1:T-h-1},\theta) = \prod_{t=T-h}^{T}\left(\frac{1}{M}\sum_{j=1}^{M}\tilde{w}_t^j W_{t-1}^j\right).$$

Setting $h = T-1$, we can deduce from (8.22) that

$$\mathbb{E}\left[\hat{p}(Y_{1:T}|\theta)|\mathcal{F}_{0,M}\right] = \frac{1}{M}\sum_{j=1}^{M} p(Y_{1:T}|s_0^j,\theta)W_0^j, \quad (8.23)$$

where $s_0^j \sim p(s_0)$ and $W_0^j = 1$. Thus,

$$\mathbb{E}\big[\hat{p}(Y_{1:T}|\theta)\big] = \mathbb{E}\left[\mathbb{E}\big[\hat{p}(Y_{1:T}|\theta)|\mathcal{F}_{0,M}\big]\right] \quad (8.24)$$

$$= \int p(Y_{1:T}|s_0,\theta)p(s_0)ds_0$$

$$= p(Y_{1:T}|\theta)$$

as desired.

We now have to verify (8.22). We proceed by induction. First note that

$$\mathbb{E}\left[\hat{p}(y_t|Y_{1:t-1},\theta)|\mathcal{F}_{t-1,M}\right] \tag{8.25}$$

$$= \frac{1}{M}\sum_{j=1}^{M}\mathbb{E}\left[\tilde{w}_t^j|\mathcal{F}_{t-1,M}\right]W_{t-1}^j$$

$$= \frac{1}{M}\sum_{j=1}^{M}\left[\int p(y_t|\tilde{s}_t^j,\theta)p(\tilde{s}_t^j|s_{t-1}^j,\theta)d\tilde{s}_t^j\right]W_{t-1}^j$$

$$= \frac{1}{M}\sum_{j=1}^{M}p(y_t|s_{t-1}^j,\theta)W_{t-1}^j.$$

Setting $t = T$ in (8.25) we have verified that (8.22) is correct for $h = 0$. To complete the proof, we show that if (8.22) holds for h, it also has to hold for $h + 1$:

$$\mathbb{E}\left[\hat{p}(Y_{T-h-1:T}|Y_{1:T-h-2},\theta)|\mathcal{F}_{T-h-2,M}\right]$$

$$= \mathbb{E}\Bigg[\mathbb{E}\left[\hat{p}(Y_{t-h:T}|Y_{1:T-h-1},\theta)|\mathcal{F}_{T-h-1,M}\right]$$

$$\times\hat{p}(y_{T-h-1}|Y_{1:T-h-2},\theta)\Bigg|\mathcal{F}_{T-h-2,M}\Bigg].$$

$$= \frac{1}{M}\sum_{j=1}^{M}\mathbb{E}\Big[p(Y_{T-h:T}|\tilde{s}_{T-h-1}^j,\theta)W_{T-h-1}^j$$

$$\times\hat{p}(y_{T-h-1}|Y_{1:T-h-2},\theta)\Big|\mathcal{F}_{T-h-2,M}\Big]$$

$$= \frac{1}{M}\sum_{j=1}^{M}\mathbb{E}\Bigg[p(Y_{T-h:T}|\tilde{s}_{T-h-1}^j,\theta)\frac{\tilde{w}_{T-h-1}^j W_{T-h-2}^j}{\frac{1}{M}\sum_{k=1}^{M}\tilde{w}_{T-h-1}^k W_{T-h-2}^k}$$

$$\times\left(\frac{1}{M}\sum_{i=1}^{M}\tilde{w}_{T-h-1}^i W_{T-h-2}^i\right)\Bigg|\mathcal{F}_{T-h-2,M}\Bigg]$$

$$= \frac{1}{M}\sum_{j=1}^{M}\Bigg(\int p(Y_{T-h:T}|\tilde{s}_{T-h-1}^j,\theta)p(y_{T-h-1}|\tilde{s}_{T-h-1}^j,\theta)$$

$$\times p(\tilde{s}_{T-h-1}^j|s_{T-h-2}^j,\theta)d\tilde{s}_{T-h-1}^j\Bigg)W_{T-h-2}^j$$

$$= \frac{1}{M} \sum_{j=1}^{M} p(Y_{T-h-1:T}|s^j_{T-h-2}, \theta) W^j_{T-h-2}$$

Note that $\mathcal{F}_{t-h-2,M} \subset \mathcal{F}_{t-h-1,M}$. Thus, the first equality follows from the law of iterated expectations. The second equality follows from the inductive hypothesis—the assumption that (8.22) holds for h. The third equality uses the definition of the period-likelihood approximation in (8.6) of Algorithm 11 and the definition of the normalized particles weights. The average in the denominator of the particle weights cancels with the expression for the estimate of the period likelihood function $\hat{p}(y_{T-h-1}|Y_{1:T-h-2}, \theta)$, which ultimately leads to the unbiasedness result.

8.1.3 The Role of Measurement Errors

Many DSGE models, e.g., the ones considered in this book, do not assume that the observables y_t are measured with error. Instead, the number of structural shocks is chosen to be equal to the number of observables, which means that the likelihood function $p(Y_{1:T}|\theta)$ is nondegenerate. It is apparent from the formulas in Table 2.1 that the Kalman filter iterations are well defined even if the measurement error covariance matrix Σ_u in the linear Gaussian state-space model (8.2) is equal to zero, provided that the number of shocks ϵ_t is not smaller than the number of observables and the forecast error covariance matrix $F_{t|t-1}$ is invertible.

For the bootstrap particle filter the case of $\Sigma_u = 0$ presents a serious problem. The incremental weights $\tilde{w}^j_t$ in (8.7) are degenerate if $\Sigma_u = 0$ because the conditional distribution of $y_t|(s_t, \theta)$ is a pointmass. For a particle j, this pointmass is located at $y^j_t = \Psi(\tilde{s}^j_t, t; \theta)$. If the innovation ϵ^j_t is drawn from a continuous distribution in the forecasting step and the state transition equation $\Phi(s_{t-1}, \epsilon_t; \theta)$ is a smooth function of the lagged state and the innovation ϵ_t, then the probability that $y^j_t = y_t$ is zero, which means that $\tilde{w}^j_t = 0$ for all j and the particles vanish after one iteration. The intuition for this result is straightforward. The incremental weights are large for particles j for which $y_t^j = \Psi(\tilde{s}_t^j, t; \theta)$ is close to the actual y_t. Under Gaussian measurement errors, the metric for closeness is given by Σ_u^{-1}. Thus, all else equal, decreasing the measurement error variance Σ_u increases the discrepancy between y_t^j and y_t and therefore the variance of the particle weights.

Consider the following stylized example (we are omitting the j superscripts). Suppose that y_t is scalar, the measurement errors are distributed as $u_t \sim N(0, \sigma_u^2)$, $W_{t-1} = 1$, and let $\delta = y_t - \Psi(s_t, t; \theta)$. Suppose that in population the δ is distributed according to a $N(0, 1)$. In this case $v_t(s_t)$ in (8.18) can be viewed as a population approximation of the normalized weights $\tilde{W}_t$ constructed in the updating step (note that the denominator of these two objects is slightly different):

$$
\tilde{W}_t(\delta) \approx v_t(\delta) = \frac{\exp\left\{-\frac{1}{2\sigma_u^2}\delta^2\right\}}{(2\pi)^{-1/2}\int \exp\left\{-\frac{1}{2}\left(1+\frac{1}{\sigma_u^2}\right)\delta^2\right\}d\delta}
$$

$$
= \left(1+\frac{1}{\sigma_u^2}\right)^{1/2}\exp\left\{-\frac{1}{2\sigma_u^2}\delta^2\right\}.
$$

The asymptotic covariance matrix $\tilde{\Omega}_t(h)$ in (8.19) which captures the accuracy of $\tilde{h}_{t,M}$ as well as the heuristic effective sample size measure defined in (8.12) depend on the variance of the particle weights, which in population is given by

$$
\int v_t^2(\delta)d\delta = \frac{1 + 1/\sigma_u^2}{\sqrt{1 + 2/\sigma_u^2}} = \frac{1}{\sigma_u}\frac{1+\sigma_u^2}{\sqrt{2+\sigma_u^2}} \longrightarrow \infty
$$

as $\sigma_u \longrightarrow 0$. Thus, a decrease in the measurement error variance raises the variance of the particle weights and thereby decreases the effective sample size. More importantly, the increasing dispersion of the weights translates into an increase in the limit covariance matrix $\tilde{\Omega}_t(h)$ and a deterioration of the Monte Carlo approximations generated by the particle filter. In sum, all else equal, the smaller the measurement error variance, the less accurate the particle filter.

8.2 A Generic Particle Filter

In the basic version of the particle filter the time t particles were generated by simulating the state transition equation forward. However, the naive forward simulation ignores information contained in the current observation y_t and may lead to a very uneven distribution of particle weights, in particular if the measurement error variance is small or if the model has difficulties explaining the period t observation in the sense that for most particles $\tilde{s}_t^j$ the actual observation y_t lies far in the tails of the model-implied distribution of $y_t|(\tilde{s}_t^j, \theta)$. The particle filter can be generalized by allowing $\tilde{s}_t^j$ in the forecasting step to be drawn from a generic importance sampling density $g_t(\cdot|s_{t-1}^j, \theta)$, which leads to the following algorithm:

Algorithm 12 (Generic Particle Filter)

1. **Initialization.** *(Same as Algorithm 11)*

2. **Recursion.** *For $t = 1, \ldots, T$:*

   (a) **Forecasting s_t.** *Draw $\tilde{s}_t^j$ from density $g_t(\tilde{s}_t|s_{t-1}^j, \theta)$ and define the importance weights*

   $$\omega_t^j = \frac{p(\tilde{s}_t^j|s_{t-1}^j, \theta)}{g_t(\tilde{s}_t^j|s_{t-1}^j, \theta)}. \qquad (8.26)$$

   An approximation of $\mathbb{E}[h(s_t)|Y_{1:t-1}, \theta]$ is given by

   $$\hat{h}_{t,M} = \frac{1}{M} \sum_{j=1}^{M} h(\tilde{s}_t^j)\omega_t^j W_{t-1}^j. \qquad (8.27)$$

   (b) **Forecasting y_t.** *Define the incremental weights*

   $$\tilde{w}_t^j = p(y_t|\tilde{s}_t^j, \theta)\omega_t^j. \qquad (8.28)$$

   The predictive density $p(y_t|Y_{1:t-1}, \theta)$ can be approximated by

   $$\hat{p}(y_t|Y_{1:t-1}, \theta) = \frac{1}{M} \sum_{j=1}^{M} \tilde{w}_t^j W_{t-1}^j. \qquad (8.29)$$

   (c) **Updating.** *(Same as Algorithm 11)*

   (d) **Selection.** *(Same as Algorithm 11)*

3. **Likelihood Approximation.** *(Same as Algorithm 11).*

The only difference between Algorithms 11 and 12 is the introduction of the importance weights ω_t^j which appear in (8.27) as well as the definition of the incremental weights $\tilde{w}_t^j$ in (8.28). The unbiasedness result discussed in Section 8.1.2 can be easily extended to the generic particle filter. The main goal of replacing the forward iteration of the state-transition equation by an importance sampling step is to improve the accuracy of $\hat{p}(y_t|Y_{1:t-1}, \theta)$ in Step 2(b) and $\tilde{h}_{t,M}$ in Step 2(c).

We subsequently focus on the analysis of $\hat{p}(y_t|Y_{1:t-1}, \theta)$. Emphasizing the dependence of ω_t^j on both $\tilde{s}_t^j$ and s_{t-1}^j, write

$$\hat{p}(y_t|Y_{1:t-1}) - p(y_t|Y_{1:t-1}) \tag{8.30}$$

$$= \frac{1}{M}\sum_{j=1}^{M}\left(p(y_t|\tilde{s}_t^j)\omega_t^j(\tilde{s}_t^j, s_{t-1}^j) \right.$$

$$\left. -\mathbb{E}_{g_t(\cdot|s_{t-1}^j)}[p(y_t|\tilde{s}_t^j)\omega_t^j(\tilde{s}_t^j, s_{t-1}^j)] \right)W_{t-1}^j$$

$$+\frac{1}{M}\sum_{j=1}^{M}\left(\mathbb{E}_{g_t(\cdot|s_{t-1}^j)}[p(y_t|\tilde{s}_t^j)\omega_t^j(\tilde{s}_t^j, s_{t-1}^j)] \right.$$

$$\left. -p(y_t|Y_{1:t-1}) \right)W_{t-1}^j$$

$$= I + II,$$

say. Consider term II. First, notice that

$$\frac{1}{M}\sum_{j=1}^{M}\mathbb{E}_{g_t(\cdot|s_{t-1}^j)}[p(y_t|\tilde{s}_t^j)\omega_t^j(\tilde{s}_t^j, s_{t-1}^j)]W_{t-1}^j \tag{8.31}$$

$$\xrightarrow{a.s.} \mathbb{E}\left[\mathbb{E}_{g_t(\cdot|s_{t-1})}[p(y_t|\tilde{s}_t^j)\omega_t(\tilde{s}_t^j, s_{t-1})]\right]$$

$$= \int\left[\int p(y_t|\tilde{s}_t^j)\frac{p(\tilde{s}_t^j|s_{t-1})}{g_t(\tilde{s}_t^j|s_{t-1})}g_t(\tilde{s}_t^j|s_{t-1})d\tilde{s}_t^j\right]$$

$$\times p(s_{t-1}|Y_{1:t-1})ds_{t-1}$$

$$= p(y_t|Y_{1:t-1}),$$

which implies that term II converges to zero almost surely and ensures the consistency of the Monte Carlo approximation. Second, because

$$\mathbb{E}_{g_t(\cdot|s_{t-1})}[p(y_t|\tilde{s}_t^j)\omega_t(\tilde{s}_t^j, s_{t-1})] \tag{8.32}$$

$$= \int p(y_t|\tilde{s}_t^j)\frac{p(\tilde{s}_t^j|s_{t-1})}{g_t(\tilde{s}_t^j|s_{t-1})}g_t(\tilde{s}_t^j|s_{t-1})d\tilde{s}_t^j = p(y_t|s_{t-1}),$$

the variance of term II is independent of the choice of the importance density $g_t(\tilde{s}_t^j|s_{t-1}^j)$.

Now consider term I. Conditional on $\{s_{t-1}^j, W_{t-1}^j\}_{j=1}^M$ the weights W_{t-1}^j are known and the summands form a triangular array of mean-zero random variables that are independently distributed within each row. Recall that

$$p(y_t|\tilde{s}_t^j)\omega_t^j(\tilde{s}_t^j, s_{t-1}^j) = \frac{p(y_t|\tilde{s}_t^j)p(\tilde{s}_t^j|s_{t-1}^j)}{g_t(\tilde{s}_t^j|s_{t-1}^j)}. \tag{8.33}$$

Choosing a suitable importance density $g_t(\tilde{s}_t^j|s_{t-1}^j)$ that is a function of the time t observation y_t can drastically reduce the variance of term I conditional on $\{s_{t-1}^j, W_{t-1}^j\}_{j=1}^M$. Such filters are called adapted particle filters. In turn, this leads to a variance reduction of the Monte Carlo approximation of $p(y_t|Y_{1:t-1})$. A similar argument can be applied to the variance of $\tilde{h}_{t,M}$. The bootstrap particle filter simply sets $g_t(\tilde{s}_t^j|s_{t-1}^j) = p(\tilde{s}_t^j|s_{t-1}^j)$ and ignores the information in y_t. We will subsequently discuss more efficient choices of $g_t(\tilde{s}_t^j|s_{t-1}^j)$.

8.3   Adapting the Generic Filter

There exists a large literature on the implementation and the improvement of the particle filters in Algorithms 11 and 12. Detailed references to this literature are provided, for instance, in Doucet, de Freitas, and Gordon (2001); Cappé, Godsill, and Moulines (2007); Doucet and Johansen (2011); and Creal (2012). We will focus in this section on the choice of the proposal density $g_t(\tilde{s}_t^j|s_{t-1}^j)$. The starting point is the conditionally optimal importance distribution. In nonlinear DSGE models it is typically infeasible to generate draws from this distribution, but it might be possible to construct an approximately conditionally optimal proposal. Finally, we consider a conditionally linear Gaussian state-space model for which it is possible to use Kalman filter updating for a subset of state variables conditional on the remaining elements of the state vector.

8.3.1 Conditionally Optimal Importance Distribution

The conditionally optimal distribution, e.g., Liu and Chen (1998), is defined as the distribution that minimizes the Monte Carlo variation of the importance weights. However, this notion of optimality conditions on the current observation y_t as well as the $t-1$ particle s_{t-1}^j. Given (y_t, s_{t-1}^j) the weights $\tilde{w}_t^j$ are constant (as a function of $\tilde{s}_t$) if

$$g_t(\tilde{s}_t|s_{t-1}^j) = p(\tilde{s}_t|y_t, s_{t-1}^j), \tag{8.34}$$

that is, $\tilde{s}_t$ is sampled from the posterior distribution of the period t state given (y_t, s_{t-1}^j). In this case

$$\tilde{w}_t^j = \int p(y_t|s_t)p(s_t|s_{t-1}^j)ds_t. \tag{8.35}$$

In a typical (nonlinear) DSGE model application it is not possible to sample directly from $p(\tilde{s}_t|y_t, s_{t-1}^j)$. One could use an accept-reject algorithm as discussed in Künsch (2005) to generate draws from the conditionally optimal distribution. However, for this approach to work efficiently, the user needs to find a good proposal distribution within the accept-reject algorithm.

As mentioned above, our numerical illustrations below are all based on DSGE models that take the form of the linear Gaussian state-space model (8.2). In this case, one can obtain $p(\tilde{s}_t|y_t, s_{t-1}^j)$ from the Kalman filter updating step described in Table 2.1. Let

$$
\begin{aligned}
\bar{s}_{t|t-1}^j &= \Phi_1 s_{t-1}^j \\
P_{t|t-1} &= \Phi_\epsilon \Sigma_\epsilon \Phi_\epsilon' \\
\bar{y}_{t|t-1}^j &= \Psi_0 + \Psi_1 t + \Psi_2 \bar{s}_{t|t-1}^j \\
F_{t|t-1} &= \Psi_2 P_{t|t-1}\Psi_2' + \Sigma_u \\
\bar{s}_{t|t}^j &= \bar{s}_{t|t-1}^j + P_{t|t-1}\Psi_2' F_{t|t-1}^{-1}(y_t - \bar{y}_{t|t-1}^j) \\
P_{t|t} &= P_{t|t-1} - P_{t|t-1}\Psi_2' F_{t|t-1}^{-1}\Psi_2 P_{t|t-1}.
\end{aligned}
$$

The conditionally optimal proposal distribution is given by

$$\tilde{s}_t | (s_{t-1}^j, y_t) \sim N\left(\bar{s}_{t|t}^j, P_{t|t}\right). \tag{8.36}$$

We will use (8.36) as a benchmark to document how accurate a well-adapted particle filter could be. In applications with nonlinear DSGE models, in which it is not possible to sample directly from $p(\tilde{s}_t | y_t, s_{t-1}^j)$, the documented level of accuracy is typically not attainable.

8.3.2 Approximately Conditionally Optimal Distributions

In a typical DSGE model application, sampling from the conditionally optimal importance distribution is infeasible or computationally too costly. Alternatively, one could try to sample from an approximately conditionally optimal importance distribution. For instance, if the DSGE model nonlinearity arises from a higher-order perturbation solution and the nonlinearities are not too strong, then an approximately conditionally optimal importance distribution could be obtained by applying the one-step Kalman filter updating in (8.36) to the first-order approximation of the DSGE model. More generally, as suggested in Guo, Wang, and Chen (2005), one could use the updating steps of a conventional nonlinear filter, such as an extended Kalman filter, unscented Kalman filter, or a Gaussian quadrature filter, to construct an efficient proposal distribution. Approximate filters for nonlinear DSGE models have been developed by Andreasen (2013) and Kollmann (2015).

8.3.3 Conditional Linear Gaussian Models

Certain DSGE models have a conditional linear structure that can be exploited to improve the efficiency of the particle filter. These models include the class of Markov-switching linear rational expectations (MS-LRE) models analyzed in Farmer, Waggoner, and Zha (2009) as well as models that are linear conditional on exogenous stochastic volatility processes, e.g., the linearized DSGE model with heteroskedastic structural shocks estimated by Justiniano and Primiceri (2008) and the long-run risks model studied in Schorfheide, Song, and Yaron (2014).

For concreteness, consider an MS-LRE model obtained by replacing the fixed target-inflation rate π^* in the monetary policy rule (1.24) with a time-varying process $\pi_t^*(m_t)$ of the form

$$\pi_t^* = m_t\pi_L^* + (1 - m_t)\pi_H^*, \quad \mathbb{P}\{m_t = l | m_{t-1} = l\} = \eta_{ll}, \quad (8.37)$$

where $l \in \{0, 1\}$. This model was estimated in Schorfheide (2005).[1] Log-linearizing the model with Markov-switching target inflation rate leads to a MS-LRE similar to (2.1), except that the log-linearized monetary policy rule now contains an intercept that depends on m_t. The solution to an MS-LRE model can be expressed as

$$
\begin{aligned}
y_t &= \Psi_0(m_t) + \Psi_1(m_t)t + \Psi_2(m_t)s_t + u_t, & (8.38) \\
& \quad u_t \sim N(0, \Sigma_u), \\
s_t &= \Phi_0(m_t) + \Phi_1(m_t)s_{t-1} + \Phi_\epsilon(m_t)\epsilon_t, \quad \epsilon_t \sim N(0, \Sigma_\epsilon),
\end{aligned}
$$

where m_t follows a discrete Markov-switching process. In (8.38) we allow for Markov switches in all coefficient matrices, which may arise if not only the intercepts but also the slope coefficients of the linear rational expectations system depend on m_t as, for instance, in Davig and Leeper (2007) and Bianchi (2013). Solution methods for general MS-LRE models are provided by Farmer, Waggoner, and Zha (2009).

The state-space representation in (8.38) is linear conditional on m_t. In a slight abuse of notation, we abbreviate the transition kernel for m_t by $p(m_t|m_{t-1})$ and use the notation $p(m_t|Y_{1:t})$ for the distribution of m_t given $Y_{1:t}$. The joint distribution of (m_t, s_t) can be factorized as follows:

$$p(m_t, s_t|Y_{1:t}) = p(m_t|Y_{1:t})p(s_t|m_t, Y_{1:t}). \quad (8.39)$$

In conditionally linear Gaussian state-space models, the distribution $p(s_t|m_t, Y_{1:t})$ is normal:

$$s_t|(m_t, Y_{1:t}) \sim N\left(\bar{s}_{t|t}(m_t), P_{t|t}(m_t)\right). \quad (8.40)$$

---

[1] A richer DSGE model with a Markov-switching target inflation rate was subsequently estimated by Liu, Waggoner, and Zha (2011).

We abbreviate the density of

$$s_t|(m_t, Y_{1:t}) \quad \text{by} \quad p_N\big(s_t|\bar{s}_{t|t}(m_t), P_{t|t}(m_t)\big),$$

where the N subscript emphasizes the conditional Normal distribution. Because the vector of means $\bar{s}_{t|t}(m_t)$ and the covariance matrix $P_{t|t}(m)_t$ are sufficient statistics for the conditional distribution of s_t, we approximate $(m_t, s_t)|Y_{1:t}$ by the quadruplets $\{m_t^j, \bar{s}_{t|t}^j, P_{t|t}^j, W_t^j\}_{i=1}^N$. The swarm of particles approximates

$$\int h(m_t, s_t)p(m_t, s_t, Y_{1:t})d(m_t, s_t) \tag{8.41}$$

$$= \int \left[\int h(m_t, s_t)p(s_t|m_t, Y_{1:t})ds_t\right]p(m_t|Y_{1:t})dm_t$$

$$\approx \frac{1}{M}\sum_{j=1}^M \left[\int h(m_t^j, s_t^j)p_N\big(s_t|\bar{s}_{t|t}^j, P_{t|t}^j\big)ds_t\right]W_t^j.$$

The Monte Carlo approximation in (8.42) is constructed by first integrating out $s_t|m_t^j$ based on the conditional Normal distribution, which for many functions $h(m_t, s_t)$ can be done analytically, and then use Monte Carlo averaging to integrate out m_t. This approach is called Rao-Blackwellization. It is a variance reduction technique that exploits the following inequality:

$$\mathbb{V}[h(s_t, m_t)] = \mathbb{E}\big[\mathbb{V}[h(s_t, m_t)|m_t]\big] + \mathbb{V}\big[\mathbb{E}[h(s_t, m_t)|m_t]\big]$$

$$\geq \mathbb{V}\big[\mathbb{E}[h(s_t, m_t)|m_t]\big]. \tag{8.42}$$

Algorithm 12 can easily be modified to exploit the conditionally Gaussian structure and integrate out $s_t|m_t$ analytically. The modification is due to Chen and Liu (2000) who referred to the resulting algorithm as a mixture Kalman filter (see also Liu, Chen, and Logvinenko (2001)). Suppose that $\{m_{t-1}^j, \bar{s}_{t-1|t-1}^j, P_{t-1|t-1}^j, W_{t-1}^j\}$ satisfies (8.42). To forecast the states in period t, generate $\tilde{m}_t^j$ from the importance sampling distribution $g_t(\tilde{m}_t|m_{t-1}^j)$ and define the importance weights:

$$\omega_t^j = \frac{p(\tilde{m}_t^j|m_{t-1}^j)}{g_t(\tilde{m}_t^j|m_{t-1}^j)}. \tag{8.43}$$

The Kalman filter forecasting step can be used to compute the conditional mean and variances of s_t and y_t given $\tilde{m}_t^j$:

$$
\begin{aligned}
\tilde{s}_{t|t-1}^j &= \Phi_0(\tilde{m}_t^j) + \Phi_1(\tilde{m}_t^j)s_{t-1|t-1}^j & (8.44) \\
P_{t|t-1}^j &= \Phi_1(\tilde{m}_t^j)P_{t-1|t-1}^j\Phi_1(\tilde{m}_t^j)' + \Phi_\epsilon(\tilde{m}_t^j)\Sigma_\epsilon(\tilde{m}_t^j)\Phi_\epsilon(\tilde{m}_t^j)' \\
\tilde{y}_{t|t-1}^j &= \Psi_0(\tilde{m}_t^j) + \Psi_1(\tilde{m}_t^j)t + \Psi_2(\tilde{m}_t^j)\tilde{s}_{t|t-1}^j \\
F_{t|t-1}^j &= \Psi_2(\tilde{m}_t^j)P_{t|t-1}^j\Psi_2(\tilde{m}_t^j)' + \Sigma_u.
\end{aligned}
$$

Then,

$$
\int h(m_t, s_t)p(m_t, s_t|Y_{1:t-1})d(m_t, s_t) \tag{8.45}
$$

$$
= \int \left[\int h(m_t, s_t)p(s_t|m_t, Y_{1:t-1})ds_t \right] p(m_t|Y_{1:t-1})dm_t
$$

$$
\approx \frac{1}{M} \sum_{j=1}^{M} \left[\int h(m_t^j, s_t^j)p_N\big(s_t|\tilde{s}_{t|t-1}^j, P_{t|t-1}^j\big)ds_t \right] \omega_t^j W_{t-1}^j.
$$

The likelihood approximation is based on the incremental weights

$$
\tilde{w}_t^j = p_N\big(y_t|\tilde{y}_{t|t-1}^j, F_{t|t-1}^j\big)\omega_t^j. \tag{8.46}
$$

The mean $\tilde{y}_{t|t-1}^j$ and variance $F_{t|t-1}^j$ of the regime-conditional predictive distribution were defined in (8.44). Conditional on $\tilde{m}_t^j$ we can use the Kalman filter once more to update the information about s_t in view of the current observation y_t:

$$
\begin{aligned}
\tilde{s}_{t|t}^j &= \tilde{s}_{t|t-1}^j + P_{t|t-1}^j\Psi_2(\tilde{m}_t^j)'\big(F_{t|t-1}^j\big)^{-1} & (8.47) \\
&\quad \times(y_t - \bar{y}_{t|t-1}^j) \\
\tilde{P}_{t|t}^j &= P_{t|t-1}^j - P_{t|t-1}^j\Psi_2(\tilde{m}_t^j)'\big(F_{t|t-1}^j\big)^{-1}\Psi_2(\tilde{m}_t^j)P_{t|t-1}^j.
\end{aligned}
$$

Overall, this leads to the following algorithm:

Algorithm 13 (Particle Filter: Conditional Linear Models)

1. **Initialization.** *Draw the initial particles from the distribution* $m_0^j \overset{iid}{\sim} p(m_0)$, *specify* $s_{0|0}^j$ *and* $P_{0|0}^j$, *and set* $W_0^j = 1, j = 1, \ldots, M$.

2. **Recursion.** *For $t = 1, \ldots, T$:*

   (a) **Forecasting** s_t. *Draw $\tilde{m}_t^j$ from $g_t(\tilde{m}_t | m_{t-1}^j, \theta)$, calculate the importance weights ω_t^j in (8.43), and compute $\tilde{s}_{t|t-1}^j$ and $P_{t|t-1}^j$ according to (8.44). An approximation of $\mathbb{E}[h(s_t, m_t) | Y_{1:t-1}, \theta]$ is given by (8.46).*

   (b) **Forecasting** y_t. *Compute the incremental weights $\tilde{w}_t^j$ according to (8.46). The predictive density $p(y_t | Y_{1:t-1}, \theta)$ can be approximated by*

$$\hat{p}(y_t | Y_{1:t-1}, \theta) = \frac{1}{M} \sum_{j=1}^{M} \tilde{w}_t^j W_{t-1}^j. \qquad (8.48)$$

   (c) **Updating.** *Define the normalized weights*

$$\tilde{W}_t^j = \frac{\tilde{w}_t^j W_{t-1}^j}{\frac{1}{M} \sum_{j=1}^{M} \tilde{w}_t^j W_{t-1}^j} \qquad (8.49)$$

and compute $\tilde{s}_{t|t}^j$ and $\tilde{P}_{t|t}^j$ according to (8.47). An approximation of $\mathbb{E}[h(m_t, s_t) | Y_{1:t}, \theta]$ can be obtained by $\{\tilde{m}_t^j, \tilde{s}_{t|t}^j, \tilde{P}_{t|t}^j, \tilde{W}_t^j\}$ according to (8.42).

   (d) **Selection.** *(Same as Algorithm 11)*

3. **Likelihood Approximation.** *(Same as Algorithm 11).*

8.4 Additional Implementation Issues

The implementation of Algorithm 12 requires the evaluation of the density $p(s_t | s_{t-1}^j)$. In a nonlinear DSGE model the innovations ϵ_t typically enter the state-transition equation $s_t = \Phi(s_{t-1}^j, \epsilon_t)$ in a non-additive form, which makes it difficult to compute $p(s_t | s_{t-1}^j)$. We show in this section that if the proposal distribution $g_t(s_t | s_{t-1}^j)$ is implicitly generated by iterating the state-transition equation forward based on a draw $\tilde{\epsilon}_t^j$ from $g_t^\epsilon(s_{t-1}^j)$, then the computation of the importance weights ω_t^j simplifies considerably and does not require the evaluation of conditional densities of s_t. Moreover, we provide a more detailed discussion of filtering for DSGE models that do not have measurement errors. In this regard, a particle filter with resample-move steps may become useful.

8.4.1 Nonlinear and Partially Deterministic State Transitions

The implementation of Algorithm 12 requires the evaluation of the density $p(s_t|s_{t-1})$. Two difficulties arise in nonlinear DSGE model applications: first, the density is singular because some state variables, e.g., the capital stock, may evolve according to a deterministic law of motion. Second, if the state-transition equation is nonlinear and the innovations do not enter in an additively separable way, it may be difficult to evaluate the density $p(s_t|s_{t-1})$ because of a complicated change of variables. For illustrative purposes, consider a modified version of the simple state-space model of Section 4.3 with state transition equations:

$$s_{1,t} = \Phi_1(s_{t-1}, \epsilon_t), \quad s_{2,t} = \Phi_2(s_{t-1}), \quad \epsilon_t \sim N(0,1). \quad (8.50)$$

Here the transition for the state $s_{2,t}$ is deterministic (think of the capital accumulation equation in a DSGE model). Thus, the joint distribution of $s_{1,t}$ and $s_{2,t}$ is a mixture of a continuous and a discrete distribution with a pointmass at $s_{2,t} = \Phi_2(s_{t-1})$.

Now suppose we define the extended state vector $\varsigma_t = [s_t', \epsilon_t']'$ and augment the state transitions in (8.50) by the identity $\epsilon_t = \epsilon_t$. Using the independence of the innovation ϵ_t from the lagged states ς_{t-1}, we can factorize the density $p(\varsigma_t|\varsigma_{t-1})$ as

$$p(\varsigma_t|\varsigma_{t-1}) = p^\epsilon(\epsilon_t)p(s_{1,t}|s_{t-1}, \epsilon_t)p(s_{2,t}|s_{t-1}). \quad (8.51)$$

Note that $p(s_{1,t}|s_{t-1}, \epsilon_t)$ and $p(s_{2,t}|s_{t-1})$ are pointmasses at $s_{1,t} = \Phi_1(s_{t-1}, \epsilon_t)$ and $s_{2,t} = \Phi_2(s_{t-1})$, respectively. The easiest way of designing an importance distribution $g_t(\varsigma_t|\varsigma_{t-1})$ that has support in the subspace of the state space that satisfies (8.50) is to sample an innovation ϵ_t and iterate the state-transition equation forward. Let $g_t^\epsilon(\epsilon_t|s_{t-1})$ denote the importance density for ϵ_t. Then

$$g_t(\varsigma_t|\varsigma_{t-1}) = g_t^\epsilon(\epsilon_t|s_{t-1})p(s_{1,t}|s_{t-1}, \epsilon_t)p(s_{2,t}|s_{t-1}). \quad (8.52)$$

In turn,

$$\omega_t^j = \frac{p(\tilde{\varsigma}_t^j | \varsigma_{t-1}^j)}{g_t(\tilde{\varsigma}_t^j | \varsigma_{t-1}^j)} \qquad (8.53)$$

$$= \frac{p^\epsilon(\tilde{\epsilon}_t^j) p(\tilde{s}_{1,t}^j | s_{t-1}^j, \tilde{\epsilon}_t^j) p(\tilde{s}_{2,t}^j | s_{t-1}^j)}{g_t^\epsilon(\tilde{\epsilon}_t^j | s_{t-1}^j) p(\tilde{s}_{1,t}^j | s_{t-1}^j, \tilde{\epsilon}_t^j) p(\tilde{s}_{2,t}^j | s_{t-1}^j)}$$

$$= \frac{p^\epsilon(\tilde{\epsilon}_t^j)}{g_t^\epsilon(\tilde{\epsilon}_t^j | s_{t-1}^j)}.$$

Thus, the computation of ω_t^j only requires the evaluation of the densities for ϵ_t.[2] The importance sampling distribution $g_t^\epsilon(\epsilon_t | s_{t-1})$ can be constructed by applying the methods described previously to a version of the DSGE model with extended state space ς_t. We can now change the forecasting step 2.(a) of Algorithm 12 to obtain a generalized bootstrap particle filter:

Algorithm 14 (Generalized Bootstrap Particle Filter)
Replace Step 2.(a) in Algorithm 12 by:

2.(a)' **Forecasting** s_t. *Draw* $\tilde{\epsilon}_t^j$ *from density* $g_t^\epsilon(\tilde{\epsilon}_t | s_{t-1})$, *let* $\tilde{s}_t^j = \Phi(s_{t-1}, \tilde{\epsilon}_{t-1}^j)$. *The importance weights* ω_t^j *are given by (8.53).*

8.4.2 Degenerate Measurement Error Distributions

We saw in Section 8.1 that the bootstrap particle filter deteriorates as the measurement error variance decreases. If the measurement error variance $\Sigma_u = 0$, then only particles that can exactly predict the current-period observation will get non-zero weight. Under a continuous distribution of the innovations ϵ_t the probability of generating such particles

---

[2] The derivation of (8.53) may appear a bit obscure because it involves the factorization of a joint density for a degenerate probability distribution. The reader may wonder why the Jacobian term that would arise under a careful change-of-variables argument does not appear in (8.53). Notice that we are ultimately using (8.53) in an importance sampling approximation of an integral. The key insight (simplifying the notation considerably) is that if $s = \Phi(\epsilon)$ then $\mathbb{E}^s[h(s)] = \int h(s) p^s(s) ds = \int h(\Phi(\epsilon)) p^\epsilon(\epsilon) d\epsilon = \mathbb{E}^\epsilon[h(\Phi(\epsilon))]$.

in the forecasting step is zero. Our discussion of the conditionally optimal importance distribution suggests that in the absence of measurement errors, one has to solve the system of equations

$$y_t = \Psi\big(\Phi(s_{t-1}^j, \tilde{\epsilon}_t^j)\big), \tag{8.54}$$

to determine $\tilde{\epsilon}_t^j$ as a function of s_{t-1}^j and the current observation y_t. One can then define

$$\omega_t^j = p^\epsilon(\tilde{\epsilon}_t^j) \quad \text{and} \quad \tilde{s}_t^j = \Phi(s_{t-1}^j, \tilde{\epsilon}_t^j). \tag{8.55}$$

In a nonlinear state-space system, e.g., one that arises from a higher-order perturbation solution there maybe be multiple solutions to the system even if the dimension of y_t and ϵ_t are equal. Let the solutions be denoted by $\tilde{\epsilon}_t^j(k)$, $k = 1, \ldots, K$. The t subscript and j superscript indicate that the solutions depend on y_t and s_{t-1}^j. The importance distribution represented by the density $g_t^\epsilon(\tilde{\epsilon}_t^j | s_{t-1}^j)$ in (8.53) is now a multinomial distribution of the form

$$\mathbb{P}\{\tilde{\epsilon}_t^j = \tilde{\epsilon}_t^i(k)\} = \frac{p^\epsilon(\tilde{\epsilon}_t^j(j))}{\sum_{k=1}^K p^\epsilon(\tilde{\epsilon}_t^j(k))}, \quad k = 1, \ldots, K, \tag{8.56}$$

which leads to

$$\omega_t^j = \sum_{k=1}^K p^\epsilon(\tilde{\epsilon}_t^j(k)). \tag{8.57}$$

By construction, $p(y_t | \tilde{s}_t^j)$ corresponds to a pointmass at y_t for each particle j. Thus, we can define the incremental weight $\tilde{w}_t^j$ in (8.28) simply as $\tilde{w}_t^j = \omega_t^j$.

There are two computational challenges. First, one has to find *all* the (real) solutions to a nonlinear system of equations. For instance, if the DSGE model has been solved with a second-order perturbation method, then one has to solve a system of quadratic equations for each particle j to determine the $\tilde{\epsilon}_t^j(k)$'s.[3] The second computational problem can be illustrated in the context of the simple state-space model presented in Section 4.3:

$$y_t = s_{1,t} + s_{2,t}, \; s_{1,t} = \phi_2 s_{1,t-1} + \epsilon_t, \; s_{2,t} = \phi_3 s_{1,t-1} + \phi_2 s_{1,t-1}.$$

---

[3]A solution to this computational problem is provided in Foerster, Rubio-Ramirez, Waggoner, and Zha (2014).

Note that due to the absence of measurement errors, it is possible to recursively solve for the entire sequence of particles $s_{1:T}^j$ conditional on the initial draws $s_0^j = (s_{1,0}^j, s_{2,0}^j)$ and the observations $Y_{1:T}$. The particles will be reweighted based on $p^\epsilon(\tilde{\epsilon}_t^j)$ which captures the likelihood of observation y_t conditional on s_{t-1}^j. The resampling step of the filter duplicates the particles for which $p^\epsilon(\tilde{\epsilon}_t^j)$ is large. But, unlike in the case of a model with measurement errors, the duplicate particles do not mutate. If two particles i and j are identical in period τ, i.e., $s_\tau^i = s_\tau^j$, then $s_t^i = s_t^j$ for $t > \tau$. Thus, the degeneracy problem does not manifest itself in an uneven distribution of particles. Instead, it is reflected by the fact that the particle values are mostly identical. This will lead to an imprecise approximation of the likelihood function, which is not surprising as the algorithm essentially approximates the integral $\int p(Y_{1:T}|s_0)p(s_0)ds_0$ by sampling s_0^j from $p(s_0)$ and evaluating the Monte Carlo average $\frac{1}{M}\sum_{j=1}^M p(Y_{1:T}|s_0^j)$.

There are two possible remedies for the second computational challenge. The first one is to introduce a resample-move step into the particle filter, which is discussed below. The second remedy is to append the initial state s_0 to the parameter vector θ, treat $p(s_0)$ as its prior distribution, and use a posterior sampler to make inference on s_0 and θ jointly. This approach has been used, for instance, by Chang, Doh, and Schorfheide (2007) to handle the initialization of non-stationary exogenous state variables.

8.4.3 Resample-Move Steps

The resampling step of Algorithms 11 and 12 is designed to equalize the distribution of particle weights and avoid a degenerate particle distribution. However, as the discussion of the model without measurement errors in Section 8.4.2 highlighted, it is possible that an even distribution of particle weights coincides with (nearly) identical particle values (impoverishment), which leads to potentially very inaccurate Monte Carlo approximations. While the sampling of $\tilde{s}_t^j$ from the proposal distribution $g_t(\tilde{s}_t|s_{t-1}^j)$ leads to some diversity of the period t particles even if the $t-1$ particle values are identical, a mutation step that "jitters" the particle values after resampling may help to increase the diversity of particle values and improve the accuracy of the filter. This "jittering" is comparable to the mutation step in the SMC Algorithm 8, used for posterior inference on the model parameter vector θ. Thus, the resampling step of the particle filter is augmented by a "move" step as in Berzuini and Gilks (2001).

The resample-move algorithm presented below is a special case of the algorithm described in Doucet and Johansen (2011). To understand how a particle filter with resample-move step works, it is useful to abstract from the resampling first and to introduce the mutation right after the updating in Step 2.(c) of Algorithm 12. The particle mutation is based on a Markov transition kernel, which we denote by $K_{(y_t, s_{t-1})}(s_t|\tilde{s}_t)$. The transition kernel transforms the particle $\tilde{s}_t^j$ into a particle s_t^j by sampling from a conditional distribution of s_t given $\tilde{s}_t$. The transition kernel depends on the current observation y_t as well as the period $t-1$ value of the state s_{t-1}, which is indicated by the subscript. One can generate the transition kernel from a sequence of MH steps. To simplify the exposition we focus on the case of a single MH step, which requires the user to specify a proposal density $q_t(s_t|\tilde{s}_t^j)$. This proposal density could be generated, for instance, through a random walk step as in the particle mutation of the SMC sampler described in Algorithm 9.

Algorithm 15 (Mutation for Resample-Move Algorithm)

1. Draw ς_t from a density $q_t(\varsigma_t|\tilde{s}_t^j)$.

2. Set $s_t^j = \varsigma_t$ with probability

$$\alpha_t(\varsigma_t|\tilde{s}_t^j) = \min\left\{1, \frac{p(y_t|\varsigma_t)p(\varsigma_t|s_{t-1}^j)/q_t(\varsigma_t|\tilde{s}_t^j)}{p(y_t|\tilde{s}_t)p(\tilde{s}_t|s_{t-1}^j)/q_t(\tilde{s}_t^j|\varsigma_t)}\right\}$$

and $s_t^j = \tilde{s}_t^j$ otherwise.

Using the same steps as in Section 3.5.2, one can establish that the transition kernel satisfies the following invariance property:

$$\int K_{(y_t, s_{t-1})}(s_t|\tilde{s}_t)p(y_t|\tilde{s}_t)p(\tilde{s}_t|s_{t-1})d\tilde{s}_t \tag{8.58}$$
$$= p(y_t|s_t)p(s_t|s_{t-1}).$$

Suppose that particle values are sampled according to

$$\tilde{s}_t^j \sim g_t(\tilde{s}_t^j|s_{t-1}) \quad \text{and} \quad s_t^j \sim K_{(y_t,s_{t-1}^j)}(s_t^j|\tilde{s}_t^j). \qquad (8.59)$$

Then, we obtain the following approximation:

$$\int_{s_{t-1}} \int_{s_t} h(s_t)p(y_t|s_t)p(s_t|s_{t-1})p(s_{t-1}|Y_{1:t-1})ds_t ds_{t-1}$$

$$= \int_{s_{t-1}} \int_{\tilde{s}_t} \int_{s_t} h(s_t)K_{(y_t,s_{t-1})}(s_t|\tilde{s}_t)\frac{p(y_t|\tilde{s}_t)p(\tilde{s}_t|s_{t-1})}{g_t(\tilde{s}_t|s_{t-1})}$$

$$\times g_t(\tilde{s}_t|s_{t-1})ds_t d\tilde{s}_t ds_{t-1} \qquad (8.60)$$

$$\approx \frac{1}{M} \sum_{j=1}^{M} h(s_t^j)\tilde{w}_t^j W_{t-1}^j, \text{ where } \tilde{w}_t^j = \frac{p(y_t|\tilde{s}_t^j)p(\tilde{s}_t^j|s_{t-1}^j)}{g_t(\tilde{s}_t^j|s_{t-1}^j)}.$$

To complete the heuristic derivations for the resample-move algorithm, notice that we can introduce a resampling step before the mutation step in which we generate draws $(\hat{s}_t^j, \hat{s}_{t-1}^j)$ from a multinomial distribution characterized by the support points and weights $\{(\tilde{s}_t^j, s_{t-1}^j), \tilde{W}_t^j\}$ with $\tilde{W}_t^j \propto \tilde{w}_t^j W_{t-1}^j$. Resampling before an MCMC step will always lead to greater sample diversity than performing the steps in the other order. After the resampling we can set the weights $W_t^j = 1$ and draw $s_t^j \sim K_{(y_t,\hat{s}_{t-1}^j)}(s_t|\hat{s}_t^j)$, which leads to the following approximation:

$$\int_{s_{t-1}} \int_{s_t} h(s_t)p(y_t|s_t)p(s_t|s_{t-1})p(s_{t-1}|Y_{1:t-1})ds_t ds_{t-1}$$

$$\approx \frac{1}{M} \sum_{j=1}^{M} h(s_t^j)W_t^j. \qquad (8.61)$$

The sequential importance sampling algorithm with resample-move step can be summarized as follows:

Algorithm 16 (Particle Filter with Resample-Move Step)
Replace Step 2.(d) of Algorithm 12 by:

2.(d)' **Resample-Move Step:**

> (i) *Resample the particles via multinomial resampling. Let $\{(\hat{s}_t^j, \hat{s}_{t-1}^j)\}_{i=1}^{N}$ denote N iid draws from a multinomial distribution characterized by support points and weights $\{\{(\tilde{s}_t^j, s_{t-1}^j), \tilde{W}_t^j\}$ and set $W_t^j = 1$.*

> (ii) *Use Algorithm 15 to generate draws s_t^j from Markov-transition kernel $K_{(y_t, \hat{s}_{t-1}^j)}(s_t | \hat{s}_t^j)$.*

8.5 Adapting s_{t-1} Draws to the Current Observation

In Section 8.3 we discussed in general terms how to improve the performance of the basic bootstrap particle filter by using a more general proposal distribution for the state $s_t | s_{t-1}$ that is adapted to the current observation y_t. When constructing a Monte Carlo approximation of

$$\int \int h(s_t) p(y_t | s_t) p(s_t | s_{t-1}) p(s_{t-1} | Y_{1:t-1}) ds_{t-1} ds_t, \quad (8.62)$$

we realized that taking into account $p(y_t | s_t)$ when generating a proposal distribution for s_t, which we denoted by $g_t(s_t | s_{t-1})$, can lead to drastic improvements in efficiency. However, because of the recursive structure of the particle filter, thus far we made no attempt to also adapt the proposal density for s_{t-1} to the current observation y_t. We now discuss two algorithms that do, namely the auxiliary particle filter developed by Pitt and Shephard (1999) and the efficient importance sampling (EIS) filter of DeJong, Liesenfeld, Moura, Richard, and Dharmarajan (2013). In a nutshell, the idea is to factorize

$$\begin{aligned} &p(y_t | s_t) p(s_t | s_{t-1}) p(s_{t-1} | Y_{1:t-1}) \quad\quad (8.63)\\ &= \; p(s_t, s_{t-1} | y_t, Y_{1:t-1}) p(y_t | Y_{1:t-1}) \end{aligned}$$

and to construct an importance sampling approximation of (8.62) by generating joint draws of (s_t, s_{t-1}) from a carefully chosen proposal distribution $g_t(s_t, s_{t-1})$.

8.5.1 Auxiliary Particle Filter

The original version of the auxiliary particle filter used auxiliary variables and contained two resampling steps. However, subsequent research has shown that a single resampling step is preferable and that it is not necessary to introduce auxiliary variables. We present a version of the auxiliary particle filter that has the same structure as Algorithm 12 and uses only one resampling step. Our description of the algorithm follows Doucet and Johansen (2011). The proposal density $g_t(s_t, s_{t-1})$ is factorized as follows:

$$g_t(s_t, s_{t-1}) = g_t(s_t|s_{t-1})\tilde{p}(s_{t-1}|y_t, Y_{1:t-1}). \tag{8.64}$$

The density $g_t(s_t|s_{t-1})$ could be chosen to $p(s_t, s_{t-1})$ as in the bootstrap particle filter, or it could be chosen based on the same considerations as in Section 8.3. The subsequent exposition will focus on the construction of $\tilde{p}(s_{t-1}|y_t, Y_{1:t-1})$.

Let $\tilde{p}(y_t|s_{t-1})$ be an approximation of the one-step-ahead predictive density $p(y_t|s_{t-1})$. The density $\tilde{p}(y_t|s_{t-1})$ can be obtained, for instance, by iterating the state-transition equation forward (based on the s_{t-1}^j's and draws of ϵ_t), averaging the simulated s_t's to form an $\bar{s}_{t|t}^j$ and using a modified version of the measurement equation to form a fat-tailed density $\tilde{p}(y_t|\bar{s}_{t|t}^j)$. Using the predictive density $\tilde{p}(y_t|s_{t-1})$ we can form the auxiliary posterior distribution

$$\tilde{p}(s_{t-1}|Y_{1:t}) = \frac{\tilde{p}(y_t|s_{t-1})p(s_{t-1}|Y_{1:t-1})}{\tilde{p}(y_t|Y_{1:t-1})}. \tag{8.65}$$

The auxiliary marginal data density is defined as

$$\tilde{p}(y_t|Y_{1:t-1}) = \int \tilde{p}(y_t|s_{t-1})p(s_{t-1}|Y_{1:t-1})ds_{t-1}. \tag{8.66}$$

A complication arises from the fact that the numerator of the importance weights $p(s_t, s_{t-1}|y_t, Y_{1:t})/g_t(s_t, s_{t-1})$ cannot be directly evaluated.

The auxiliary particle filter is based on two sets of weights. The first set of weights tracks the distribution $\tilde{p}(s_{t-1}|Y_{1:t})$ and the second set of weights is needed to approximate the posterior of interest $p(s_t|Y_{1:t})$. We begin the derivations with the assumption that the $t-1$ particle swarm $\{s_{t-1}^j, W_{t-1}^j\}_{j=1}^M$ approximates the auxiliary posterior distribution

$$\frac{1}{M} \sum_{j=1}^M h(s_{t-1}^j) W_{t-1}^j \approx \int h(s_{t-1}) \tilde{p}(s_{t-1}|Y_{1:t}) ds_{t-1} \quad (8.67)$$

and then manipulate the particle swarm to obtain an approximation of $\tilde{p}(s_t|Y_{1:t+1})$. Once the recursion for $\{s_t^j, W_t^j\}_{j=1}^M$ is established, we discuss the Monte Carlo approximation of $h(s_t)$ and the likelihood increment $p(y_t|Y_{t-1})$.

Suppose that the time t particles $\tilde{s}_t^j$ are sampled from the importance density $g_t(\tilde{s}_t|s_{t-1}^j)$. Define the incremental weights

$$\tilde{w}_t^j = p(y_t|\tilde{s}_t^j) \frac{p(\tilde{s}_t^j|s_{t-1}^j)}{g_t(\tilde{s}_t^j|s_{t-1}^j)} \frac{\tilde{p}(y_{t+1}|\tilde{s}_t^j)}{\tilde{p}(y_t|s_{t-1}^j)}. \quad (8.68)$$

These weights replace the incremental weights in (8.28) of Algorithm 12. Using the definitions of $\tilde{p}(s_{t-1}|Y_{1:t})$ and $\tilde{w}_t^j$ in (8.65) and (8.68), respectively, we deduce that

$$\frac{1}{M} \sum_{j=1}^M h(s_t^j) \tilde{w}_t^j W_{t-1}^j \quad (8.69)$$

$$\approx \int \int h(s_t) p(y_t|s_t) \frac{p(s_t|s_{t-1}) \tilde{p}(y_{t+1}|s_t)}{g_t(s_t|s_{t-1}) \tilde{p}(y_t|s_{t-1})}$$
$$\times g_t(s_t|s_{t-1}) \tilde{p}(s_{t-1}|Y_{1:t}) ds_{t-1} ds_t$$

$$= \frac{1}{\tilde{p}(y_t|Y_{1:t-1})} \int h(s_t) p(y_t|s_t) \tilde{p}(y_{t+1}|s_t)$$
$$\times \left[\int p(s_t|s_{t-1}) p(s_{t-1}|Y_{1:t-1}) ds_{t-1} \right] ds_t.$$

$$= \frac{1}{\tilde{p}(y_t|Y_{1:t-1})} \int h(s_t) \tilde{p}(y_{t+1}|s_t) p(y_t|s_t) p(s_t|Y_{1:t-1}) ds_t$$

$$= \frac{p(y_t|Y_{1:t-1})}{\tilde{p}(y_t|Y_{1:t-1})} \int h(s_t) \tilde{p}(y_{t+1}|s_t) p(s_t|Y_{1:t}) ds_t.$$

The first equality follows from (8.65) and the third equality utilizes Bayes Theorem to obtain a posterior for s_t given $(y_t, Y_{1:t-1})$. The factor in front of the last integral is a nuisance, but it cancels once we take ratios. Define (this derivation ignores the distinction between the updated normalized weights $\tilde{W}_t^j$ and the weights W_t^j after the resampling step in the particle filter algorithms)

$$W_t^j = \frac{\tilde{w}_t^j W_{t-1}^j}{\frac{1}{M} \sum_{j=1}^{M} \tilde{w}_t^j W_{t-1}^j} \tag{8.70}$$

and notice that

$$\frac{1}{M} \sum_{j=1}^{M} h(s_t^j) W_t^j \approx \frac{\int h(s_t) \tilde{p}(y_{t+1}|s_t) p(s_t|Y_{1:t}) ds_t}{\int \tilde{p}(y_{t+1}|s_t) p(s_t|Y_{1:t}) ds_t}$$

$$= \int h(s_t) \tilde{p}(s_t|Y_{1:t+1}) ds_t, \tag{8.71}$$

which is the time t version of (8.67).

A second set of weights is necessary, because unlike in the original Algorithm 12 the particle swarm $\{\tilde{s}_t^j, W_t^j\}$ does not deliver approximations to the objects of interest, which are the density of the state $p(s_t|Y_{1:t})$ and the predictive likelihood $p(y_t|Y_{1:t-1})$. Dividing $\tilde{w}_t^j$ in (8.68) by $\tilde{p}(y_{t+1}|\tilde{s}_t^j)$ yields the alternative weights:

$$\bar{w}_t^j = p(y_t|\tilde{s}_t^j) \frac{p(\tilde{s}_t^j|s_{t-1}^j)}{g_t(\tilde{s}_t^j|s_{t-1}^j)} \frac{1}{\tilde{p}(y_t|s_{t-1}^j)}, \tag{8.72}$$

$$\bar{W}_t^j = \frac{\bar{w}_t^j W_{t-1}^j}{\frac{1}{M} \sum_{j=1}^{M} \bar{w}_t^j W_{t-1}^j}.$$

Using the same steps as in (8.69) one can verify that

$$\frac{1}{M} \sum_{j=1}^{M} h(\tilde{s}_t^j) \bar{w}_t^j W_{t-1}^j \tag{8.73}$$

$$\approx \frac{p(y_t|Y_{1:t-1})}{\tilde{p}(y_t|Y_{1:t-1})} \int h(s_t) p(s_t|Y_{1:t}) ds_t.$$

It follows immediately that the posterior of $s_t|Y_{1:t}$ can be approximated according to:

$$\frac{1}{M} \sum_{j=1}^{M} h(s_t^j) \bar{W}_t^j \approx \int h(s_t) p(s_t|Y_{1:t}) ds_t. \tag{8.74}$$

The factor $p(y_t|Y_{1:t-1})/\tilde{p}(y_t|Y_{1:t-1})$ cancels due to the definition of $\bar{W}_t^j$ in (8.72) as a ratio.

In the generic particle filter we approximated the likelihood increments by averaging the unnormalized particle weights. For the auxiliary particle filter the two sets of particle weights deliver the following approximations:

$$\frac{1}{M}\sum_{j=1}^{M}\tilde{w}_t^j W_{t-1}^j \approx p(y_t|Y_{1:t-1})\frac{\tilde{p}(y_{t+1}|Y_{1:t})}{\tilde{p}(y_t|Y_{1:t-1})}, \quad (8.75)$$

$$\frac{1}{M}\sum_{j=1}^{M}\bar{w}_t^j W_{t-1}^j \approx \frac{p(y_t|Y_{1:t-1})}{\tilde{p}(y_t|Y_{1:t-1})}. $$

Thus, neither of the two Monte Carlo averages deliver the desired object directly. Correcting the average of the $\bar{w}_t^j$ requires an estimate of $\tilde{p}(y_t|Y_{1:t-1})$, which can be obtained from:

$$\frac{1}{M}\sum_{j=1}^{M}\frac{1}{\tilde{p}(y_t|s_{t-1}^j)}W_{t-1}^j \quad (8.76)$$

$$\approx \int \frac{1}{\tilde{p}(y_t|s_{t-1})}\frac{\tilde{p}(y_t|s_{t-1})p(s_{t-1}|Y_{1:t-1})}{\tilde{p}(y_t|Y_{1:t-1})}ds_{t-1}$$

$$= \frac{1}{\tilde{p}(y_t|Y_{1:t-1})}. $$

Here we used (8.65) and (8.67). Thus, we obtain

$$\left(\frac{1}{M}\sum_{j=1}^{M}\frac{1}{\tilde{p}(y_t|s_{t-1}^j)}W_{t-1}^j\right)^{-1}\left(\frac{1}{M}\sum_{j=1}^{M}\bar{w}_t^j W_{t-1}^j\right)$$

$$\approx p(y_t|Y_{1:t-1}). \quad (8.77)$$

Alternatively, note that

$$\left(\frac{1}{M}\sum_{j=1}^{M}\bar{w}_T^j W_{T-1}^j\right)\left\{\prod_{t=1}^{T-1}\left(\frac{1}{M}\sum_{j=1}^{M}\tilde{w}_t^j W_{t-1}^j\right)\right\} \quad (8.78)$$

$$\approx p(y_T|Y_{1:T-1})p(y_{T-1}|Y_{1:T-2})\cdots p(y_2|y_1)p(y_1)\frac{1}{\tilde{p}(y_1)}$$

$$= \frac{p(Y_{1:T})}{\tilde{p}(y_1)},$$

which can be adjusted by an estimate of $\tilde{p}(y_1)$ to obtain a likelihood function approximation.

The potential advantage of the auxiliary particle filter is that the incremental weights, $\bar{w}_t^j$, are more stable than in the generic particle filter even under the bootstrap proposal density $g_t(\cdot|s_{t-1}^j) = p(\cdot|s_{t-1}^j)$. In this case $\bar{w}_t^j = p(y_t|\tilde{s}_t^j)/\tilde{p}(y_t|s_{t-1}^j)$ which potentially has much lower variance than $p(y_t|\tilde{s}_t^j)$. As in any importance sampling approximation, it is important that the density $\tilde{p}(y_t|s_{t-1}^j)$ has fatter tails than $p(y_t|\tilde{s}_t^j)$. The auxiliary particle filter can be summarized as follows:

Algorithm 17 (Auxiliary Particle Filter)

1. **Initialization.** *Draw the initial particles from the distribution* $s_0^j \overset{iid}{\sim} p(s_0)$ *and set* $\tilde{w}_0^j = \tilde{p}(y_1|s_0^j)$ *and* $W_0^j = \tilde{w}_0^j / \frac{1}{M}\sum_{j=1}^{M} \tilde{w}_0^j.$

2. **Recursion.** *For* $t = 1, \ldots, T$:

    (a) **Importance Sampling.** *Draw* $\tilde{s}_t^j$ *from* $g_t(\tilde{s}_t|s_{t-1}^j, \theta)$ *and compute the incremental weights* $\tilde{w}_t^j$ *defined in (8.68) and* $\bar{w}_t^j$ *in (8.72). Also compute the normalized weights* $\tilde{W}_t^j \propto \tilde{w}_t^j$ *and* $\bar{W}_t^j \propto \bar{w}_t^j$.

    (b) **Forecasting** y_t. *The predictive density* $p(y_t|Y_{1:t-1}, \theta)$ *can be approximated by (8.77).*

    (c) **Updating.** *An approximation of* $\mathbb{E}[h(s_t)|Y_{1:t}, \theta]$ *is given by (8.74).*

    (d) **Selection.** *(Same as Algorithm 11)*

3. **Likelihood Approximation.** *The approximation of the log-likelihood function can be obtained based on (8.77) or (8.78).*

8.5.2   EIS Filter

A second filter that adapts the proposal distribution of s_{t-1} to y_t was developed by DeJong, Liesenfeld, Moura, Richard, and Dharmarajan (2013). The algorithm is based on the assumption that at the end of iteration $t - 1$ one inherits a continuous filtering approximation $\hat{p}(s_{t-1}|Y_{1:t-1})$ (as opposed to the discrete approximation generated by the particle filter). The importance sampling step in iteration targets the density

$$\varphi_t(s_t, s_{t-1}) = p(y_t|s_t)p(s_t|s_{t-1})\hat{p}(s_{t-1}|Y_{1:t-1}),$$

using a joint proposal density for s_{t-1} and s_t, denoted by $g_t(s_t, s_{t-1})$, which is factorized as

$$g_t(s_t, s_{t-1}) = g_t(s_t)g_t(s_{t-1}|s_t).$$

The proposal density is constructed by approximating the target distribution $\varphi_t(s_t, s_{t-1})$ with a parametric class of distributions. The parameterization is selected to minimize the Monte Carlo variance of the importance sampling ratio $\varphi_t(s_t, s_{t-1})/g_t(s_t)g_t(s_{t-1}|s_t)$, which is what the authors refer to as efficient importance sampling. The iterations of the algorithm turn the approximation $\hat{p}(s_{t-1}|Y_{1:t-1})$ into an approximation $\hat{p}(s_t|Y_{1:t})$. For the actual implementation of the EIS filter we refer the reader to DeJong, Liesenfeld, Moura, Richard, and Dharmarajan (2013), who provide numerical illustrations of their method in the context of small-scale DSGE models.

8.6 Application to the Small-Scale DSGE Model

To illustrate the particle filtering techniques, we will use the bootstrap PF, the conditionally optimal PF, and the auxiliary PF to evaluate the likelihood function associated with the small-scale New Keynesian DSGE model. We do so for two parameter vectors, which are denoted by θ^m and θ^l and tabulated in Table 8.1. The value θ^m is chosen by searching among the posterior draws $\{\theta^i\}_{i=1}^N$ (see Section 4.2) for the draw associated with the highest likelihood. Note that this value is neither the posterior mode (because the mode is determined by the product of likelihood and prior) nor necessarily the maximum of the likelihood function (because the posterior sampler does not necessarily visit the area of the parameter space in which the likelihood function is maximized). The log likelihood at θ^m is $\ln p(Y|\theta^m) = -306.49$. The second parameter value, θ^l, is chosen to be associated with a lower log-likelihood value. Based on our choice, $\ln p(Y|\theta^l) = -313.36$.

Table 8.1: Small-Scale Model: Parameter Values

Parameter	θ^m	θ^l	Parameter	θ^m	θ^l
τ	2.09	3.26	κ	0.98	0.89
ψ_1	2.25	1.88	ψ_2	0.65	0.53
ρ_r	0.81	0.76	ρ_g	0.98	0.98
ρ_z	0.93	0.89	$r^{(A)}$	0.34	0.19
$\pi^{(A)}$	3.16	3.29	$\gamma^{(Q)}$	0.51	0.73
σ_r	0.19	0.20	σ_g	0.65	0.58
σ_z	0.24	0.29	$\ln p(Y|\theta)$	-306.5	-313.4

To put the likelihood differentials into perspective, twice the log-likelihood differential, 13.8, can be compared to the 5% χ^2 critical value for the hypothesis $\theta = \theta^m$ vs. $\theta = \theta^l$ is 22.4. Thus, while the data prefer θ^m, they do not provide overwhelming evidence against θ^l.

The particle filters generate approximations of the period t contribution of the likelihood function, $\hat{p}(y_t|Y_{1:t-1}, \theta)$, and the distribution of the filtered states, $\hat{p}(s_t|Y_{1:t}, \theta)$. Because we are using the linearized version of the small-scale DSGE model, we can compare the approximations $\hat{p}(\cdot)$ to the exact densities $p(\cdot)$ obtained from the Kalman filter. We begin with a single run of the filters over the period 1983:I to 2002:IV. This is the period that has been previously used to estimate the DSGE model. We compare the output of the Kalman filter, the bootstrap PF, and the conditionally optimal PF. To facilitate the use of particle filters, we augment the measurement equation of the DSGE model by independent measurement errors, whose standard deviations we set to be 20% of the standard deviation of the observables.[4] We use 40,000 particles for the bootstrap PF and 400 particles for the conditionally optimal PF. We expect the conditionally optimal PF to deliver much more precise approximations than the bootstrap PF, which is why we use a substantially smaller number of particles.

Throughout this chapter, the bootstrap PF can be viewed

---

[4]The measurement error standard deviations are 0.1160 for output growth, 0.2942 for inflation, and 0.4476 for the interest rates.

as providing a lower bound on the accuracy of particle-filter-based likelihood approximation, because this filter can be easily implemented in DSGE model applications provided that the measurement equation contains measurement errors. As mentioned in Section 8.3, the conditionally optimal filter is typically not implementable for nonlinear DSGE models, but an approximate version that utilizes some other nonlinear filter to generate the proposal distribution may be implementable. Thus, we view it as a realistic upper bound on the accuracy that can be achieved with particle filters in DSGE model applications.

Figure 8.1 depicts the sequence of log-likelihood increments as well as the mean $\mathbb{E}[\hat{g}_t | Y_{1:t}]$, where $\hat{g}_t$ is the exogenous government spending in percentage deviations from its steady state. The log-likelihood approximation generated by the conditionally optimal PF is visually indistinguishable from the exact log likelihood. The bootstrap PF approximation deviates from the actual log likelihood more strongly, in particular in periods in which the likelihood is low, e.g., around 1986 and 1991. The results for the filtered demand shock are similar: the approximation of $\mathbb{E}[g_t | Y_{1:t}, \theta^m]$ obtained from the conditionally optimal PF is fairly accurate, whereas there is a substantial discrepancy between the estimated path of $\hat{g}_t$ produced by the Kalman filter and the bootstrap PF. A gap of about 2 percentages opens up in 1991, at the same time when the log likelihood drops below -10. Due to the persistence in the $\hat{g}_t$ process ($\rho_g = 0.98$), the gap does not close for the remainder of the sample.

To assess the accuracy of the particle filter approximation of the likelihood function, we now run the filters $N_{run} = 100$ times and examine the sampling properties of the discrepancy

$$\hat{\Delta}_1 = \ln \hat{p}(Y_{1:T}|\theta) - \ln p(Y_{1:T}|\theta). \qquad (8.79)$$

The results are depicted in Figure 8.2. The left panel compares the accuracy of the bootstrap filter for θ^m and θ^l. Conditional on θ^m, most of the simulated values for $\hat{\Delta}_1$ fall in the range from -8 to 5 log-likelihood units. At θ^l the dispersion of $\hat{\Delta}_1$ is much larger and more skewed toward the left, encompassing values from -20 to 5. The deterioration of fit

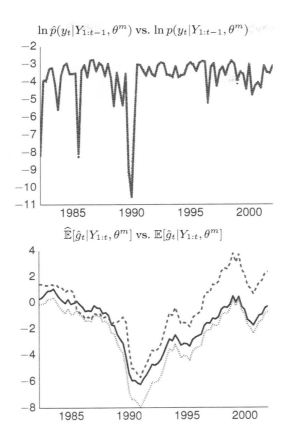

Figure 8.1: Small-Scale Model: Log-Likelihood Approximation and Filtered $\hat{g}_t$. The results depicted in the figure are based on a single run of the bootstrap PF (dashed), the conditionally optimal PF (dotted), and the Kalman filter (solid).

is associated with a deterioration in the approximation accuracy. This is not surprising because the bootstrap PF generates proposal draws for s_t through forward simulation of the state-transition equation. The worse the fit of the model, the greater the mismatch between the proposal distribution and the target posterior distribution of s_t.

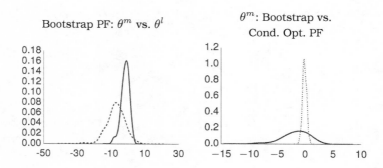

Figure 8.2: Small-Scale Model: Distribution of Log-Likelihood Approximation Errors (Part 1). Density estimate of $\hat{\Delta}_1 = \ln \hat{p}(Y_{1:T}|\theta) - \ln p(Y_{1:T}|\theta)$ based on $N_{run} = 100$ runs of the PF. Solid lines depict densities for $\theta = \theta^m$ and bootstrap PF ($M = 40,000$); dashed line depicts density for $\theta = \theta^l$ and bootstrap PF ($M = 40,000$); dotted line depicts density for $\theta = \theta^m$ and conditionally optimal PF ($M = 400$).

The right panel of Figure 8.2 compares the distribution of $\hat{\Delta}_1$ for the bootstrap and the conditionally optimal PF at θ^m. The latter is a lot more precise than the former and the empirical distribution of $\hat{\Delta}_1$ is tightly centered around zero. The biases and standard deviations of $\hat{\Delta}_1$ for the two filters are summarized in Table 8.2. Conditional on θ^m, the standard deviation of $\hat{\Delta}_1$ is about six times larger for the bootstrap PF than for the conditionally optimal PF. Changing the parameter to θ^l increases the standard deviation by a factor of 2.3 (1.4) for the bootstrap PF (conditionally optimal PF). Thus, the bootstrap PF is much more sensitive to the fit of the model specification than the conditionally optimal PF.

As an alternative to the bootstrap PF and the conditionally optimal PF we also consider the auxiliary PF. To configure the auxiliary PF we set $g_t(\tilde{s}_t^j|s_{t-1}^j) = p(\tilde{s}_t^j|s_{t-1}^j)$ and $\tilde{p}(y_t|s_{t-1}^j)$ is a normal distribution with mean $\mathbb{E}[y_t|s_{t-1}^j]$ and a variance that equals the measurement error variance scaled by a factor of 10. The distribution of log-likelihood approximation errors $\hat{\Delta}_1$ is plotted in Figure 8.3.[5] Visually, results from the aux-

---

[5]The log-likelihood approximations based on (8.77) and (8.78) are numer-

Table 8.2: Small-Scale Model: PF Summary Statistics

	Bootstrap	Cond. Opt.	Auxiliary
Number of Particles M	40,000	400	40,000
Number of Repetitions	100	100	100
High Posterior Density: $\theta = \theta^m$			
Bias $\hat{\Delta}_1$	-1.39	-0.10	-2.83
StdD $\hat{\Delta}_1$	2.03	0.37	1.87
Bias $\hat{\Delta}_2$	0.32	-0.03	-0.74
Low Posterior Density: $\theta = \theta^l$			
Bias $\hat{\Delta}_1$	-7.01	-0.11	-6.44
StdD $\hat{\Delta}_1$	4.68	0.44	4.19
Bias $\hat{\Delta}_2$	-0.70	-0.02	-0.50

Notes: The likelihood discrepancies $\hat{\Delta}_1$ and $\hat{\Delta}_2$ are defined in (8.79) and (8.80). Results are based on $N_{run} = 100$ runs of the particle filters.

iliary PF and the bootstrap PF are very similar. For θ^m the downward bias is a bit more pronounced for the auxiliary PF, whereas for θ^l the distribution of $\hat{\Delta}_1$ is less skewed to the left. The last column of Table 8.2 reports sample moments for $\hat{\Delta}_1$ and $\hat{\Delta}_2$. While the auxiliary PF is able to reduce the variability of the log-likelihood discrepancies, the small-sample bias for $\hat{\Delta}_1$ increases by a factor of 2 for θ^m compared to the bootstrap PF.

In Chapters 9 and 10 we will embed a particle filter into a posterior sampler. This is necessary to implement posterior inference for a nonlinear DSGE model. The key requirement for such algorithms to generate draws that can be used to consistently approximate moments and quantiles of the posterior distribution of θ based on a finite number of particles M is that the particle filter generates an unbiased approximation of the likelihood function $p(Y_{1:T}|\theta)$ and its increments $p(y_t|Y_{1:t-1}, \theta)$. While particle filter likelihood approximations are unbiased in theory, in practice the sampling distribution

---

ically very similar. In the figures and tables we report the former.

High Post. Density Param θ^m Low Post. Density Param θ^l

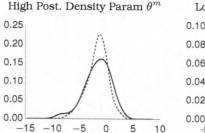 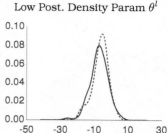

Figure 8.3: Small-Scale Model: Distribution of Log-Likelihood Approximation Errors (Part 2). Density estimates of $\hat{\Delta}_1 = \ln \hat{p}(Y|\theta) - \ln p(Y|\theta)$ based on $N_{run} = 100$ runs of the particle filters. Solid lines depict densities for bootstrap PF; dashed lines correspond to auxiliary PF. The number of particles is $M = 40,000$.

of the approximation may be highly skewed and fat-tailed, such that finite sample averages across a modest number of repetitions may appear biased. This may translate into slow convergence (or failure of convergence) of posterior samplers that rely on particle filter approximations.

We previously focused on the distribution of the log-likelihood approximation $\ln \hat{p}(Y_{1:T}|\theta)$ in Figure 8.2. It is quite apparent that the particle filters provide a downward-biased estimate of $\ln p(Y_{1:T}|\theta)$. The negative bias is expected from Jensen's inequality if the approximation of the likelihood function is unbiased, because the logarithmic transformation is concave. Assessing the bias of $\hat{p}(Y_{1:T}|\theta)$ is numerically delicate because exponentiating a log-likelihood value of around -300 leads to a missing value. Instead, we will consider the following statistic:

$$
\begin{aligned}
\hat{\Delta}_2 &= \frac{\hat{p}(Y_{1:T}|\theta)}{p(Y_{1:T}|\theta)} - 1 \\
&= \exp[\ln \hat{p}(Y_{1:T}|\theta) - \ln p(Y_{1:T}|\theta)] - 1.
\end{aligned}
\tag{8.80}
$$

The computation of $\hat{\Delta}_2$ requires us to exponentiate the difference in log-likelihood values, which is feasible if the particle filter approximation is reasonably accurate. If the particle filter approximation is unbiased, then the sampling mean of $\hat{\Delta}_2$ is equal to zero.

By construction, $\hat{\Delta}_2$ is bounded below by -1. The right panel of our earlier Figure 8.2 suggests that for the bootstrap PF, we expect the distribution of $\hat{\Delta}_2$ to have significant mass near -1 (note that $\exp[-5] \approx 0.007$) and a long right tail ($\exp[3] \approx 20$). Table 8.2 reports the means of $\hat{\Delta}_2$ across 100 repetitions: for the conditionally optimal PF the means given θ^m and θ^l are essentially zero. For the bootstrap PF the mean is close to zero conditional on θ^m, but substantially below zero for θ^l. The auxiliary PF is not able to reduce the small-sample bias of $\hat{\Delta}_2$ compared to the bootstrap PF. In fact, at θ^m the bias of the auxiliary PF is more than twice as large (in absolute terms) as the bias of the bootstrap filter.

By construction, the accuracy of the bootstrap PF is very sensitive to outliers in the observations. To the extent that outliers are unlikely under the entertained DSGE model, the forward simulation of the state vector is unlikely to yield many proposed states $\tilde{s}_t^j$ that can rationalize the observation y_t. This leads to an uneven distribution of particle weights and inaccurate Monte Carlo approximations. The recent Great Recession in 2008–09 was a large outlier from the perspective of DSGE models (as well as other popular time series models). Holding the parameter values θ^m and θ^l fixed, we now run the filters on the sample 2003:I to 2013:IV. Results are depicted in Figure 8.4.

The top left panel of Figure 8.4 depicts the sequence of log-likelihood increments. In 2008:IV, which is when output growth collapsed, the log-likelihood increment is substantially lower than in any other period. The conditionally optimal PF still does well in tracking the actual likelihood, whereas the bootstrap PF approximation becomes highly inaccurate. The bootstrap PF underestimates the likelihood increment by about 250 units on a log scale. Interestingly, the bootstrap PF recovers fairly quickly in subsequent periods. The top right panel depicts 90% bands for the approximations of the likelihood increments across 100 repetitions. The width of the band for the bootstrap PF is generally less than 1 unit on the log scale. The bottom panel shows the log standard deviation of the log-likelihood increments. For the condition-

Mean of Log-Likelihood Increments $\ln \hat{p}(y_t|Y_{1:t-1}, \theta^m)$

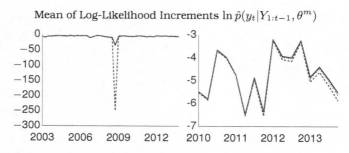

Log Standard Dev. of Log-Likelihood Increments

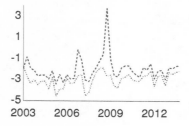

Figure 8.4: Small-Scale Model: Particle Filtering during the Great Recession and Beyond. Solid lines represent results from Kalman filter. Dashed lines correspond to bootstrap PF ($M = 40,000$) and dotted lines correspond to conditionally optimal PF ($M = 400$). Results are based on $N_{run} = 100$ runs of the filters.

ally optimal PF the log standard deviation stays fairly stable over time, though there appears to be a slight increase after 2008. For the bootstrap PF, the standard deviations are generally larger than for the conditionally optimal PF and there is a large spike in 2008:Q4.

8.7 Application to the SW Model

Our second application of the particle filter considers the SW model. From a computational perspective, the SW model differs from the small-scale DSGE model in terms of the number of observables used in the estimation and with respect to the number of latent state variables. For the estimation of the small-scale New Keynesian model we used three observables and the model has one endogenous state variable and three exogenous shocks. The SW model is estimated based on seven variables and it has more than a dozen state variables. We will examine the extent to which the increased model size leads to a deterioration of the accuracy of the particle filter approximation. The large state space makes it more difficult to accurately integrate out the hidden state variables with the filter, and the relatively large number of observables creates a potential for model misspecification, which in turn may lead to a deterioration of the bootstrap PF. Recall that the bootstrap PF is sensitive to the accuracy of forecasts of y_t based on the distribution $s_{t-1}|Y_{1:t-1}$.

As in the previous section, we compute the particle filter approximations conditional on two sets of parameter values, θ^m and θ^l, which are summarized in Table 8.3. θ^m is the parameter vector associated with the highest likelihood value among the draws that we previously generated with our posterior sampler. θ^l is a parameter vector that attains a lower likelihood value. The log-likelihood difference between the two parameter vectors is approximately 13. The standard deviations of the measurement errors are chosen to be approximately 20% of the sample standard deviation of the time series.[6] We run the filter $N_{run} = 100$ times over the period 1966:Q1 to 2004:Q4.

Figure 8.5 depicts density plots of the log-likelihood discrepancy $\hat{\Delta}_1$ for the bootstrap PF and the conditionally optimal PF. A comparison to Figure 8.2 highlights that the accuracy of the PF deteriorates substantially by moving from a small-scale DSGE model to a medium-scale DSGE model. The results depicted in the top row of Figure 8.5 are based on 40,000 particles for the bootstrap particle filter, which is the same number of particles used for the small-scale DSGE model. According to Table 8.4, the bias of $\hat{\Delta}_1$ at θ^m is -238.49 and the standard deviation is 68.28. The corresponding sample moments obtained for the small-scale model are -1.39

---

[6]The standard deviations for the measurement errors are: 0.1731 (output growth), 0.1394 (consumption growth), 0.4515 (investment growth), 0.1128 (wage growth), 0.5838 (log hours), 0.1230 (inflation), 0.1653 (interest rates).

Table 8.3: SW Model: Parameter Values

	θ^m	θ^l		θ^m	θ^l
$\tilde{\beta}$	0.159	0.182	$\bar{\pi}$	0.774	0.571
$\bar{l}$	-1.078	0.019	α	0.181	0.230
σ	1.016	1.166	Φ	1.342	1.455
φ	6.625	4.065	h	0.597	0.511
ξ_w	0.752	0.647	σ_l	2.736	1.217
ξ_p	0.861	0.807	ι_w	0.259	0.452
ι_p	0.463	0.494	ψ	0.837	0.828
r_π	1.769	1.827	ρ	0.855	0.836
r_y	0.090	0.069	$r_{\Delta y}$	0.168	0.156
ρ_a	0.982	0.962	ρ_b	0.868	0.849
ρ_g	0.962	0.947	ρ_i	0.702	0.723
ρ_r	0.414	0.497	ρ_p	0.782	0.831
ρ_w	0.971	0.968	ρ_{ga}	0.450	0.565
μ_p	0.673	0.741	μ_w	0.892	0.871
σ_a	0.375	0.418	σ_b	0.073	0.075
σ_g	0.428	0.444	σ_i	0.350	0.358
σ_r	0.144	0.131	σ_p	0.101	0.117
σ_w	0.311	0.382	$\ln p(Y|\theta)$	-943.0	-956.1

Notes: $\tilde{\beta} = 100(\beta^{-1} - 1)$.

and 2.03.

Increasing the number of particles from 40,000 to 400,000 improves the accuracy of the filter somewhat as shown in the bottom row of Figure 8.5, but also increases the computational time. For the conditionally optimal PF we used 4,000 particles, which is ten times more than for the small-scale DSGE model. Compared to the bootstrap PF, there is a substantial gain from using the refined proposal distribution. According to Table 8.4 the small-sample bias of $\hat{\Delta}_1$ drops by more than a factor of 20 and the standard deviation is reduced by more than a factor of 15 relative to the bootstrap PF with 40,000 particles. Unlike for the small-scale DSGE model, the likelihood approximation of the conditionally optimal PF appears to be biased in the small sample: the means

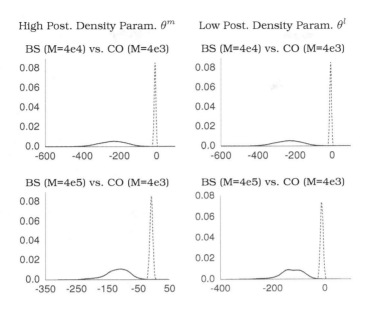

Figure 8.5: SW Model: Distribution of Log-Likelihood Approximation Errors. Density estimates of $\hat{\Delta}_1 = \ln \hat{p}(Y|\theta) - \ln p(Y|\theta)$ based on $N_{run} = 100$. Solid densities summarize results for the bootstrap (BS) PF; dashed densities summarize results for the conditionally optimal (CO) PF.

of $\hat{\Delta}_2$ are -0.87 and -0.97 for θ^m and θ^l, respectively.

The left panel of Figure 8.6 plots the filtered exogenous shock process $\hat{g}_t$ from a single run of the Kalman filter, the bootstrap PF, and the conditionally optimal PF. In the first half of the sample, the conditionally optimal PF tracks $\mathbb{E}[\hat{g}_t|Y_{1:t}]$ very closely. In the early 1980s, a gap between the conditionally optimal PF approximation and the true mean of $\hat{g}_t$ opens up and for a period of about 40 quarters, the bootstrap PF approximation follows the path of $\mathbb{E}[\hat{g}_t|Y_{1:t}]$ more closely. The right panel of the figure shows the standard deviation of the two particle filter approximations across 100 repetitions. The conditionally optimal PF produces a more accurate approximation than the bootstrap PF, but both ap-

Table 8.4: SW Model: PF Summary Statistics

	Bootstrap		Cond. Opt.	
No. of Particles M	40,000	400,000	4,000	40,000
No. of Repetitions	100	100	100	100
High Posterior Density: $\theta = \theta^m$				
Bias $\hat{\Delta}_1$	−238.49	−118.20	−8.55	−2.88
StdD $\hat{\Delta}_1$	68.28	35.69	4.43	2.49
Bias $\hat{\Delta}_2$	−1.00	−1.00	−0.87	−0.41
Low Posterior Density: $\theta = \theta^l$				
Bias $\hat{\Delta}_1$	−253.89	−128.13	−11.48	−4.91
StdD $\hat{\Delta}_1$	65.57	41.25	4.98	2.75
Bias $\hat{\Delta}_2$	−1.00	−1.00	−0.97	−0.64

Notes: Results are based on $N_{run} = 100$. The likelihood discrepancies $\hat{\Delta}_1$ and $\hat{\Delta}_2$ are defined in (8.79) and (8.80).

proximations are associated with considerable variability. For the conditionally optimal PF, the smallest value of the standard deviation of $\hat{\mathbb{E}}[\hat{g}_t | Y_{1:t}]$ is 0.4 and the largest value is 1.4.

8.8 Computational Considerations

The illustrations in Sections 8.6 and 8.7 highlighted that a careful specification of the proposal distribution in Algorithm 12 is very important. Because of the ease of implementation, the results for the bootstrap PF provide a lower bound on the accuracy of particle filter approximations for DSGE model likelihood functions, whereas the results from the conditionally optimal PF provide an upper bound that in applications with nonlinear DSGE models is generally not attainable. As discussed in Section 8.3.2, an approximate conditionally optimal filter could be obtained by using an extended Kalman filter or an unscented Kalman filter to construct an efficient proposal distribution. If the nonlinearities in the DSGE model are mild, then a Kalman filter updating step applied to a linearized version of the DSGE model could be used to obtain

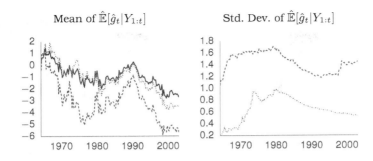

Figure 8.6: SW Model: Filtered Government Spending Process $\hat{g}_t$. Mean and standard deviations of $\hat{\mathbb{E}}[\hat{g}_t|Y_{1:t}]$ are computed across $N_{run} = 100$ runs of the filters. The mean for the Kalman filter appears in solid, results for the bootstrap PF ($M = 40,000$) are represented by dashed lines, and results for the conditionally optimal PF ($M = 4,000$) are dotted.

a good proposal distribution. While the computation of efficient proposal distribution requires additional time, it makes it possible to reduce the number of particles, which can speed up the particle filter considerably.

While it is possible to parallelize the forecasting steps of the particle filter algorithms, a massive parallelization is difficult because of the high communication costs in the subsequent updating and selection steps. In fact, the speed of the resampling routine may become the biggest bottleneck and it is important to use a fast routine, e.g., stratified resampling. DSGE model solutions often generate redundant state variables. In high-dimensional systems it is useful to reduce the dimension of the state vector to its minimum. This reduces the memory requirements to store the particles and it avoids numerical difficulties that may arise from singularities in the distribution of the states.

Chapter 9

Combining Particle Filters with MH Samplers

We previously focused on the particle filter approximation of the likelihood function of a potentially nonlinear DSGE model. In order to conduct Bayesian inference, the approximate likelihood function has to be embedded into a posterior sampler. We begin by combining the particle filtering methods of Chapter 8 with the MCMC methods of Chapter 4. In a nutshell, we replace the actual likelihood functions that appear in the formula for the acceptance probability $\alpha(\vartheta|\theta^{i-1})$ in Algorithm 5 with particle filter approximations $\hat{p}(Y|\theta)$. This idea was first proposed for the estimation of nonlinear DSGE models by Fernández-Villaverde and Rubio-Ramírez (2007). We refer to the resulting algorithm as PFMH algorithm. It is a special case of a larger class of algorithms called particle Markov chain Monte Carlo (PMCMC). The theoretical properties of PMCMC methods were established in Andrieu, Doucet, and Holenstein (2010). Applications of PFMH algorithms in other areas of econometrics are discussed in Flury and Shephard (2011).

9.1   The PFMH Algorithm

The statistical theory underlying the PFMH algorithm is very complex and beyond the scope of this book. We refer the interested reader to Andrieu, Doucet, and Holenstein (2010) for a careful exposition. Below we will sketch the main idea behind the algorithm. The exposition is based on Flury and Shephard (2011). We will distinguish between $\{p(Y|\theta), p(\theta|Y), p(Y)\}$

and $\{\hat{p}(Y|\theta), \hat{p}(\theta|Y), \hat{p}(Y)\}$. The first triplet consists of the exact likelihood function $p(Y|\theta)$ and the resulting posterior distribution and marginal data density defined as

$$p(\theta|Y) = \frac{p(Y|\theta)p(\theta)}{p(Y)}, \quad p(Y) = \int p(Y|\theta)p(\theta)d\theta. \quad (9.1)$$

The second triplet consists of the particle filter approximation of the likelihood function denoted by $\hat{p}(Y|\theta)$ and the resulting posterior and marginal data density:

$$\hat{p}(\theta|Y) = \frac{\hat{p}(Y|\theta)p(\theta)}{\hat{p}(Y)}, \quad \hat{p}(Y) = \int \hat{p}(Y|\theta)p(\theta)d\theta. \quad (9.2)$$

By replacing the exact likelihood function $p(\theta|Y)$ with the particle filter approximation $\hat{p}(Y|\theta)$ in Algorithm 5, one might expect to obtain draws from the approximate posterior $\hat{p}(\theta|Y)$ instead of the exact posterior $p(\theta|Y)$. The surprising implication of the theory developed in Andrieu, Doucet, and Holenstein (2010) is that the distribution of draws from the PFMH algorithm that replaces $p(Y|\theta)$ by $\hat{p}(Y|\theta)$ in fact does converge to the exact posterior. The algorithm takes the following form:

Algorithm 18 (PFMH Algorithm) *For $i = 1$ to N:*

1. *Draw ϑ from a density $q(\vartheta|\theta^{i-1})$.*

2. *Set $\theta^i = \vartheta$ with probability*

$$\alpha(\vartheta|\theta^{i-1}) = \min\left\{1, \frac{\hat{p}(Y|\vartheta)p(\vartheta)/q(\vartheta|\theta^{i-1})}{\hat{p}(Y|\theta^{i-1})p(\theta^{i-1})/q(\theta^{i-1}|\vartheta)}\right\}$$

and $\theta^i = \theta^{i-1}$ otherwise. The likelihood approximation $\hat{p}(Y|\vartheta)$ is computed using Algorithm 12.

Any of the particle filters described in Chapter 8 could be used in the PFMH algorithm. Suppose we use the generic filter described in Algorithm 12. At each iteration the filter generates draws $\tilde{s}_t^j$ from the proposal distribution $g_t(\cdot|s_{t-1}^j)$. Let $\tilde{S}_t = (\tilde{s}_t^1, \ldots, \tilde{s}_t^M)'$ and denote the entire sequence of draws by $\tilde{S}_{1:T}^{1:M}$. In the selection step we are using multinomial resampling to determine the ancestor for each particle in the next iteration. Thus, we can define a random variable A_t^j that contains this ancestry information. For instance, suppose that during the resampling particle $j = 1$ was assigned the value $\tilde{s}_t^{10}$ then $A_t^1 = 10$. Let $A_t = \left(A_t^1, \ldots, A_t^N\right)$ and use $A_{1:T}$ to denote the sequence of A_t's.

The PFMH algorithm operates on a probability space that includes the parameter vector θ as well as $\tilde{S}_{1:T}$ and $A_{1:T}$. We use $U_{1:T}$ to denote the sequence of random vectors that are used to generate $\tilde{S}_{1:T}$ and $A_{1:T}$. $U_{1:T}$ can be thought of as an array of iid uniform random numbers. The transformation of $U_{1:T}$ into $(\tilde{S}_{1:T}, A_{1:T})$ typically depends on θ and $Y_{1:T}$ because the proposal distribution $g_t(\tilde{s}_t | s_{t-1}^j)$ in Algorithm 12 depends on the current observation y_t as well as the parameter vector θ which enters measurement and state-transitions equations; see (8.1).

Consider, for instance, the conditionally optimal particle filter for a linear state-space model described in Section 8.3.1. The implementation of this filter requires sampling from a $N(\bar{s}_{t|t}^j, P_{t|t})$ distribution for each particle j. The mean of this distribution depends on y_t and both mean and covariance matrix depend on θ through the system matrices of the state-space representation (8.2). Draws from this distribution can in principle be obtained, by sampling iid uniform random variates, using a probability integral transform to convert them into iid draws from a standard normal distribution, and then converting them into draws from a $N(\bar{s}_{t|t}^j, P_{t|t}^j)$. Likewise, in the selection step, the multinomial resampling could be implemented based on draws from iid uniform random variables. Therefore, we can express the particle filter approximation of the likelihood function as

$$\hat{p}(Y_{1:T} | \theta) = g(Y_{1:T} | \theta, U_{1:T}), \tag{9.3}$$

where

$$U_{1:T} \sim p(U_{1:T}) = \prod_{t=1}^{T} p(U_t). \tag{9.4}$$

The PFMH algorithm can be interpreted as operating on an enlarged probability space for the triplet $(Y_{1:T}, \theta, U_{1:T})$. Define the joint distribution

$$p_g\left(Y_{1:T}, \theta, U_{1:T}\right) = g(Y_{1:T} | \theta, U_{1:T}) p\left(U_{1:T}\right) p(\theta). \tag{9.5}$$

The PFMH algorithm samples from the joint posterior

$$p_g(\theta, U_{1:T}|Y_{1:T}) \propto g(Y|\theta, U_{1:T})p(U_{1:T})p(\theta) \qquad (9.6)$$

and discards the draws of $(U_{1:T})$. For this procedure to be valid, it has to be the case that marginalizing the joint posterior $p_g(\theta, U_{1:T}|Y_{1:T})$ with respect to $(U_{1:T})$ yields the exact posterior $p(\theta|Y_{1:T})$. In other words, we require that the particle filter produces an unbiased simulation approximation of the likelihood function for all values of θ:

$$\mathbb{E}[\hat{p}(Y_{1:T}|\theta)] \qquad (9.7)$$
$$= \int g(Y_{1:T}|\theta, U_{1:T})p(U_{1:T})dU_{1:T} = p(Y_{1:T}|\theta).$$

In Section 8.1.2 we verified that the particle filter does indeed satisfy the unbiasedness requirement.

It turns out that the acceptance probability for the MH algorithm that operates on the enlarged probability space can be directly expressed in terms of the particle filter approximation $\hat{p}(Y_{1:T}|\theta)$. On the enlarged probability space, one needs to generate a proposed draw for both θ and $U_{1:T}$. We denote these draws by ϑ and $U_{1:T}^*$. The proposal distribution for $(\vartheta, U_{1:T}^*)$ in the MH algorithm is given by $q(\vartheta|\theta^{(i-1)})p(U_{1:T}^*)$. There is no need to keep track of the draws $(U_{1:T}^*)$, because the acceptance probability for Algorithm 18 can be written as follows (omitting the time subscripts):

$$\alpha(\vartheta|\theta^{i-1}) \qquad (9.8)$$
$$= \min\left\{1, \frac{\frac{g(Y|\vartheta, U^*)p(U^*)p(\vartheta)}{q(\vartheta|\theta^{(i-1)})p(U^*)}}{\frac{g(Y|\theta^{(i-1)}, U^{(i-1)})p(U^{(i-1)})p(\theta^{(i-1)})}{q(\theta^{(i-1)}|\theta^*)p(U^{(i-1)})}}\right\}$$
$$= \min\left\{1, \frac{\hat{p}(Y|\vartheta)p(\vartheta)/q(\vartheta|\theta^{(i-1)})}{\hat{p}(Y|\theta^{(i-1)})p(\theta^{(i-1)})/q(\theta^{(i-1)}|\vartheta)}\right\}.$$

The terms $p(U^*)$ and $p(U^{(i-1)})$ cancel from the expression in the first line of (9.8) and it suffices to record the particle filter likelihood approximations $\hat{p}(Y|\vartheta)$ and $\hat{p}(Y|\theta^{(i-1)})$.

9.2 Application to the Small-Scale DSGE Model

We now apply the PFMH algorithm to the small-scale New Keynesian model, which is estimated over the period 1983:I to 2002:IV. We use the 1-block RWMH-V algorithm and combine it with the Kalman filter, the bootstrap PF, and the conditionally optimal PF. According to the theory sketched in the previous section the PFMH algorithm should accurately approximate the posterior distribution of the DSGE model parameters. Our results are based on $N_{run} = 20$ runs of each algorithm. In each run we generate $N = 100,000$ posterior draws and discard the first $N_0 = 50,000$. As in Section 8.6, we use $M = 40,000$ particles for the bootstrap filter and $M = 400$ particles for the conditionally optimal filter. A single run of the RWMH-V algorithm takes 1 minute and 30 seconds with the Kalman filter, approximately 40 minutes with the conditionally optimal PF, and approximately 1 day with the bootstrap PF.

The results are summarized in Table 9.1. Most notably, despite the inaccurate likelihood approximation of the bootstrap PF documented in Section 8.6, the PFMH works remarkably well. Columns 2 to 4 of the table report posterior means which are computed by pooling the draws generated by the 20 runs of the algorithms. Except for some minor discrepancies in the posterior mean for τ and $r^{(A)}$, which are parameters with a high posterior variance, the posterior mean approximations are essentially identical for all three likelihood evaluation methods. Columns 5 to 7 contain the inefficiency factors $\text{InEff}_N(\bar{\theta})$ for each parameter and the last three columns of Table 9.1 contain the standard deviations of the posterior mean estimates across the 20 runs. Not surprisingly, the posterior sampler that is based on the bootstrap PF is the least accurate. The standard deviations are two to four times as large as for the samplers that utilize either the Kalman filter or the conditionally optimal PF. Under the Kalman filter the inefficiency factors range from 35 to about 150, whereas under the bootstrap particle filter they range from 575 to 1,890. As stressed in Section 9.1 the most important requirement for PFMH algorithms is that the particle filter approximation is unbiased—it does not have to be exact.

Table 9.1: Small-Scale Model: PFMH Accuracy

	Mean ($\bar{\theta}_N$)			Inefficiency Factors			StdD ($\bar{\theta}_N$)		
	KF	CO-PF	BS-PF	KF	CO-PF	BS-PF	KF	CO-PF	BS-PF
τ	2.63	2.62	2.64	66.17	126.76	1360.22	0.020	0.028	0.091
κ	0.82	0.81	0.82	128.00	97.11	1887.37	0.007	0.006	0.026
ψ_1	1.88	1.88	1.87	113.46	159.53	749.22	0.011	0.013	0.029
ψ_2	0.64	0.64	0.63	61.28	56.10	681.85	0.011	0.010	0.036
ρ_r	0.75	0.75	0.75	108.46	134.01	1535.34	0.002	0.002	0.007
ρ_g	0.98	0.98	0.98	94.10	88.48	1613.77	0.001	0.001	0.002
ρ_z	0.88	0.88	0.88	124.24	118.74	1518.66	0.001	0.001	0.005
$r^{(A)}$	0.44	0.44	0.44	148.46	151.81	1115.74	0.016	0.016	0.044
$\pi^{(A)}$	3.32	3.33	3.32	152.08	141.62	1057.90	0.017	0.016	0.045
$\gamma^{(Q)}$	0.59	0.59	0.59	106.68	142.37	899.34	0.006	0.007	0.018
σ_r	0.24	0.24	0.24	35.21	179.15	1105.99	0.001	0.002	0.004
σ_g	0.68	0.68	0.67	98.22	64.18	1490.81	0.003	0.002	0.011
σ_z	0.32	0.32	0.32	84.77	61.55	575.90	0.001	0.001	0.003
$\ln \hat{p}(Y)$	−357.14	−357.17	−358.32				0.040	0.038	0.949

Notes: Results are based on $N_{run} = 20$ runs of the PF-RWMH-V algorithm. Each run of the algorithm generates $N = 100,000$ draws and the first $N_0 = 50,000$ are discarded. The likelihood function is computed with the Kalman filter (KF), bootstrap particle filter (BS-PF, $M = 40,000$), or conditionally optimal particle filter (CO-PF, $M = 400$). We report means and standard deviations of posterior mean approximations $\bar{\theta}_N$ for the $N_{run} = 20$ runs.

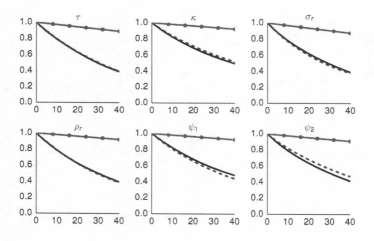

Figure 9.1: Autocorrelation of PFMH Draws. The figure depicts autocorrelation functions computed from the output of the 1 Block RWMH-V algorithm based on the Kalman filter (solid), the conditionally optimal particle filter (dashed), and the bootstrap particle filter (solid with dots).

In Figure 9.1 we depict autocorrelation functions for parameter draws computed based on the output of the PFMH algorithms. As a benchmark, the figure also contains autocorrelation functions obtained from the sampler that uses the exact likelihood function computed with the Kalman filter. While under the conditionally optimal particle filter the persistence of the Markov chain for the DSGE model parameters is comparable to the persistence under the Kalman filter, the use of the bootstrap particle filter raises the serial correlation of the parameter draws drastically, which leads to the less precise Monte Carlo approximations reported in Table 9.1.

9.3 Application to the SW Model

We now use the PF-RWMH-V algorithm to estimate the SW model. Unlike in Section 6.2, where we used a more diffuse prior distribution to estimate the SW model, we now revert back to the prior originally specified by Smets and Wouters (2007). This prior is summarized in Table A-2 in the Appendix. As shown in Herbst and Schorfheide (2014), under the original prior distribution the RWMH algorithm is much better behaved than under our diffuse prior, because it leads to a posterior distribution that does not exhibit multiple modes. The estimation sample is 1966:I to 2004:IV. Using the RWMH-V algorithm, we estimate the model posteriors using the Kalman filter and the conditionally optimal PF, running each algorithm $N_{run} = 20$ times. The bootstrap particle filters with $M = 40,000$ and $M = 400,000$ particles turned out to be too inaccurate to deliver reliable posterior estimates.

Table 9.2 shows the results for the Kalman filter and the conditionally optimal PF. While the MCMC chains generated using the KF and CO-PF generate roughly the same means for the parameter draws on average, the variability across the chains is much higher for the CO-PF. According to inefficiency factors, the KF chains are about ten times more efficient than the CO-PF.

The results are summarized in Table 9.2. Due to the computational complexity of the PF-RWMH-V algorithm, the results reported in the table are based on $N = 10,000$ instead of $N = 100,000$ draws from the posterior distribution. We used the conditionally optimal PF with $M = 40,000$ particles and a single-block RWMH-V algorithm in which we scaled the posterior covariance matrix that served as covariance matrix of the proposal distribution by $c^2 = 0.25^2$ for the KF and $c^2 = 0.05^2$ for the conditionally optimal PF. This leads to acceptance rates of 33% for the KF and 24% for the conditionally optimal PF.

In our experience, the noisy approximation of the likelihood function through the PF makes it necessary to reduce the variance of the proposal distribution to maintain a targeted acceptance rate. In the SW application the proposed moves using the PF approximation are about five times smaller than under the exact KF likelihood function. This increases the persistence of the Markov chain and leads to a reduction in accuracy. Because of the difference in precision of PF approximations at different points in the param-

Table 9.2: SW Model: PFMH Accuracy

| | Mean ($\bar{\theta}_N$) | | Ineff. Factors | | StdD ($\bar{\theta}_N$) | |
	KF	CO-PF	KF	CO-PF	KF	CO-PF
$\tilde{\beta}$	0.14	0.14	172.58	3732.90	0.007	0.034
$\bar{\pi}$	0.73	0.74	185.99	4343.83	0.016	0.079
$\bar{l}$	0.51	0.37	174.39	3133.89	0.130	0.552
α	0.19	0.20	149.77	5244.47	0.003	0.015
σ_c	1.49	1.45	86.27	3557.81	0.013	0.086
Φ	1.47	1.45	134.34	4930.55	0.009	0.056
φ	5.34	5.35	138.54	3210.16	0.131	0.628
h	0.70	0.72	277.64	3058.26	0.008	0.027
ξ_w	0.75	0.75	343.89	2594.43	0.012	0.034
σ_l	2.28	2.31	162.09	4426.89	0.091	0.477
ξ_p	0.72	0.72	182.47	6777.88	0.008	0.051
ι_w	0.54	0.53	241.80	4984.35	0.016	0.073
ι_p	0.48	0.50	205.27	5487.34	0.015	0.078
ψ	0.45	0.44	248.15	3598.14	0.020	0.078
r_π	2.09	2.09	98.32	3302.07	0.020	0.116
ρ	0.80	0.80	241.63	4896.54	0.006	0.025
r_y	0.13	0.13	243.85	4755.65	0.005	0.023
$r_{\Delta y}$	0.21	0.21	101.94	5324.19	0.003	0.022

Notes: $\tilde{\beta} = 100(\beta^{-1} - 1)$. Results are based on $N_{run} = 20$ runs of the PF-RWMH-V algorithm. Each run of the algorithm generates $N = 10,000$ draws. The likelihood function is computed with the Kalman filter (KF) or conditionally optimal particle filter (CO-PF). The CO-PF uses $M = 40,000$ particles to compute the likelihood. We report means and standard deviations of posterior mean approximations $\bar{\theta}_N$ for the $N_{run} = 20$ runs.

Table 9.2: (Continued) SW Model: PFMH Accuracy

	Mean $(\bar{\theta}_N)$		Ineff. Factors		StdD $(\bar{\theta}_N)$	
	KF	CO-PF	KF	CO-PF	KF	CO-PF
ρ_a	0.96	0.96	153.46	1358.87	0.002	0.005
ρ_b	0.22	0.21	325.98	4468.10	0.018	0.068
ρ_g	0.97	0.97	57.08	2687.56	0.002	0.011
ρ_i	0.71	0.70	219.11	4735.33	0.009	0.044
ρ_r	0.54	0.54	194.73	4184.04	0.020	0.094
ρ_p	0.80	0.81	338.69	2527.79	0.022	0.061
ρ_w	0.94	0.94	135.83	4851.01	0.003	0.019
ρ_{ga}	0.41	0.37	196.38	5621.86	0.025	0.133
μ_p	0.66	0.66	300.29	3552.33	0.025	0.087
μ_w	0.82	0.81	218.43	5074.31	0.011	0.052
σ_a	0.34	0.34	128.00	5096.75	0.005	0.034
σ_b	0.24	0.24	186.13	3494.71	0.004	0.016
σ_g	0.51	0.49	208.14	2945.02	0.006	0.021
σ_i	0.43	0.44	115.42	6093.72	0.006	0.043
σ_r	0.14	0.14	193.37	3408.01	0.004	0.016
σ_p	0.13	0.13	194.22	4587.76	0.003	0.013
σ_w	0.22	0.22	211.80	2256.19	0.004	0.012
$\ln \hat{p}(Y)$	-964	-1018			0.298	9.139

Notes: $\tilde{\beta} = 100(\beta^{-1} - 1)$. Results are based on $N_{run} = 20$ runs of the PF-RWMH-V algorithm. Each run of the algorithm generates $N = 10,000$ draws. The likelihood function is computed with the Kalman filter (KF) or conditionally optimal particle filter (CO-PF). The CO-PF uses $M = 40,000$ particles to compute the likelihood. We report means and standard deviations of posterior mean approximations $\bar{\theta}_N$ for the $N_{run} = 20$ runs.

eter space, the RWMH-V acceptance rate varies much more across chains. For example, the standard deviation of the acceptance rate for the CO-PF PMCMC is 0.09, about ten times larger than for the KF runs.

While the pooled posterior means using the KF and the conditionally optimal PF reported in Table 9.1 are very similar, the standard deviation of the means across runs is three to five times larger if the PF approximation of the likelihood function is used. Because the PF approximation of the log-likelihood function is downward-biased, the log marginal data density approximation obtained with the PF is much smaller than the one obtained with the KF.

Reducing the number of particles for the conditionally optimal PF to 4,000 or switching to the bootstrap PF with 40,000 or 400,000 particles was not successful in the sense that the acceptance rate quickly dropped to zero. Reducing the variance of the proposal distribution did not solve the problem because to obtain a nontrivial acceptance rate the step-size had to be so small that the sampler would not be able to traverse the high posterior density region of the parameter space in a reasonable amount of time. In view of the accuracy of the likelihood approximation reported in Table 8.4, this is not surprising. The PF approximations are highly volatile and even though the PF approximation is unbiased in theory, finite sample averages appear to be severely biased.

If the variation in the likelihood approximation, conditional on a particular value of θ, is much larger than the variation that we would observe along a Markov chain (evaluating the likelihood for the sequence θ^i, $i = 1, \ldots, N$) that is generated by using the exact likelihood function, the sampler is likely to get stuck, meaning the acceptance rate for proposed draws drops to zero, for the following reason. Once the PF has generated an estimate $\hat{p}(Y|\theta^i)$ that exceeds $p(Y|\theta^i)$ by a wide margin, it becomes extremely difficult to move to a nearby $\tilde{\theta}$. A θ^i and a $\tilde{\theta}$ that are close to each other tend to be associated with similar exact likelihood values. Because most of the PF evaluations underestimate $p(Y|\tilde{\theta})$ and because previously $\hat{p}(Y|\theta^i)$ overestimated $p(Y|\theta^i)$, the acceptance probability will drop to essentially zero.

9.4 Computational Considerations

We implement the PFMH algorithm on a single machine, utilizing up to twelve cores. Efficient parallelization of the algorithm is difficult, because it is challenging to parallelize MCMC algorithms and it is not profitable to use distributed memory parallelization for the filter. For the small-scale DSGE model it takes 30:20:33 [hh:mm:ss] hours to generate 100,000 parameter draws using the bootstrap PF with 40,000 particles. Under the conditionally optimal filter we only use 400 particles, which reduces the run time to 00:39:20 minutes. Thus, with the conditionally optimal filter, the PFMH algorithm runs about fifty times faster and delivers highly accurate approximations of the posterior means. For the SW model the computational time is substantially larger. It took 05:14:20:00 [dd:hh:mm:ss] days to generate 10,000 draws using the conditionally optimal PF with 40,000 particles.

In practical applications with nonlinear DSGE models the conditionally optimal PF that we used in our numerical illustrations is typically not available and has to be replaced by one of the other filters, possibly an approximately conditionally optimal PF. Having a good understanding of the accuracy of the PF approximation is crucial. Thus, we recommend assessing the variance of the likelihood approximation at various points in the parameter space as we did in Sections 8.6 and 8.7 and tailoring the filter until it is reasonably accurate. To put the accuracy of the filter approximation into perspective, one could compare it to the variation in the likelihood function of a linearized DSGE model fitted to the same data, along a sequence of posterior draws θ^i. If the variation in the likelihood function due to the PF approximation is larger than the variation generated by moving through the parameter space, the PF-MH algorithm is unlikely to produce reliable results.

In general, likelihood evaluations for nonlinear DSGE models are computationally very costly. Rather than spending computational resources on tailoring the proposal density for the PF to reduce the number of particles, one can also try to lower the number of likelihood evaluations in the MH algorithm. Smith (2012) developed a PFMH algorithm based on surrogate transitions. In summary, the algorithm proceeds as follows: Instead of evaluating the posterior density (and thereby the DSGE model likelihood function) for every proposal draw ϑ, one first evaluates the likelihood function for an approximate model, e.g., a linearized DSGE model, or one uses a fast approximate filter, e.g., an extended Kalman filter, to obtain a likelihood value for the nonlinear model. Using the surrogate likelihood, one can compute the acceptance probability α. For ϑ's rejected in this step, one never has to execute the time-consuming PF computations. If the proposed draw ϑ is accepted in the first stage, then a second randomization that requires the evaluation of the actual likelihood is necessary to determine whether $\theta^i = \vartheta$ or $\theta^i = \theta^{i-1}$. If the surrogate transition is well tailored, then the acceptance probability in the second step is high and the overall algorithm accelerates the posterior sampler by reducing the number of likelihood evaluations for poor proposals ϑ.

Chapter 10

Combining Particle Filters with SMC Samplers

Following recent work by Chopin, Jacob, and Papaspiliopoulos (2012), we now combine the SMC algorithm of Chapter 5 with the particle filter approximation of the likelihood function developed in Chapter 8 to develop an SMC^2 algorithm.

10.1 An SMC^2 Algorithm

As with the PFMH algorithm, our goal is to obtain a posterior sampler for the DSGE model parameters for settings in which the likelihood function of the DSGE model cannot be evaluated with the Kalman filter. The starting point is the SMC Algorithm 8. However, we make a number of modifications to our previous algorithm. Some of these modifications are important, others are merely made to simplify the exposition. First and foremost, we add data sequentially to the likelihood function rather than tempering the entire likelihood function: we consider the sequence of posteriors $\pi_n^D(\theta) = p(\theta|Y_{1:t_n})$, defined in (5.3), where $t_n = \lfloor \phi_n T \rfloor$. The advantage of using data tempering is that the particle filter can deliver an unbiased estimate of the incremental weight $p(Y_{t_{n-1}+1:t_n}|\theta)$ in the correction step—see Section 8.1.2—whereas the estimate of a concave transformation $p(Y_{1:T}|\theta)^{\phi_n - \phi_{n-1}}$ tends to be biased. Moreover, in general one has to evaluate the likelihood only for t_n observations instead of all T observations, which can speed up computations considerably.

Second, the evaluation of the incremental and the full likelihood function in the correction and mutation steps of Algorithm 8 are replaced by the evaluation of the respective particle filter approximations. Using the same notation as in (9.3), we write the particle approximations as

$$\hat{p}(y_{t_{n-1}+1:t_n}|Y_{1:t_{n-1}},\theta) = g(y_{t_{n-1}+1:t_n}|Y_{1:t_{n-1}},\theta,U_{1:t_n}),$$
$$\hat{p}(Y_{1:t_n}|\theta_n) = g(Y_{1:t_n}|\theta_n,U_{1:t_n}). \quad (10.1)$$

As before, $U_{1:t_n}$ is an array of *iid* uniform random variables generated by the particle filter with density $p(U_{1:t_n})$; see (9.4). The approximation of the likelihood increment also depends on the entire sequence $p(U_{1:t_n})$: the particle approximation of $p(s_{t_{n-1}+1}|Y_{1:t_{n-1}},\theta)$ is dependent on the approximation of $p(s_{t_{n-1}}|Y_{1:t_{n-1}},\theta)$. The distribution of $U_{1:t_n}$ neither depends on θ nor on $Y_{1:t_n}$ and can be factorized as

$$p(U_{1:t_n}) = p(U_{1:t_1})p(U_{t_1+1:t_2})\cdots p(U_{t_{n-1}+1:t_n}). \quad (10.2)$$

To describe the particle system, we follow the convention of Chapter 5 and index the parameter vector θ by the stage n of the SMC algorithm and write θ_n. The particles generated by the SMC sampler are indexed $i = 1, \ldots, N$ and the particles generated by the particle filter are indexed $j = 1, \ldots, M$. At stage n we have a particle system $\{\theta_n^i, W_n^i\}_{i=1}^N$ that represents the posterior distribution $p(\theta_n|Y_{1:t_n})$. Moreover, for each θ_n^i we have a particle system that represents the distribution $p(s_t|Y_{1:t_n},\theta_n^i)$. To distinguish the weights used for the particle values that represent the conditional distribution of θ_t from the weights used to characterize the conditional distribution of s_t, we denote the latter by $\mathcal{W}$ instead of W. Moreover, because the distribution of the states is conditional on the value of θ, we use i,j superscripts: $\{s_t^{i,j}, \mathcal{W}_t^{i,j}\}_{j=1}^M$. The particle system can be arranged in the matrix form given in Table 10.1.

Finally, to streamline the notation used in the description of the algorithm, we assume that during each stage n exactly one observation is added to the likelihood function. Thus, we can write θ_t instead of θ_n and $Y_{1:t}$ instead of $Y_{1:t_n}$ and the number of stages is $N_\phi = T$. Moreover, we resample the θ particles at every iteration of the algorithm (which means we do not have to keep track of the resampling indicator ρ_t) and we only use one MH step in the mutation phase.

Table 10.1: SMC^2 Particle System after Stage n

Parameter	State			
(θ_n^1, W_n^1)	$(s_{t_n}^{1,1}, \mathcal{W}_{t_n}^{1,1})$	$(s_{t_n}^{1,2}, \mathcal{W}_{t_n}^{1,2})$	$\cdots$	$(s_{t_n}^{1,M}, \mathcal{W}_{t_n}^{1,M})$
(θ_n^2, W_n^2)	$(s_{t_n}^{2,1}, \mathcal{W}_{t_n}^{2,1})$	$(s_{t_n}^{2,2}, \mathcal{W}_{t_n}^{2,2})$	$\cdots$	$(s_{t_n}^{2,M}, \mathcal{W}_{t_n}^{2,M})$
$\vdots$	$\vdots$	$\vdots$	$\ddots$	$\vdots$
(θ_n^N, W_n^N)	$(s_{t_n}^{N,1}, \mathcal{W}_{t_n}^{N,1})$	$(s_{t_n}^{N,2}, \mathcal{W}_{t_n}^{N,2})$	$\cdots$	$(s_{t_n}^{N,M}, \mathcal{W}_{t_n}^{N,M})$

Algorithm 19 (SMC^2)

1. **Initialization.** *Draw the initial particles from the prior:*
   $\theta_0^i \overset{iid}{\sim} p(\theta)$ *and* $W_0^i = 1$, $i = 1, \ldots, N$.

2. **Recursion.** *For* $t = 1, \ldots, T$,

   (a) **Correction.** *Reweight the particles from stage* $t - 1$
   by defining the incremental weights

   $$\tilde{w}_t^i = \hat{p}(y_t | Y_{1:t-1}, \theta_{t-1}^i) = g(y_t | Y_{1:t-1}, \theta_{t-1}^i, U_{1:t}^i)$$
   (10.3)

   and the normalized weights

   $$\tilde{W}_t^i = \frac{\tilde{w}_n^i W_{t-1}^i}{\frac{1}{N} \sum_{i=1}^{N} \tilde{w}_t^i W_{t-1}^i}, \quad i = 1, \ldots, N.$$
   (10.4)

   An approximation of $\mathbb{E}_{\pi_t}[h(\theta)]$ *is given by*

   $$\tilde{h}_{t,N} = \frac{1}{N} \sum_{i=1}^{N} \tilde{W}_t^i h(\theta_{t-1}^i).$$
   (10.5)

   (b) **Selection.** *Resample the particles via multinomial*
   resampling. Let $\{\hat{\theta}_t^i\}_{i=1}^{M}$ *denote* M *iid draws from*
   a multinomial distribution characterized by support
   points and weights $\{\theta_{t-1}^i, \tilde{W}_t^i\}_{j=1}^{M}$ *and set* $W_t^i =$
   1. *Define the vector of ancestors* $\mathcal{A}_t$ *with elements*
   $\mathcal{A}_t^i$ *by setting* $\mathcal{A}_t^i = k$ *if the ancestor of resampled*

particle i is particle k, that is, $\hat{\theta}_t^i = \theta_{t-1}^k$.
An approximation of $\mathbb{E}_{\pi_t}[h(\theta)]$ is given by

$$\hat{h}_{t,N} = \frac{1}{N} \sum_{j=1}^{N} W_t^i h(\hat{\theta}_t^i). \qquad (10.6)$$

(c) **Mutation.** *Propagate the particles $\{\hat{\theta}_t^i, W_t^i\}$ via 1 step of an MH algorithm. The proposal distribution is given by*

$$q(\vartheta_t^i | \hat{\theta}_t^i) p(U_{1:t}^{*i}) \qquad (10.7)$$

and the acceptance probability can be expressed as

$$\alpha(\vartheta_t^i | \hat{\theta}_t^i) = \min \left\{ 1, \ \frac{\hat{p}(Y_{1:t}|\vartheta_t^i) p(\vartheta_t^i)/q(\vartheta_t^i|\hat{\theta}_t^i)}{\hat{p}(Y_{1:t}|\hat{\theta}_t^i) p(\hat{\theta}_t^i)/q(\hat{\theta}_t^i|\vartheta_t^i)} \right\}. \qquad (10.8)$$

An approximation of $\mathbb{E}_{\pi_t}[h(\theta)]$ is given by

$$\bar{h}_{t,N} = \frac{1}{N} \sum_{i=1}^{N} h(\theta_t^i) W_t^i. \qquad (10.9)$$

3. *For $t = T$ the final importance sampling approximation of $\mathbb{E}_{\pi}[h(\theta)]$ is given by:*

$$\bar{h}_{T,N} = \sum_{i=1}^{N} h(\theta_T^i) W_T^i. \qquad (10.10)$$

A formal analysis of SMC^2 algorithms is provided in Chopin, Jacob, and Papaspiliopoulos (2012). We will provide a heuristic explanation of why the algorithm correctly approximates the target posterior distribution and comment on some aspects of the implementation. At the end of iteration $t-1$ the algorithm has generated particles $\{\theta_{t-1}^i, W_{t-1}^i\}_{i=1}^N$. For each parameter value θ_{t-1}^i there is also a particle filter approximation of the likelihood function $\hat{p}(Y_{1:t-1}|\theta_{t-1}^i)$, a swarm of particles $\{s_{t-1}^{i,j}, \mathcal{W}_{t-1}^{i,j}\}_{j=1}^M$ that represents the distribution $p(s_{t-1}|Y_{1:t-1}, \theta_{t-1}^i)$, and the sequence of random vectors $U_{1:t-1}^i$

that underlies the simulation approximation of the particle filter. To gain an understanding of the algorithm it is useful to focus on the triplets $\{\theta^i_{t-1}, U^i_{1:t-1}, W^i_{t-1}\}^N_{i=1}$. Suppose that

$$\int \int h(\theta, U_{1:t-1})p(U_{1:t-1})p(\theta|Y_{1:t-1})dU_{1:t-1}d\theta$$

$$\approx \frac{1}{N} \sum_{i=1}^{N} h(\theta^i_{t-1}, U^i_{1:t-1})W^i_{t-1}. \tag{10.11}$$

This implies that we obtain the familiar approximation for functions $h(\cdot)$ that do not depend on $U_{1:t-1}$

$$\int h(\theta)p(\theta|Y_{1:t-1})d\theta \approx \frac{1}{N} \sum_{i=1}^{N} h(\theta^i_{t-1})W^i_{t-1}. \tag{10.12}$$

Correction Step. The incremental likelihood $\hat{p}(y_t|Y_{1:t-1}, \theta^i_{t-1})$ can be evaluated by iterating the particle filter forward for one period, starting from $\{s^{i,j}_{t-1}, \mathcal{W}^{i,j}_{t-1}\}^M_{j=1}$. Using the notation in (10.1), the particle filter approximation of the likelihood increment can be written as

$$\hat{p}(y_t|Y_{1:t-1}, \theta^i_{t-1}) = g(y_t|Y_{1:t-1}, U^i_{1:t}, \theta^i_{t-1}). \tag{10.13}$$

The value of the likelihood function for $Y_{1:t}$ can be tracked recursively as follows:

$$\begin{aligned}
\hat{p}(Y_{1:t}|\theta^i_{t-1}) &= \hat{p}(y_t|Y_{1:t-1}, \theta^i_{t-1})\hat{p}(Y_{1:t-1}|\theta^i_{t-1}) \tag{10.14}\\
&= g(y_t|Y_{1:t}, U^i_{1:t}, \theta^i_{t-1})g(Y_{1:t-1}|U^i_{1:t-1}, \theta^i_{t-1})\\
&= g(Y_{1:t}|U^i_{1:t}, \theta^i_{t-1}).
\end{aligned}$$

The last equality follows because conditioning the density $g(Y_{1:t-1}|U^i_{1:t-1}, \theta^i_{t-1})$ also on U_t does not change the particle filter approximation of the likelihood function for $Y_{1:t-1}$.

By induction, we can deduce from (10.11) that the Monte Carlo average $\frac{1}{N}\sum_{i=1}^{N} h(\theta^i_{t-1})\tilde{w}^i_t W^i_{t-1}$ approximates the following integral:

$$\int \int h(\theta)g(y_t|Y_{1:t-1}, U_{1:t}, \theta)p(U_{1:t})p(\theta|Y_{1:t-1})dU_{1:t}d\theta$$

$$= \int h(\theta) \left[\int g(y_t|Y_{1:t-1}, U_{1:t}, \theta)p(U_{1:t})dU_{1:t} \right]$$

$$\times p(\theta|Y_{1:t-1})d\theta.$$

Provided that the particle filter approximation of the likelihood increment is unbiased, that is,

$$\int g(y_t|Y_{1:t-1}, U_{1:t}, \theta)p(U_{1:t})dU_{1:t} = p(y_t|Y_{1:t-1}, \theta) \quad (10.15)$$

for each θ, we deduce that $\tilde{h}_{t,N}$ is a consistent estimator of $\mathbb{E}_{\pi_t}[h(\theta)]$.

Selection Step. The selection step Algorithm 19 is very similar to Algorithm 8. To simplify the description of the SMC^2 algorithm, we are resampling in every iteration. Moreover, we are keeping track of the ancestry information in the vector $\mathcal{A}_t$. This is important, because for each resampled particle i we not only need to know its value $\hat{\theta}_t^i$ but we also want to track the corresponding value of the likelihood function $\hat{p}(Y_{1:t}|\hat{\theta}_t^i)$ as well as the particle approximation of the state, given by $\{s_t^{i,j}, W_t^{i,j}\}$, and the set of random numbers $U_{1:t}^i$. In the implementation of the algorithm, the likelihood values are needed for the mutation step and the state particles are useful for a quick evaluation of the incremental likelihood in the correction step of iteration $t+1$ (see above). The $U_{1:t}^i$'s are not required for the actual implementation of the algorithm but are useful to provide a heuristic explanation for the validity of the algorithm.

Mutation Step. The mutation step essentially consists of one iteration of the PFMH algorithm described in Section 9.1. For each particle i there is a proposed value ϑ_t^i, an associated particle filter approximation $\hat{p}(Y_{1:t}|\vartheta_t^i)$ of the likelihood, and a sequence of random vectors $U_{1:t}^*$ drawn from the distribution $p(U_{1:t})$ in (10.2). As in (9.8), the densities $p(U_{1:t}^i)$ and $p(U_{1:t}^*)$ cancel from the formula for the acceptance probability $\alpha(\vartheta_t^i|\hat{\theta}_t^i)$. For the implementation it is important to record the likelihood value as well as the particle system for the state s_t for each particle θ_t^i.

10.2   Application to the Small-Scale DSGE Model

We now present an application of the SMC^2 algorithm to the small-scale DSGE model. The results in this section can be compared to the results obtained in Section 9.2. Because the SMC^2 algorithm requires an unbiased approximation of the likelihood function, we will use data tempering instead of likelihood tempering as in Section 5.3. Overall, we compare the output of four algorithms: SMC^2 based on the conditionally optimal PF; SMC^2 based on the bootstrap PF; SMC based on the Kalman filter likelihood function using data tempering; and SMC based on the Kalman filter likelihood function using likelihood tempering. In order to approximate the likelihood function with the particle filter, we are using $M = 40,000$ particles for the bootstrap PF and $M = 400$ particles for the conditionally optimal PF. The approximation of the posterior distribution is based on $N = 4,000$ particles for θ, $N_\phi = T + 1 = 81$ stages under data tempering, and $N_{blocks} = 3$ blocks for the mutation step.

Table 10.2 summarizes the results from running each algorithm $N_{run} = 20$ times. We report pooled posterior means from the output of the 20 runs as well as inefficiency factors $\text{InEff}_N(\bar{\theta})$ and the standard deviation of the posterior mean approximations across the 20 runs. The results in the column labeled KF(L) are based on the Kalman filter likelihood evaluation and obtained from the same algorithm that was used in Section 5.3. The results in column KF(D) are also based on the Kalman filter, but the SMC algorithm uses data tempering instead of likelihood tempering. The columns CO-PF and BS-BF contain SMC^2 results based on the conditionally optimal and the bootstrap PF, respectively. The pooled means of the DSGE model parameters computed from output of the KF(L), KF(D), and CO-PF algorithms are essentially identical. The log marginal data density approximations are less accurate than the posterior mean approximations and vary for the first three algorithms from -358.75 to -356.33.

A comparison of the standard deviations and the inefficiency factors indicates that moving from likelihood tempering to data tempering leads to a deterioration of accuracy. For instance, the standard deviation of the log marginal data den-

Table 10.2: Small-Scale Model: SMC^2 Accuracy

	Posterior Mean (Pooled)				Inefficiency Factors				Std. Dev. of Means			
	KF(L)	KF(D)	CO-PF	BS-PF	KF(L)	KF(D)	CO-PF	BS-PF	KF(L)	KF(D)	CO-PF	BS-PF
τ	2.65	2.67	2.68	2.53	1.51	10.41	47.60	6570	0.01	0.03	0.07	0.76
κ	0.81	0.81	0.81	0.70	1.40	8.36	40.60	7223	0.00	0.01	0.01	0.18
ψ_1	1.87	1.88	1.87	1.89	3.29	18.27	22.56	4785	0.01	0.01	0.02	0.27
ψ_2	0.66	0.66	0.67	0.65	2.72	10.02	43.30	4197	0.01	0.02	0.03	0.34
ρ_r	0.75	0.75	0.75	0.72	1.31	11.39	60.18	14979	0.00	0.01	0.01	0.08
ρ_g	0.98	0.98	0.98	0.95	1.32	4.28	250.34	21736	0.00	0.00	0.00	0.04
ρ_z	0.88	0.88	0.88	0.84	3.16	15.06	35.35	10802	0.00	0.00	0.00	0.05
$r^{(A)}$	0.45	0.46	0.44	0.46	1.09	26.58	73.78	7971	0.00	0.02	0.04	0.42
$\pi^{(A)}$	3.32	3.31	3.31	3.56	2.15	40.45	158.64	6529	0.01	0.03	0.06	0.40
$\gamma^{(Q)}$	0.59	0.59	0.59	0.64	2.35	32.35	133.25	5296	0.01	0.03	0.06	0.16
σ_r	0.24	0.24	0.24	0.26	0.75	7.29	43.96	16084	0.00	0.01	0.03	0.06
σ_g	0.68	0.68	0.68	0.73	1.30	1.48	20.20	5098	0.00	0.00	0.00	0.08
σ_z	0.32	0.32	0.32	0.42	2.32	3.63	26.98	41284	0.00	0.00	0.00	0.11
$\ln p(Y)$	−358.75	−357.34	−356.33	−340.47					0.120	1.191	4.374	14.49

Notes: Results are based on $N_{run} = 20$ runs of the SMC^2 algorithm with $N = 4,000$ particles. D is data tempering and L is likelihood tempering. KF is Kalman filter. CO-PF is conditionally optimal PF with $M = 400$. BS-PF is bootstrap PF with $M = 40,000$. CO-PF and BS-PF use data tempering.

sity increases from 0.12 to 1.19. As discussed in Section 5.3 in DSGE model applications it is important to use a convex tempering schedule that adds very little likelihood information in the initial stages. The implied tempering schedule of our sequential estimation procedure is linear and adds a full observation in stage $n = 1$ (recall that $n = 0$ corresponds to sampling from the prior distribution). Replacing the Kalman filter evaluation of the likelihood function by the conditionally optimal particle filter increases the standard deviations further. Compared to KF(D) the standard deviations of the posterior mean approximations increase by factors ranging from 1.5 to 5. The inefficiency factors for the KF(D) algorithm range from 1.5 to 40, whereas they range from 20 to 250 for CO-PF. A comparison with Table 9.1 indicates that the SMC algorithm is more sensitive to the switch from the Kalman filter likelihood to the particle filter approximation. Using the conditionally optimal particle filter, there seems to be no deterioration in accuracy of the RWMH algorithm. Finally, replacing the conditionally optimal PF by the bootstrap PF leads to an additional deterioration in accuracy. Compared to KF(D) the standard deviations for the BS-PF approach are an order of magnitude larger and the smallest inefficiency factor is 4,200. Nonetheless, the pooled posterior means are fairly close to those obtained from the other three algorithms.

10.3 Computational Considerations

The SMC^2 results reported in Table 10.2 are obtained by utilizing forty processors. We parallelized the likelihood evaluations $\hat{p}(Y_{1:t}|\theta_t^i)$ for the θ_t^i particles rather than the particle filter computations for the swarms $\{s_t^{i,j}, \mathcal{W}_t^{i,j}\}_{j=1}^M$. The likelihood evaluations are computationally costly and do not require communication across processors. The run time for the SMC^2 with conditionally optimal PF ($N = 4,000$, $M = 400$) is 23:24 [mm:ss] minutes, whereas the algorithm with bootstrap PF ($N = 4,000$ and $M = 40,000$) runs for 08:05:35 [hh:mm:ss] hours. The bootstrap PF performs poorly in terms of accuracy and run time.

After running the particle filter for the sample $Y_{1:t-1}$ one could in principle save the particle swarm for the final state

s_{t-1} for each θ_t^i. In the period t forecasting step, this information can then be used to quickly evaluate the likelihood increment. In our experience with the small-scale DSGE model, the sheer memory size of the objects (in the range of 10–20 gigabytes) precluded us from saving the $t-1$ state particle swarms in a distributed parallel environment in which memory transfers are costly. Instead, we re-computed the entire likelihood for $Y_{1:t}$ in each iteration.

Our sequential (data-tempering) implementation of the SMC^2 algorithm suffers from particle degeneracy in the initial stages, i.e., for small sample sizes. Instead of initially sampling from the prior distribution, one could initialize the algorithm by using an importance sampler with a student-t proposal distribution that approximates the posterior distribution obtained conditional on a small set of observations, e.g., $Y_{1:2}$ or $Y_{1:5}$, as suggested in Creal (2007).

Appendix A

Model Descriptions

A.1 Smets-Wouters Model

The log-linearized equilibrium conditions of the Smets and Wouters (2007) model take the following form:

$$\hat{y}_t = c_y \hat{c}_t + i_y \hat{i}_t + z_y \hat{z}_t + \varepsilon_t^g \tag{A.1}$$

$$\hat{c}_t = \frac{h/\gamma}{1+h/\gamma} \hat{c}_{t-1} + \frac{1}{1+h/\gamma} \mathbb{E}_t \hat{c}_{t+1} \tag{A.2}$$
$$+ \frac{wl_c(\sigma_c - 1)}{\sigma_c(1+h/\gamma)} (\hat{l}_t - \mathbb{E}_t \hat{l}_{t+1})$$
$$- \frac{1-h/\gamma}{(1+h/\gamma)\sigma_c} (\hat{r}_t - \mathbb{E}_t \hat{\pi}_{t+1}) - \frac{1-h/\gamma}{(1+h/\gamma)\sigma_c} \varepsilon_t^b$$

$$\hat{i}_t = \frac{1}{1+\beta\gamma^{(1-\sigma_c)}} \hat{i}_{t-1} + \frac{\beta\gamma^{(1-\sigma_c)}}{1+\beta\gamma^{(1-\sigma_c)}} \mathbb{E}_t \hat{i}_{t+1} \tag{A.3}$$
$$+ \frac{1}{\varphi\gamma^2(1+\beta\gamma^{(1-\sigma_c)})} \hat{q}_t + \varepsilon_t^i$$

$$\hat{q}_t = \beta(1-\delta)\gamma^{-\sigma_c} \mathbb{E}_t \hat{q}_{t+1} - \hat{r}_t + \mathbb{E}_t \hat{\pi}_{t+1} \tag{A.4}$$
$$+ (1 - \beta(1-\delta)\gamma^{-\sigma_c}) \mathbb{E}_t \hat{r}_{t+1}^k - \varepsilon_t^b$$

$$\hat{y}_t = \Phi(\alpha \hat{k}_t^s + (1-\alpha)\hat{l}_t + \varepsilon_t^a) \tag{A.5}$$

$$\hat{k}_t^s = \hat{k}_{t-1} + \hat{z}_t \tag{A.6}$$

$$\hat{z}_t = \frac{1-\psi}{\psi} \hat{r}_t^k \tag{A.7}$$

$$\hat{k}_t = \frac{(1-\delta)}{\gamma}\hat{k}_{t-1} + (1 - (1-\delta)/\gamma)\hat{i}_t \tag{A.8}$$
$$+(1 - (1-\delta)/\gamma)\varphi\gamma^2(1 + \beta\gamma^{(1-\sigma_c)})\varepsilon_t^i$$

$$\hat{\mu}_t^p = \alpha(\hat{k}_t^s - \hat{l}_t) - \hat{w}_t + \varepsilon_t^a \tag{A.9}$$

$$\hat{\pi}_t = \frac{\beta\gamma^{(1-\sigma_c)}}{1 + \iota_p\beta\gamma^{(1-\sigma_c)}}\mathbb{E}_t\hat{\pi}_{t+1} + \frac{\iota_p}{1 + \beta\gamma^{(1-\sigma_c)}}\hat{\pi}_{t-1} \tag{A.10}$$
$$-\frac{(1 - \beta\gamma^{(1-\sigma_c)}\xi_p)(1 - \xi_p)}{(1 + \iota_p\beta\gamma^{(1-\sigma_c)})(1 + (\Phi - 1)\varepsilon_p)\xi_p}\hat{\mu}_t^p + \varepsilon_t^p$$

$$\hat{r}_t^k = \hat{l}_t + \hat{w}_t - \hat{k}_t^s \tag{A.11}$$

$$\hat{\mu}_t^w = \hat{w}_t - \sigma_l\hat{l}_t - \frac{1}{1 - h/\gamma}(\hat{c}_t - h/\gamma\hat{c}_{t-1}) \tag{A.12}$$

$$\hat{w}_t = \frac{\beta\gamma^{(1-\sigma_c)}}{1 + \beta\gamma^{(1-\sigma_c)}}(\mathbb{E}_t\hat{w}_{t+1} \tag{A.13}$$
$$+\mathbb{E}_t\hat{\pi}_{t+1}) + \frac{1}{1 + \beta\gamma^{(1-\sigma_c)}}(\hat{w}_{t-1} - \iota_w\hat{\pi}_{t-1})$$
$$-\frac{1 + \beta\gamma^{(1-\sigma_c)}\iota_w}{1 + \beta\gamma^{(1-\sigma_c)}}\hat{\pi}_t$$
$$-\frac{(1 - \beta\gamma^{(1-\sigma_c)}\xi_w)(1 - \xi_w)}{(1 + \beta\gamma^{(1-\sigma_c)})(1 + (\lambda_w - 1)\epsilon_w)\xi_w}\hat{\mu}_t^w + \varepsilon_t^w$$

$$\hat{r}_t = \rho\hat{r}_{t-1} + (1 - \rho)(r_\pi\hat{\pi}_t + r_y(\hat{y}_t - \hat{y}_t^*)) \tag{A.14}$$
$$+r_{\Delta y}((\hat{y}_t - \hat{y}_t^*) - (\hat{y}_{t-1} - \hat{y}_{t-1}^*)) + \varepsilon_t^r.$$

The exogenous shocks evolve according to

$$\varepsilon_t^a = \rho_a\varepsilon_{t-1}^a + \eta_t^a \tag{A.15}$$
$$\varepsilon_t^b = \rho_b\varepsilon_{t-1}^b + \eta_t^b \tag{A.16}$$
$$\varepsilon_t^g = \rho_g\varepsilon_{t-1}^g + \rho_{ga}\eta_t^a + \eta_t^g \tag{A.17}$$
$$\varepsilon_t^i = \rho_i\varepsilon_{t-1}^i + \eta_t^i \tag{A.18}$$
$$\varepsilon_t^r = \rho_r\varepsilon_{t-1}^r + \eta_t^r \tag{A.19}$$
$$\varepsilon_t^p = \rho_r\varepsilon_{t-1}^p + \eta_t^p - \mu_p\eta_{t-1}^p \tag{A.20}$$
$$\varepsilon_t^w = \rho_w\varepsilon_{t-1}^w + \eta_t^w - \mu_w\eta_{t-1}^w. \tag{A.21}$$

The counterfactual no-rigidity prices and quantities evolve according to

$$\hat{y}_t^* = c_y\hat{c}_t^* + i_y\hat{i}_t^* + z_y\hat{z}_t^* + \varepsilon_t^g \tag{A.22}$$

$$\hat{c}_t^* = \frac{h/\gamma}{1+h/\gamma}\hat{c}_{t-1}^* + \frac{1}{1+h/\gamma}\mathbb{E}_t\hat{c}_{t+1}^* \tag{A.23}$$
$$+\frac{wl_c(\sigma_c-1)}{\sigma_c(1+h/\gamma)}(\hat{l}_t^* - \mathbb{E}_t\hat{l}_{t+1}^*)$$
$$-\frac{1-h/\gamma}{(1+h/\gamma)\sigma_c}r_t^* - \frac{1-h/\gamma}{(1+h/\gamma)\sigma_c}\varepsilon_t^b$$

$$\hat{i}_t^* = \frac{1}{1+\beta\gamma^{(1-\sigma_c)}}\hat{i}_{t-1}^* + \frac{\beta\gamma^{(1-\sigma_c)}}{1+\beta\gamma^{(1-\sigma_c)}}\mathbb{E}_t\hat{i}_{t+1}^*$$
$$+\frac{1}{\varphi\gamma^2(1+\beta\gamma^{(1-\sigma_c)})}\hat{q}_t^* + \varepsilon_t^i \tag{A.24}$$

$$\hat{q}_t^* = \beta(1-\delta)\gamma^{-\sigma_c}\mathbb{E}_t\hat{q}_{t+1}^* - r_t^* \tag{A.25}$$
$$+(1-\beta(1-\delta)\gamma^{-\sigma_c})\mathbb{E}_t r_{t+1}^{k*} - \varepsilon_t^b$$

$$\hat{y}_t^* = \Phi(\alpha k_t^{s*} + (1-\alpha)\hat{l}_t^* + \varepsilon_t^a) \tag{A.26}$$

$$\hat{k}_t^{s*} = k_{t-1}^* + z_t^* \tag{A.27}$$

$$\hat{z}_t^* = \frac{1-\psi}{\psi}\hat{r}_t^{k*} \tag{A.28}$$

$$\hat{k}_t^* = \frac{(1-\delta)}{\gamma}\hat{k}_{t-1}^* + (1-(1-\delta)/\gamma)\hat{i}_t \tag{A.29}$$
$$+(1-(1-\delta)/\gamma)\varphi\gamma^2(1+\beta\gamma^{(1-\sigma_c)})\varepsilon_t^i$$

$$\hat{w}_t^* = \alpha(\hat{k}_t^{s*} - \hat{l}_t^*) + \varepsilon_t^a \tag{A.30}$$

$$\hat{r}_t^{k*} = \hat{l}_t^* + \hat{w}_t^* - \hat{k}_t^* \tag{A.31}$$

$$\hat{w}_t^* = \sigma_l\hat{l}_t^* + \frac{1}{1-h/\gamma}(\hat{c}_t^* + h/\gamma\hat{c}_{t-1}^*). \tag{A.32}$$

The steady state (ratios) that appear in the measurement equation or the log-linearized equilibrium conditions are given by

$$\gamma = \bar{\gamma}/100 + 1 \tag{A.33}$$

$$\pi^* = \bar{\pi}/100 + 1 \tag{A.34}$$

$$\bar{r} = 100(\beta^{-1}\gamma^{\sigma_c}\pi^* - 1) \tag{A.35}$$

$$r_{ss}^k = \gamma^{\sigma_c}/\beta - (1 - \delta) \tag{A.36}$$

$$w_{ss} = \left(\frac{\alpha^\alpha(1-\alpha)^{(1-\alpha)}}{\Phi r_{ss}^k{}^\alpha}\right)^{\frac{1}{1-\alpha}} \tag{A.37}$$

$$i_k = (1 - (1 - \delta)/\gamma)\gamma \tag{A.38}$$

$$l_k = \frac{1-\alpha}{\alpha}\frac{r_{ss}^k}{w_{ss}} \tag{A.39}$$

$$k_y = \Phi l_k^{(\alpha-1)} \tag{A.40}$$

$$i_y = (\gamma - 1 + \delta)k_y \tag{A.41}$$

$$c_y = 1 - g_y - i_y \tag{A.42}$$

$$z_y = r_{ss}^k k_y \tag{A.43}$$

$$wl_c = \frac{1}{\lambda_w}\frac{1-\alpha}{\alpha}\frac{r_{ss}^k k_y}{c_y}. \tag{A.44}$$

The measurement equations take the form:

$$YGR_t = \bar{\gamma} + \hat{y}_t - \hat{y}_{t-1} \tag{A.45}$$

$$INF_t = \bar{\pi} + \hat{\pi}_t$$

$$FFR_t = \bar{r} + \hat{R}_t$$

$$CGR_t = \bar{\gamma} + \hat{c}_t - \hat{c}_{t-1}$$

$$IGR_t = \bar{\gamma} + \hat{i}_t - \hat{i}_{t-1}$$

$$WGR_t = \bar{\gamma} + \hat{w}_t - \hat{w}_{t-1}$$

$$HOURS_t = \bar{l} + \hat{l}_t.$$

Table A-1: SW Model: Diffuse Prior

	Type	Para (1)	Para (2)		Type	Para (1)	Para (2)
φ	N	4.00	4.50	α	N	0.30	0.15
σ_c	N	1.50	1.11	ρ_a	U	0.00	1.00
h	U	0.00	1.00	ρ_b	U	0.00	1.00
ξ_w	U	0.00	1.00	ρ_g	U	0.00	1.00
σ_l	N	2.00	2.25	ρ_i	U	0.00	1.00
ξ_p	U	0.00	1.00	ρ_r	U	0.00	1.00
ι_w	U	0.00	1.00	ρ_p	U	0.00	1.00
ι_p	U	0.00	1.00	ρ_w	U	0.00	1.00
ψ	U	0.00	1.00	μ_p	U	0.00	1.00
Φ	N	1.25	0.36	μ_w	U	0.00	1.00
r_π	N	1.50	0.75	ρ_{ga}	U	0.00	1.00
ρ	U	0.00	1.00	σ_a	IG	0.10	2.00
r_y	N	0.12	0.15	σ_b	IG	0.10	2.00
$r_{\Delta y}$	N	0.12	0.15	σ_g	IG	0.10	2.00
π	G	0.62	0.30	σ_i	IG	0.10	2.00
$\tilde{\beta}$	G	0.25	0.30	σ_r	IG	0.10	2.00
l	N	0.00	6.00	σ_p	IG	0.10	2.00
γ	N	0.40	0.30	σ_w	IG	0.10	2.00

Notes: $\tilde{\beta} = 100(\beta^{-1} - 1)$. Para (1) and Para (2) correspond to the mean and standard deviation of the Beta (B), Gamma (G), and Normal (N) distributions and to the upper and lower bounds of the support for the Uniform (U) distribution. For the Inv. Gamma (IG) distribution, Para (1) and Para (2) refer to s and ν, where $p(\sigma|\nu, s) \propto \sigma^{-\nu-1}e^{-\nu s^2/2\sigma^2}$. The following parameters are fixed during the estimation: $\delta = 0.025$, $g_y = 0.18$, $\lambda_w = 1.50$, $\varepsilon_w = 10.0$, and $\varepsilon_p = 10$.

Table A-2: SW Model: Original Prior

	Type	Para (1)	Para (2)		Type	Para (1)	Para (2)
φ	N	4.00	1.50	α	N	0.30	0.05
σ_c	N	1.50	0.37	ρ_a	B	0.50	0.20
h	B	0.70	0.10	ρ_b	B	0.50	0.20
ξ_w	B	0.50	0.10	ρ_g	B	0.50	0.20
σ_l	N	2.00	0.75	ρ_i	B	0.50	0.20
ξ_p	B	0.50	0.10	ρ_r	B	0.50	0.20
ι_w	B	0.50	0.15	ρ_p	B	0.50	0.20
ι_p	B	0.50	0.15	ρ_w	B	0.50	0.20
ψ	B	0.50	0.15	μ_p	B	0.50	0.20
Φ	N	1.25	0.12	μ_w	B	0.50	0.20
r_π	N	1.50	0.25	ρ_{ga}	B	0.50	0.20
ρ	B	0.75	0.10	σ_a	IG	0.10	2.00
r_y	N	0.12	0.05	σ_b	IG	0.10	2.00
$r_{\Delta y}$	N	0.12	0.05	σ_g	IG	0.10	2.00
π	G	0.62	0.10	σ_i	IG	0.10	2.00
$\tilde{\beta}$	G	0.25	0.10	σ_r	IG	0.10	2.00
l	N	0.00	2.00	σ_p	IG	0.10	2.00
γ	N	0.40	0.10	σ_w	IG	0.10	2.00

Notes: $\tilde{\beta} = 100(\beta^{-1} - 1)$. Para (1) and Para (2) correspond to the mean and standard deviation of the Beta (B), Gamma (G), and Normal (N) distributions and to the upper and lower bounds of the support for the Uniform (U) distribution. For the Inv. Gamma (IG) distribution, Para (1) and Para (2) refer to s and ν, where $p(\sigma|\nu, s) \propto \sigma^{-\nu-1} e^{-\nu s^2/2\sigma^2}$.

A.2   Leeper-Plante-Traum Fiscal Policy Model

The log-linearized equilibrium conditions of the Leeper, Plante, and Traum (2010) are given by:

$$\hat{u}_t^b - \frac{\gamma(1+h)}{1-h}\hat{C}_t + \frac{\gamma h}{1-h}\hat{C}_{t-1} - \frac{\tau^c}{1+\tau^c}\hat{\tau}_t^c \tag{A.46}$$

$$= \hat{R}_t - \frac{\tau^c}{1+\tau^c}\mathbb{E}_t\hat{\tau}_{t+1}^c + \mathbb{E}_t u_{t+1}^b - \frac{\gamma}{1-h}\mathbb{E}_t\hat{C}_{t+1}$$

$$\hat{u}_t^l + (1+\kappa)\hat{l}_t + \frac{\tau^c}{1+\tau^c}\hat{\tau}_t^c \tag{A.47}$$

$$= \hat{Y}_t - \frac{\tau^l}{1+\tau^l}\hat{\tau}_t^l - \frac{\gamma}{1-h}\hat{C}_t + \frac{\gamma h}{1-h}\hat{C}_{t-1}$$

$$\hat{q}_t = \mathbb{E}_t\hat{u}_{t+1}^b - \frac{\gamma}{1-h}\mathbb{E}_t\hat{C}_{t+1} + \frac{\gamma(1+h)}{1-h}\hat{C}_t \tag{A.48}$$

$$- \frac{\tau^c}{1+\tau^c}\mathbb{E}_t\tau_{t+1}^c - \hat{u}_t^b - \frac{\gamma h}{1-h}\hat{C}_{t-1}$$

$$+ \frac{\tau^c}{1+\tau^c}\hat{\tau}_t^c + \beta(1-\tau^k)\alpha\frac{Y}{K}\mathbb{E}_t\hat{Y}_{t+1}$$

$$- \beta(1-\tau^k)\alpha\frac{Y}{K}\hat{K}_t - \beta\tau^k\alpha\frac{Y}{K}\mathbb{E}_t\hat{\tau}_{t+1}^k$$

$$- \beta\delta_1\mathbb{E}_t\hat{\nu}_{t+1} + \beta(1-\delta_0)E_t\hat{q}_{t+1}$$

$$Y_t = \frac{\tau^k}{1-\tau^k}\hat{\tau}_t^k + \hat{K}_{t+1} + \hat{q}_t + \left(1+\frac{\delta_2}{\delta_0}\right)\hat{\nu}_t \tag{A.49}$$

$$0 = \frac{1}{s''(1)}\hat{q}_t + (1-\beta)\hat{I}_t + \hat{I}_{t-1} + \beta\mathbb{E}_t\hat{u}_t^i \tag{A.50}$$

$$+ \beta\mathbb{E}_t\hat{u}_{t+1}^i$$

$$Y\hat{Y}_t = C\hat{C}_t + G\hat{G}_t + I\hat{I}_t \tag{A.51}$$

$$\hat{K}_t = (1-\delta_0)K_{t-1} + \delta_1\hat{\nu}_t + \delta_0 I_t \tag{A.52}$$

$$\frac{B}{\beta}\hat{R}_{t-1} + \frac{B}{\beta}\hat{B}_{t-1} + G\hat{G}_t + Z\hat{Z}_t \tag{A.53}$$

$$= B\hat{B}_t + \tau^k\alpha Y(\hat{\tau}_t^k + \hat{Y}_t) + \tau^l(1-\alpha)Y(\hat{\tau}_t^l + \hat{Y}_t)$$

$$+ \tau^c C(\hat{\tau}_t^c + \hat{C}_t)$$

$$\hat{Y}_t = \hat{u}_t^a + \alpha\nu_t + \alpha\hat{K}_{t-1} + (1-\alpha)\hat{L}_t. \tag{A.54}$$

The fiscal policy rules and the law of motion of the exogenous shock processes are provided in the main text (Section 6.3).

Table A-3: LPT Model: Posterior Moments (Part 2)

	Based on LPT Prior		Based on Diff. Prior	
	Mean	[5%, 95%] Int.	Mean	[5%, 95%] Int.
Endogenous Propagation Parameters				
γ	2.5	[1.82, 3.35]	2.5	[1.81, 3.31]
κ	2.4	[1.70, 3.31]	2.5	[1.74, 3.37]
h	0.57	[0.46, 0.68]	0.57	[0.46, 0.67]
s''	7.0	[6.08, 7.98]	6.9	[6.06, 7.89]
δ_2	0.25	[0.16, 0.39]	0.24	[0.16, 0.37]
Endogenous Propagation Parameters				
ρ_a	0.96	[0.93, 0.98]	0.96	[0.93, 0.98]
ρ_b	0.65	[0.60, 0.69]	0.65	[0.60, 0.69]
ρ_l	0.98	[0.96, 1.00]	0.98	[0.96, 1.00]
ρ_i	0.48	[0.38, 0.57]	0.47	[0.37, 0.57]
ρ_g	0.96	[0.94, 0.98]	0.96	[0.94, 0.98]
ρ_{tk}	0.93	[0.89, 0.97]	0.94	[0.88, 0.98]
ρ_{tl}	0.98	[0.95, 1.00]	0.93	[0.86, 0.98]
ρ_{tc}	0.93	[0.89, 0.97]	0.97	[0.94, 0.99]
ρ_z	0.95	[0.91, 0.98]	0.95	[0.91, 0.98]
σ_b	7.2	[6.48, 8.02]	7.2	[6.47, 8.00]
σ_l	3.2	[2.55, 4.10]	3.2	[2.55, 4.08]
σ_i	5.7	[4.98, 6.47]	5.6	[4.98, 6.40]
σ_a	0.64	[0.59, 0.70]	0.64	[0.59, 0.70]

Appendix B

Data Sources

B.1 Small-Scale New Keynesian DSGE Model

The data from the estimation comes from Lubik and Schorfheide (2006). Here we detail the construction of the extended
sample (2003:I to 2013:IV) for Section 8.6.

1. **Per Capita Real Output Growth** Take the level of real
   gross domestic product, (FRED mnemonic "GDPC1"),
   call it GDP_t. Take the quarterly average of the Civilian
   Non-institutional Population (FRED mnemonic "CNP16OV"
   / BLS series "LNS10000000"), call it POP_t. Then,

   Per Capita Real Output Growth
   $$= 100 \left[\ln \left(\frac{GDP_t}{POP_t} \right) - \ln \left(\frac{GDP_{t-1}}{POP_{t-1}} \right) \right].$$

2. **Annualized Inflation.** Take the CPI price level, (FRED
   mnemonic "CPIAUCSL"), call it CPI_t. Then,

   $$\text{Annualized Inflation} = 400 \ln \left(\frac{CPI_t}{CPI_{t-1}} \right).$$

3. **Federal Funds Rate.** Take the effective federal funds
   rate (FRED mnemonic "FEDFUNDS"), call it FFR_t. Then,

   $$\text{Federal Funds Rate} = FFR_t.$$

B.2 Smets-Wouters Model

The data cover 1966:Q1 to 2004:Q4. The construction follows
that of Smets and Wouters (2007). Output data come from the
NIPA; other sources are noted in the exposition.

1. **Per Capita Real Output Growth.** Take the level of real gross domestic product (FRED mnemonic "GDPC1"), call it GDP_t. Take the quarterly average of the Civilian Non-institutional Population (FRED mnemonic "CNP16OV" / BLS series "LNS10000000"), normalized so that its 1992Q3 value is 1, call it POP_t. Then,

   Per Capita Real Output Growth
   $$= \quad 100 \left[\ln \left(\frac{GDP_t}{POP_t} \right) - \ln \left(\frac{GDP_{t-1}}{POP_{t-1}} \right) \right].$$

2. **Per Capita Real Consumption Growth.** Take the level of personal consumption expenditures (FRED mnemonic "PCEC"), call it $CONS_t$. Take the level of the GDP price deflator (FRED mnemonic "GDPDEF"), call it $GDPP_t$. Then,

   Per Capita Real Consumption Growth
   $$= \quad 100 \left[\ln \left(\frac{CONS_t}{GDPP_t POP_t} \right) \right.$$
   $$\left. - \ln \left(\frac{CONS_{t-1}}{GDPP_{t-1} POP_{t-1}} \right) \right].$$

3. **Per Capita Real Investment Growth.** Take the level of fixed private investment (FRED mnemonic "FPI"), call it INV_t. Then,

   Per Capita Real Investment Growth
   $$= \quad 100 \left[\ln \left(\frac{INV_t}{GDPP_t POP_t} \right) \right.$$
   $$\left. - \ln \left(\frac{INV_{t-1}}{GDPP_{t-1} POP_{t-1}} \right) \right].$$

4. **Per Capita Real Wage Growth.** Take the BLS measure of compensation per hour for the nonfarm business sector (FRED mnemonic "COMPNFB" / BLS series "PRS85006103"), call it W_t. Then,

   Per Capita Real Wage Growth
   $$= \quad 100 \left[\ln \left(\frac{W_t}{GDPP_t} \right) - \ln \left(\frac{W_{t-1}}{GDPP_{t-1}} \right) \right].$$

5. **Per Capita Hours Index.** Take the index of average weekly nonfarm business hours (FRED mnemonic / BLS series "PRS85006023"), call it $HOURS_t$. Take the number of employed civilians (FRED mnemonic "CE16OV"), normalized so that its 1992Q3 value is 1, call it EMP_t. Then,

$$\text{Per Capita Hours} = 100\ln\left(\frac{HOURS_t EMP_t}{POP_t}\right).$$

The series is then demeaned.

6. **Inflation.** Take the GDP price deflator, then,

$$\text{Inflation} = 100\ln\left(\frac{GDPP_t}{GDPP_{t-1}}\right).$$

7. **Federal Funds Rate.** Take the effective federal funds rate (FRED mnemonic "FEDFUNDS"), call it FFR_t. Then,

$$\text{Federal Funds Rate} = FFR_t/4.$$

B.3   Leeper-Plante-Traum Fiscal Policy Model

The data cover 1960:Q1 to 2008:Q1. The construction follows that of Leeper, Plante, and Traum (2010). Output data come from the NIPA; other sources are noted in the exposition. Each series has a (seperate) linear trend removed prior to estimation.

1. **Real Investment.** Take nominal personal consumption on durable goods (FRED mnemonic "PCDG"), call it $PCED_t$ and deflate it by the GDP deflator for personal consumption (FRED mnemonic "DPCERD3Q086SBEA"), call it P_t. Take the number of employed civilians (FRED mnemonic "CE16OV"), normalized so that its 1992Q3 value is 1, call it POP_t. Then,

$$\text{Real Investment} = 100\ln\left(\frac{PCED_t/P_t}{POP_t}\right).$$

2. **Real Consumption.**Take nominal personal consumption on durable goods (FRED mnemonic "PCNG"), call it PCE_t and deflate it by the GDP deflator for personal consumption (FRED mnemonic "DPCERD3Q086SBEA"), call it P_t. Take the number of employed civilians (FRED mnemonic "CE16OV"), normalized so that its 1992Q3 value is 1, call it POP_t. Then,

$$\text{Real Consumption} = 100 \ln \left(\frac{PCE_t/P_t}{POP_t} \right).$$

3. **Real Hours Worked.** Take the index of average weekly nonfarm business hours (FRED mnemonic / BLS series "PRS85006023"), call it $HOURS_t$. Take the number of employed civilians (FRED mnemonic "CE16OV"), normalized so that its 1992Q3 value is 1, call it EMP_t. Then,

$$\text{Real Hours Worked} = 100 \ln \left(\frac{HOURS_t EMP_t}{POP_t} \right).$$

4. **Real Consumption Tax Revenues.** Take federal govenment current tax receipts from production and imports (FRED mnemonic "W007RC1Q027SBEA"), call it $CTAX_t$. Then,

$$\text{Real Consumption Tax Revenues}$$
$$= \quad 100 \ln \left(\frac{CTAX_t/P_t}{POP_t} \right).$$

5. **Real Labor Tax Revenues.** Take personal current tax revenues (FRED mnemonic "A074RC1Q027SBEA"), call it IT_t, take wage and salary accruals (FRED mnemonic "WASCUR"), call it W_t, and take proprietors' incomes (FRED mnemonic "A04RC1Q027SBEA"), call it PRI_t. Take rental income (FRED mnemoic "RENTIN"), call it $RENT_t$, take corporate profits (FRED mnemonic "CPROFIT"), call it $PROF_t$, and take interest income (FRED mnemonic "W255RC1Q027SBEA"), call it INT_t. Define capital income, CI_t, as

$$CI_t = RENT_t + PROF_T + INT_t + PRI/2.$$

Define the average personal income tax rate as

$$\tau_t^p = \frac{IT_t}{W_t + PRI_t/2 + CI_t}.$$

Take contributions for government social insurance (FRED mnemonic "W780RC1Q027SBEA"), call it CSI_t, and take compensation for employees (FRED mnemonic "A57RC1Q027SBEA"), call it EC_t. Define the average labor income tax rate as

$$\tau_t^l = \frac{\tau_t^p(W_t + PRI_t) + CSI_t}{EC_t + PRI_t/2}.$$

Take the tax base $BASE_t = PCE_t + PCED_t$. Then,

$$\text{Real Labor Tax Revenues} = 100 \ln\left(\frac{\tau_t^l BASE_t/P_t}{POP_t}\right).$$

6. **Real Capital Tax Revenues.** Take taxes on corporate income (FRED mnemonic "B075RC1Q027SBEA"), call it CT_t, and take property taxes (FRED mnemonic "B249RC1Q027SBEA"), and call it PT_t. Define the average capital income tax rate as

$$\tau^k = \frac{\tau^p CI_t + CT_t}{CI_t + PT_t}.$$

Then,

$$\text{Real Capital Tax Revenues} = 100 \ln\left(\frac{\tau_t^k BASE_t/P_t}{POP_t}\right).$$

7. **Real Government Expenditure.** Take government consumption expenditure (FRED mnemonic "FGEXPND"), call it GC_t. Take government gross investment (FRED mnemonic "A787RC1Q027SBEA"), call it GI_t. Take government net purchases of non-produced assets, (FRED mnemonic "AD08RC1A027NBEA"), call it GP_t. Finally, take government consumption of fixed capital (FRED mnemonic "A918RC1Q027SBEA"), call it GCK_t. Define $G_t = GC_t + GI_t + GP_t - GCK_t$. Then,

$$\text{Real Government Expenditure} = 100 \ln\left(\frac{G_t/P_t}{POP_t}\right).$$

8. **Real Government Transfers.** Take current transfer payments (FRED mnemonic "A084RC1Q027SBEA"), call it $TRANSPAY_t$, and take current transfer receipts (FRED mnemonic "A577RC1Q027SBEA"), call it $TRANSREC_t$. Define net current transfers as

$$CURRTRANS_t = TRANSPAY_t - TRANSREC_t.$$

Take capital transfer payments (FRED mnemonic "W069RC1Q027SBEA") call it $CAPTRANSPAY_t$ and take capital transfer receipts (FRED mnemonic "B232RC1Q027SBEA"), call it $CAPTRANSREC_t$. Define net capital transfers as

$$
\begin{aligned}
CAPTRANS_t \\
= CAPTRANSPAY_t - CAPTRANSREC_t.
\end{aligned}
$$

Take current tax receipts (FRED mnemonic "W006RC1Q027SBEA"), call it $TAXREC_t$, take income receipts on assets (FRED mnemonic "W210RC1Q027SBEA"), call it $INCREC_t$, and take the current surplus of government enterprises (FRED mnemonic "A108RC1Q027SBEA"), call it $GOVSRP_t$. Define the total tax revenue, T_t, as the sum on consumption, labor, and capital tax revenues. Define the tax residual as

$$
\begin{aligned}
TAXRESID_t &= TAXREC + INCREC \\
&+ CSI_t + GOVSRP_t - T_t.
\end{aligned}
$$

Define

$$
\begin{aligned}
TR_t &= CURRTRANS_t + CAPTRANS_t \\
&- TAXRESID_t.
\end{aligned}
$$

Then

$$\text{Real Government Transfers} = 100 \ln\left(\frac{TR_t/P_t}{POP_t}\right).$$

9. **Real Government Debt.** Take interest payments (FRED mnemonic "A091RC1Q027SBEA"), call it $INTPAY_t$. Define net borrowing as

$$NB_t = G_t + INT_t + TR_t - T_t.$$

Take the adjusted monetary base (FRED mnemonic "AMBSL"), take quarterly averages, then call it M_t. Then define government debt—starting in 1947—as

$$B_t = NB_t - \Delta M_t + B_{t-1}.$$

The value B_{1947Q1} is from Cox and Hirschhorn (1983). Then,

$$\text{Real Government Debt} = 100\ln\left(\frac{B_t/P_t}{POP_t}\right).$$

Bibliography

ALTUG, S. (1989): "Time-to-Build and Aggregate Fluctuations: Some New Evidence," *International Economic Review*, 30(4), 889–920.

AN, S., AND F. SCHORFHEIDE (2007): "Bayesian Analysis of DSGE Models," *Econometric Reviews*, 26(2-4), 113–172.

ANDERSON, G. (2000): "A Reliable and Computationally Efficient Algorithm for Imposing the Saddle Point Property in Dynamic Models," *Manuscript*, Federal Reserve Board of Governors.

ANDREASEN, M. M. (2013): "Non-Linear DSGE Models and the Central Difference Kalman Filter," *Journal of Applied Econometrics*, 28(6), 929–955.

ANDRIEU, C., A. DOUCET, AND R. HOLENSTEIN (2010): "Particle Markov Chain Monte Carlo Methods," *Journal of the Royal Statistical Society Series B*, 72(3), 269–342.

ARDIA, D., N. BASTÜRK, L. HOOGERHEIDE, AND H. K. VAN DIJK (2012): "A Comparative Study of Monte Carlo Methods for Efficient Evaluation of Marginal Likelihood," *Computational Statistics and Data Analysis*, 56(11), 3398–3414.

ARULAMPALAM, S., S. MASKELL, N. GORDON, AND T. CLAPP (2002): "A Tutorial on Particle Filters for Online Nonlinear/Non-Gaussian Bayesian Tracking," *IEEE Transactions on Signal Processing*, 50(2), 174–188.

ARUOBA, B., P. CUBA-BORDA, AND F. SCHORFHEIDE (2014): "Macroeconomic Dynamics Near the ZLB: A Tale of Two Countries," *NBER Working Paper*, 19248.

ARUOBA, S. B., L. BOCOLA, AND F. SCHORFHEIDE (2013): "Assessing DSGE Model Nonlinearities," *NBER Working Paper*, 19693.

ARUOBA, S. B., J. FERNÁNDEZ-VILLAVERDE, AND J. F. RUBIO-RAMÍREZ (2006): "Comparing Solution Methods for Dynamic Equilibrium Economies," *Journal of Economic Dynamics and Control*, 30(12), 2477–2508.

BERZUINI, C., AND W. GILKS (2001): "RESAMPLE-MOVE Filtering with Cross-Model Jumps," in *Sequential Monte Carlo Methods in Practice*, ed. by A. Doucet, N. de Freitas, and N. Gordon, pp. 117–138. Springer Verlag.

BIANCHI, F. (2013): "Regime Switches, Agents' Beliefs, and Post–World War II U.S. Macroeconomic Dynamics," *Review of Economic Studies*, 80(2), 463–490.

BINDER, M., AND H. PESARAN (1997): "Multivariate Linear Rational Expectations Models: Characterization of the Nature of the Solutions and Their Fully Recursive Computation," *Econometric Theory*, 13(6), 877–888.

BLANCHARD, O. J., AND C. M. KAHN (1980): "The Solution of Linear Difference Models under Rational Expectations," *Econometrica*, 48(5), 1305–1312.

CANOVA, F., AND L. SALA (2009): "Back to Square One: Identification Issues in DSGE Models," *Journal of Monetary Economics*, 56, 431–449.

CAPPÉ, O., S. J. GODSILL, AND E. MOULINES (2007): "An Overview of Existing Methods and Recent Advances in Sequential Monte Carlo," *Proceedings of the IEEE*, 95(5), 899–924.

CAPPÉ, O., E. MOULINES, AND T. RYDEN (2005): *Inference in Hidden Markov Models*. Springer Verlag.

CHANG, Y., T. DOH, AND F. SCHORFHEIDE (2007): "Non-stationary Hours in a DSGE Model," *Journal of Money, Credit, and Banking*, 39(6), 1357–1373.

CHEN, R., AND J. LIU (2000): "Mixture Kalman Filters," *Journal of the Royal Statistical Society Series B*, 62, 493–508.

CHIB, S., AND E. GREENBERG (1995): "Understanding the Metropolis-Hastings Algorithm," *American Statistician*, 49, 327–335.

CHIB, S., AND I. JELIAZKOV (2001): "Marginal Likelihoods from the Metropolis Hastings Output," *Journal of the American Statistical Association*, 96(453), 270–281.

CHIB, S., AND S. RAMAMURTHY (2010): "Tailored Randomized Block MCMC Methods with Application to DSGE Models," *Journal of Econometrics*, 155(1), 19–38.

CHOPIN, N. (2002): "A Sequential Particle Filter for Static Models," *Biometrika*, 89(3), 539–551.

———— (2004): "Central Limit Theorem for Sequential Monte Carlo Methods and its Application to Bayesian Inference," *Annals of Statistics*, 32(6), 2385–2411.

CHOPIN, N., P. E. JACOB, AND O. PAPASPILIOPOULOS (2012): "SMC^2: An Efficient Algorithm for Sequential Analysis of State-Space Models," *arXiv:1101.1528*.

CHRISTIANO, L. J. (2002): "Solving Dynamic Equilibrium Models by a Methods of Undetermined Coefficients," *Computational Economics*, 20(1–2), 21–55.

CHRISTIANO, L. J., M. EICHENBAUM, AND C. L. EVANS (2005): "Nominal Rigidities and the Dynamic Effects of a Shock to Monetary Policy," *Journal of Political Economy*, 113(1), 1–45.

COX, W., AND E. HIRSCHHORN (1983): "The Market Value of US Government Debt," *Journal of Monetary Economics*, 11, 261–272.

CREAL, D. (2007): "Sequential Monte Carlo Samplers for Bayesian DSGE Models," *Manuscript, University Chicago Booth.*

——— (2012): "A Survey of Sequential Monte Carlo Methods for Economics and Finance," *Econometric Reviews*, 31(3), 245–296.

CURDIA, V., AND R. REIS (2009): "Correlated Disturbances and U.S. Business Cycles," *Working Paper.*

——— (2010): "Correlated Disturbances and U.S. Business Cycles," *Manuscript, Columbia University and FRB New York.*

DAVIG, T., AND E. M. LEEPER (2007): "Generalizing the Taylor Principle," *American Economic Review*, 97(3), 607–635.

DEJONG, D. N., B. F. INGRAM, AND C. H. WHITEMAN (2000): "A Bayesian Approach to Dynamic Macroeconomics," *Journal of Econometrics*, 98(2), 203–223.

DEJONG, D. N., R. LIESENFELD, G. V. MOURA, J.-F. RICHARD, AND H. DHARMARAJAN (2013): "Efficient Likelihood Evaluation of State-Space Representations," *Review of Economic Studies*, 80(2), 538–567.

DEL MORAL, P. (2004): *Feynman-Kac Formulae.* Springer Verlag.

——— (2013): *Mean Field Simulation for Monte Carlo Integration.* Chapman & Hall/CRC.

DEL NEGRO, M., R. B. HASEGAWA, AND F. SCHORFHEIDE (2014): "Dynamic Prediction Pools: An Investigation of Financial Frictions and Forecasting Performance," *NBER Working Paper*, 20575.

DEL NEGRO, M., AND F. SCHORFHEIDE (2008): "Forming Priors for DSGE Models (and How it Affects the Assessment of Nominal Rigidities)," *Journal of Monetary Economics*, 55(7), 1191–1208.

——— (2013): "DSGE Model-Based Forecasting," in *Handbook of Economic Forecasting*, ed. by G. Elliott, and A. Timmermann, vol. 2, forthcoming. North Holland.

DOUCET, A., N. DE FREITAS, AND N. GORDON (eds.) (2001): *Sequential Monte Carlo Methods in Practice*. Springer Verlag.

DOUCET, A., AND A. M. JOHANSEN (2011): "A Tutorial on Particle Filtering and Smoothing: Fifteen Years Later," in *Handook of Nonlinear Filtering*, ed. by D. Crisan, and B. Rozovsky. Oxford University Press.

DURBIN, J., AND S. J. KOOPMAN (2001): *Time Series Analysis by State Space Methods*. Oxford University Press.

DURHAM, G., AND J. GEWEKE (2014): "Adaptive Sequential Posterior Simulators for Massively Parallel Computing Environments," in *Advances in Econometrics*, ed. by I. Jeliazkov, and D. Poirier, vol. 34, chap. 6, pp. 1–44. Emerald Group Publishing Limited.

FARMER, R., D. WAGGONER, AND T. ZHA (2009): "Understanding Markov Switching Rational Expectations Models," *Journal of Economic Theory*, 144(5), 1849–1867.

FERNÁNDEZ-VILLAVERDE, J., G. GORDON, P. GUERRÓN-QUINTANA, AND J. F. RUBIO-RAMÍREZ (2015): "Nonlinear Adventures at the Zero Lower Bound," *Journal of Economic Dynamics and Control*, 57(August), 182–204.

FERNANDEZ-VILLAVERDE, J., AND J. F. RUBIO-RAMIREZ (2004): "Comparing Dynamic Equilibrium Models to Data: A Bayesian Approach," *Journal of Econometrics*, 123(1), 153–187.

FERNÁNDEZ-VILLAVERDE, J., AND J. F. RUBIO-RAMÍREZ (2007): "Estimating Macroeconomic Models: A Likelihood Approach," *Review of Economic Studies*, 74(4), 1059–1087.

——— (2013): "Macroeconomics and Volatility: Data, Models, and Estimation," in *Advances in Economics and Econometrics: Tenth World Congress*, ed. by D. Acemoglu, M. Arellano, and E. Dekel, vol. 3, pp. 137–183. Cambridge University Press.

FLURY, T., AND N. SHEPHARD (2011): "Bayesian Inference Based Only on Simulated Likelihood: Particle Filter Analysis of Dynamic Economic Models," *Econometric Theory*, 27, 933–956.

FOERSTER, A., J. F. RUBIO-RAMIREZ, D. F. WAGGONER, AND T. ZHA (2014): "Perturbation Methods for Markov-Switching DSGE Models," *Manuscript, FRB Kansas City and Atlanta*.

GALI, J. (2008): *Monetary Policy, Inflation, and the Business Cycle: An Introduction to the New Keynesian Framework*. Princeton University Press.

GEWEKE, J. (1989): "Bayesian Inference in Econometric Models Using Monte Carlo Integration," *Econometrica*, 57(6), 1317–1399.

——— (1999): "Using Simulation Methods for Bayesian Econometric Models: Inference, Development, and Communication," *Econometric Reviews*, 18(1), 1–126.

——— (2005): *Contemporary Bayesian Econometrics and Statistics*. John Wiley & Sons.

GIROLAMI, M., AND B. CALDERHEAD (2011): "Riemann Manifold Langevin and Hamilton Monte Carlo Methods (with discussion)," *Journal of the Royal Statistical Society Series B*, 73, 123–214.

GORDON, N., D. SALMOND, AND A. F. SMITH (1993): "Novel Approach to Nonlinear/Non-Gaussian Bayesian State Estimation," *Radar and Signal Processing, IEE Proceedings F*, 140(2), 107–113.

GUO, D., X. WANG, AND R. CHEN (2005): "New Sequential Monte Carlo Methods for Nonlinear Dynamic Systems," *Statistics and Computing*, 15, 135–147.

GUST, C., D. LOPEZ-SALIDO, AND M. E. SMITH (2012): "The Empirical Implications of the Interest-Rate Lower Bound," *Manuscript, Federal Reserve Board*.

HALPERN, E. F. (1974): "Posterior Consistency for Coefficient Estimation and Model Selection in the General Linear Hypothesis," *Annals of Statistics*, 2(4), 703-712.

HAMILTON, J. D. (1989): "A New Approach to the Economic Analysis of Nonstationary Time Series and the Business Cycle," *Econemetrica*, 57(2), 357-384.

———— (1994): *Time Series Analysis*. Princeton University Press.

HAMMERSLEY, J., AND D. HANDSCOMB (1964): *Monte Carlo Methods*. Methuen and Company.

HASTINGS, W. (1970): "Monte Carlo Sampling Methods Using Markov Chains and Their Applications," *Biometrika*, 57, 97-109.

HERBST, E. (2011): "Gradient and Hessian-based MCMC for DSGE Models," *Unpublished Manuscript, University of Pennsylvania*.

HERBST, E., AND F. SCHORFHEIDE (2014): "Sequential Monte Carlo Sampling for DSGE Models," *Journal of Applied Econometrics*, 19(7), 1073-1098.

HOETING, J. A., D. MADIGAN, A. E. RAFTERY, AND C. T. VOLINSKY (1999): "Bayesian Model Averaging: A Tutorial," *Statistical Science*, 14(4), 382-417.

HOLMES, M. (1995): *Introduction to Perturbation Methods*. Cambridge University Press.

IRELAND, P. N. (2004): "A Method for Taking Models to the Data," *Journal of Economic Dynamics and Control*, 28(6), 1205-1226.

ISKREV, N. (2010): "Local Identification of DSGE Models," *Journal of Monetary Economics*, 2, 189-202.

JOHNSON, R. (1970): "Asymptotic Expansions Associated with Posterior Distributions," *Annals of Mathematical Statistics*, 41, 851-864.

JUDD, K. (1998): *Numerical Methods in Economics*. MIT Press.

JUSTINIANO, A., AND G. E. PRIMICERI (2008): "The Time-Varying Volatility of Macroeconomic Fluctuations," *American Economic Review*, 98(3), 604–641.

KANTAS, N., A. DOUCET, S. SINGH, J. MACIEJOWSKI, AND N. CHOPIN (2014): "On Particle Methods for Parameter Estimation in State-Space Models," *arXiv Working Paper*, 1412.8659v1.

KASS, R. E., AND A. E. RAFTERY (1995): "Bayes Factors," *Journal of the American Statistical Association*, 90(430), 773–795.

KIM, J., S. KIM, E. SCHAUMBURG, AND C. A. SIMS (2008): "Calculating and Using Second-Order Accurate Solutions of Discrete Time Dynamic Equilibrium Models," *Journal of Economic Dynamics and Control*, 32, 3397–3414.

KIM, J., AND F. RUGE-MURCIA (2009): "How Much Inflation Is Necessary to Grease the Wheels," *Journal of Monetary Economics*, 56, 365–377.

KING, R. G., C. I. PLOSSER, AND S. REBELO (1988): "Production, Growth, and Business Cycles: I The Basic Neoclassical Model," *Journal of Monetary Economics*, 21(2-3), 195–232.

KING, R. G., AND M. W. WATSON (1998): "The Solution of Singular Linear Difference Systems under Rational Expectations," *International Economic Review*, 39(4), 1015–1026.

KLEIN, P. (2000): "Using the Generalized Schur Form to Solve a Multivariate Linear Rational Expectations Model," *Journal of Economic Dynamics and Control*, 24(10), 1405–1423.

KLOEK, T., AND H. K. VAN DIJK (1978): "Bayesian Estimates of Equation System Parameters: An Application of Integration by Monte Carlo," *Econometrica*, 46, 1–20.

KOENKER, R. (2005): *Quantile Regression*. Cambridge University Press.

KOENKER, R., AND G. BASSETT (1978): "Regression Quantiles," *Econometrica*, 46(1), 33–50.

KOHN, R., P. GIORDANI, AND I. STRID (2010): "Adaptive Hybrid Metropolis-Hastings Samplers for DSGE Models," *Working Paper*.

KOLLMANN, R. (2015): "Tractable Latent State Filtering for Non-Linear DSGE Models Using a Second-Order Approximation and Pruning," *Computational Economics*, 45(2), 239–260.

KOMUNJER, I., AND S. NG (2011): "Dynamic Identification of DSGE Models," *Econometrica*, 79(6), 1995–2032.

KOOP, G. (2003): *Bayesian Econometrics*. John Wiley & Sons.

KÜNSCH, H. R. (2005): "Recursive Monte Carlo Filters: Algorithms and Theoretical Analysis," *Annals of Statistics*, 33(5), 1983–2021.

KYDLAND, F. E., AND E. C. PRESCOTT (1982): "Time to Build and Aggregate Fluctuations," *Econometrica*, 50(6), 1345–1370.

LANCASTER, T. (2004): *An Introduction to Modern Bayesian Econometrics*. Blackwell Publishing.

LEAMER, E. E. (1978): *Specification Searches*. John Wiley & Sons.

LEEPER, E. M., M. PLANTE, AND N. TRAUM (2010): "Dynamics of Fiscaling Financing in the United States," *Journal of Econometrics*, 156, 304–321.

LIU, J. S. (2001): *Monte Carlo Strategies in Scientific Computing*. Springer Verlag.

LIU, J. S., AND R. CHEN (1998): "Sequential Monte Carlo Methods for Dynamic Systems," *Journal of the American Statistical Association*, 93(443), 1032–1044.

LIU, J. S., R. CHEN, AND T. LOGVINENKO (2001): "A Theoretical Franework for Sequential Importance Sampling with Resampling," in *Sequential Monte Carlo Methods in Practice*, ed. by A. Doucet, N. de Freitas, AND N. Gordon, pp. 225–246. Springer Verlag.

LIU, Z., D. F. WAGGONER, AND T. ZHA (2011): "Sources of Macroeconomic Fluctuations: A Regime-switching DSGE Approach," *Quantitative Economics*, 2, 251–301.

LUBIK, T., AND F. SCHORFHEIDE (2003): "Computing Sunspot Equilibria in Linear Rational Expectations Models," *Journal of Economic Dynamics and Control*, 28(2), 273–285.

——— (2006): "A Bayesian Look at the New Open Macroeconomics," *NBER Macroeconomics Annual 2005*.

MALIAR, L., AND S. MALIAR (2015): "Merging Simulation and Projection Approaches to Solve High-Dimensional Problems with an Application to a New Keynesian Model," *Quantitative Economics*, 6(1), 1–47.

METROPOLIS, N., A. ROSENBLUTH, M. ROSENBLUTH, A. TELLER, AND E. TELLER (1953): "Equations of State Calculations by Fast Computing Machines," *Journal of Chemical Physics*, 21, 1087–1091.

MIN, C.-K., AND A. ZELLNER (1993): "Bayesian and Non-Bayesian Methods for Combining Models and Forecasts with Applications to Forecasting International Growth Rates," *Journal of Econometrics*, 56(1-2), 89–118.

MÜLLER, U. (2011): "Measuring Prior Sensitivity and Prior Informativeness in Large Bayesian Models," *Manuscript, Princeton University*.

MURRAY, L. M., A. LEE, AND P. E. JACOB (2014): "Parallel Resampling in the Particle Filter," *arXiv Working Paper*, 1301.4019v2.

NEAL, R. (2010): "MCMC using Hamiltonian Dynamics," in *Handbook of Markov Chain Monte Carlo*, ed. by S. Brooks, A. Gelman, G. Jones, and X.-L. Meng, pp. 113–162. Chapman & Hall, CRC Press.

OTROK, C. (2001): "On Measuring the Welfare Costs of Business Cycles," *Journal of Monetary Economics*, 47(1), 61–92.

PHILLIPS, D., AND A. SMITH (1994): "Bayesian Model Comparison via Jump Diffusions," *Technical Report: Imperial College of Science, Technology, and Medicine, London*, 94-02.

PITT, M. K., AND N. SHEPHARD (1999): "Filtering via Simulation: Auxiliary Particle Filters," *Journal of the American Statistical Association*, 94(446), 590–599.

PITT, M. K., R. D. S. SILVA, P. GIORDANI, AND R. KOHN (2012): "On Some Properties of Markov Chain Monte Carlo Simulation Methods Based on the Particle Filter," *Journal of Econometrics*, 171, 134–151.

QI, Y., AND T. P. MINKA (2002): "Hessian-based Markov Chain Monte-Carlo Algorithms," *Unpublished Manuscript*.

RÍOS-RULL, J.-V., F. SCHORFHEIDE, C. FUENTES-ALBERO, M. KRYSHKO, AND R. SANTAEULALIA-LLOPIS (2012): "Methods versus Substance: Measuring the Effects of Technology Shocks," *Journal of Monetary Economics*, 59(8), 826–846.

ROBERT, C. P. (1994): *The Bayesian Choice*. Springer Verlag.

ROBERT, C. P., AND G. CASELLA (2004): *Monte Carlo Statistical Methods*. Springer.

ROBERTS, G., AND J. S. ROSENTHAL (1998): "Markov-Chain Monte Carlo: Some Practical Implications of Theoretical Results," *Canadian Journal of Statistics*, 25(1), 5–20.

ROBERTS, G., AND O. STRAMER (2002): "Langevin Diffusions and Metropolis-Hastings Algorithms," *Methodology and Computing in Applied Probability*, 4, 337–357.

ROBERTS, G. O., A. GELMAN, AND W. R. GILKS (1997): "Weak Convergence and Optimal Scaling of Random Walk Metropolis Algorithms," *Annals of Applied Probability*, 7(1), 110–120.

ROBERTS, G. O., AND S. SAHU (1997): "Updating Schemes, Correlation Structure, Blocking and Parameterization for the Gibbs Sampler," *Journal of the Royal Statistical Society. Series B (Methodological)*, 59(2), 291–317.

ROBERTS, G. O., AND R. TWEEDIE (1992): "Exponential Convergence of Langevin Diffusions and Their Discrete Approximations," *Bernoulli*, 2, 341–363.

ROTEMBERG, J. J., AND M. WOODFORD (1997): "An Optimization-Based Econometric Framework for the Evaluation of Monetary Policy," in *NBER Macroeconomics Annual 1997*, ed. by B. S. Bernanke, and J. J. Rotemberg. MIT Press.

SARGENT, T. J. (1989): "Two Models of Measurements and the Investment Accelerator," *Journal of Political Economy*, 97(2), 251–287.

SCHMITT-GROHÉ, S., AND M. URIBE (2004): "Solving Dynamic General Equilibrium Models Using a Second-Order Approximation to the Policy Function," *Journal of Economic Dynamics and Control*, 28, 755–775.

——— (2012): "What's News in Business Cycles?," *Econometrica*, 80(6), 2733–2764.

SCHORFHEIDE, F. (2000): "Loss Function-based Evaluation of DSGE Models," *Journal of Applied Econometrics*, 15, 645–670.

——— (2005): "Learning and Monetary Policy Shifts," *Review of Economic Dynamics*, 8(2), 392–419.

——— (2010): "Estimation and Evaluation of DSGE Models: Progress and Challenges," *NBER Working Paper*.

SCHORFHEIDE, F., D. SONG, AND A. YARON (2014): "Identifying Long-Run Risks: A Bayesian Mixed-Frequency Approach," *NBER Working Paper*, 20303.

SCHWARZ, G. (1978): "Estimating the Dimension of a Model," *Annals of Statistics*, 6(2), 461–464.

SIMS, C. A. (2002): "Solving Linear Rational Expectations Models," *Computational Economics*, 20, 1–20.

SIMS, C. A., D. WAGGONER, AND T. ZHA (2008): "Methods for Inference in Large Multiple-Equation Markov-Switching Models," *Journal of Econometrics*, 146(2), 255–274.

SMETS, F., AND R. WOUTERS (2003): "An Estimated Dynamic Stochastic General Equilibrium Model of the Euro Area," *Journal of the European Economic Association*, 1(5), 1123–1175.

SMETS, F., AND R. WOUTERS (2007): "Shocks and Frictions in US Business Cycles: A Bayesian DSGE Approach," *American Economic Review*, 97, 586–608.

SMITH, M. (2012): "Estimating Nonlinear Economic Models Using Surrogate Transitions," *Manuscript, RePEc*.

STRID, I. (2010): "Efficient parallelisation of Metropolis-Hastings algorithms using a prefetching approach," *Computational Statistics & Data Analysis*, 54(11), 2814–2835.

TIERNEY, L. (1994): "Markov Chains for Exploring Posterior Distributions," *Annals of Statistics*, 22(4), 1701–1728.

VAN DER VAART, A. (1998): *Asymptotic Statistics*. Cambridge University Press.

WOODFORD, M. (2003): *Interest and Prices*. Princeton University Press.

WRIGHT, J. (2008): "Bayesian Model Averaging and Exchange Rate Forecasting," *Journal of Econometrics*, 146, 329–341.

Index